Social Reform
in England, 1780-1880

Social Reform
in England 1780-1880

JOHN ROACH

St. Martin's Press

New York

To Patrick and Betty Bury
For thirty years of friendship

Library of Congress Cataloging in Publication Data

Roach, John Peter Charles.
  Social reform in England, 1780-1880.

  Bibliography: p.
  Includes index.
    1. England—Social conditions—18th century. 2. England—
Social conditions—19th century. 3. Social reformers—England—
History. 1. Title.
HN398. E5R6   301.24'0942   78-6384
ISBN 0-312-73481-6

CONTENTS

Preface

This book is an attempt to study the reasons for change in English society between 1780 and 1880. It does not set out to give a factual account of those changes which indeed would demand far more space than has been available here. During the nineteenth century a new society developed in England, based on movement rather than on stability, on cash rather than on status. That era is often dubbed 'Victorian', though in my view that title is a misnomer. When I began to explore the subject, it soon became clear to me that the process of change did not begin with the legislation of the 1830's, while at the other end of the story the death of the Queen provided no particular landmark in the sequence which I was anxious to describe. In my view the changes which were to produce the social pattern of modern industrial England began in the 1780's. They were inspired by an individualistic philosophy which worked out a certain accommodation with state power which endured till about 1880. At that point two vital changes occurred. The first was the fact that men came to expect that the state, rather than individuals or groups, should take responsibility for policy. The second was the fact that local initiatives, which had been so important all through the century under discussion, receded more and more into the background and were replaced by the growing dominance of central power. It is therefore to the hundred years from 1780 to 1880 that this book is devoted.

Much recent study of this period has begun either with the administration or with economic conditions. These aspects have obviously been brought under contribution, more especially the former, but this book does not begin from either of these standpoints. It sees social history primarily as the working out of ideas under the pressure of events. Much attention is given to the Utilitarians and to the mid-Victorian debates about individual freedom and collective claims. Religious themes run through the whole story, sometimes seen in isolation, sometimes in collaboration with secular influences of many kinds, and particularly with the ideals of self-help and of philanthropy which were so important to nineteenth-century Englishmen. The word 'Englishmen' is deliberate, since attention has been almost entirely concentrated on that part of the United Kingdom. There is hardly any discussion of Wales or Scotland, and minimal attention is given to Ireland.

The main areas which are studied are those of poverty and the poor law, public health, factory legislation, education, and prisons and punishment, and these are developed in what may seem to be a rather difficult fashion. The book has been divided into three parts, covering the years 1780-1830, 1830-1850, and 1850-1880. Within each part all these major topics which have been mentioned are pursued in relation to one another. This inevitably leads to some repetition and to much cross-referencing, but it avoids the danger, which often affects this kind of historical writing, when the separate topics are handled in more or less isolation over long periods. It seemed to me important to emphasize that what people were thinking and writing about one topic in the 1830's or the 1870's was deeply affected by what they were saying at the same time about the other areas of social concern. It is one of the historian's major tasks, in a book of this kind, to provide a cross-section across a period of time, as well as a longitudinal study of events. I believe that the three parts do have a unity of their own and that there are certain emphases distinctive to each generation.

I have made extensive use of parliamentary papers, which rank as my major source, though there are obviously many other Blue Books which I might also have consulted. The references to parliamentary papers are to the bound sets of sessional papers (see P. & .G. Ford, *A Guide to Parliamentary Papers* (3rd. ed., 1972), p. 23). I have used the set in the Cambridge University Library. In general I have confined myself to printed sources, and I have tried to use, as far as possible, books published at the time. I have not attempted to provide a full bibliography which would be extremely voluminous, but I have provided some 'Notes for further reading' at the end. I have received generous help from many people, and I wish particularly to mention Professor Norman McCord, Dr.B.I. Coleman, who read a large part of the typescript, Dr. and Mrs. J.P.T. Bury, who read the proofs, and Mr. Samuel Carr of Messrs. Batsford, who has been a very helpful and understanding publisher. The whole idea of the book owes a great deal to Dr. George Kitson Clark, who encouraged me to persist when I had almost given up the project. I wish that he had lived to see it completed and I hope that he might have approved of it.

Sheffield, 14 July 1977

J.R.

I. Introduction
The subject defined; outlines and themes

i) The Concept of social reform

J.R. Seeley's book, *Ecce Homo*, published in 1865, made a great stir in its day because it dealt with the person of Christ solely from the human standpoint. Seeley argued that the first special injunction laid upon Christians was 'to apply themselves to relieving the physical needs and distresses of their fellow creatures'.[1] The demands made by that injunction had developed considerably over eighteen hundred years as physical well-being had grown and scientific knowledge had increased. Christ commanded the Christians of the nineteenth century 'to investigate the causes of all physical evil, to master the science of health, to consider the question of education with a view to health, the question of labour with a view to health, the question of trade with a view to health; and while all these investigations are made, with free expense of energy and time and means to work out the rearrangement of human life in accordance with the results they give'.[2] Seeley coined a striking phrase to describe this whole activity—'The Enthusiasm of Humanity' and in that phrase he incapsulated the subject of this book.

This enthusiasm was a far cry from Christ's original command to his followers to heal the sick and to give alms. Seeley's concept contains too a profound shift in the fundamental idea of charity to which much attention will later be given here. To the Apostles and for centuries after, the duty of kindness to the poor was laid upon men who were briefly travelling the temporal world with their eyes fixed upon the spiritual. Both poor and rich were alike conscious of the fact that here they had no abiding city. Seeley's time man's mastery over his environment had grown so much that, even among religious men, the problems of this world were steadily looming larger than the promises of the next. For a minority at least of the population of an advanced industrial society great advances in social and economic conditions had been made. The advance of that small group brought out in even stronger contrast the wretchedness in which the majority of the population still lived, while the success which some had enjoyed in improving their material conditions inspired more and more reformers to believe that the lives of the great mass of the population were improvable. Social changes do not merely happen of themselves. They take place because some men, a creative minority, believe that they are possible and agitate to bring them about. They have to be believed in before they can happen.

Moreover in the nineteenth century such changes were taking place in a society which was itself changing with great speed. To put the transition in very broad terms, Britain changed between 1700 and 1850 from a society dominated by the traditional loyalties of village, parish and manor to a society of great towns and growing industries in which the primary ties were based on money not on tradition. Overall the process called the Industrial Revolution greatly increased the nation's total wealth, though historians have sharply disagreed about the effect of the economic changes on the various social groups, more particularly in the period before 1850. The changes produced both great wealth and widespread unsettlement as traditional industries like hand-loom weaving became obsolescent. It is not difficult to understand why Edward Lytton Bulwer wrote in 1833 that the main schools of English thought were devoted to 'the science of money making and the passionate warfare with social abuses.'[3] The collocation of these two activities is not a coincidence. The passion for money making was the passion of the first modern industrial society, in which British business men led the world. It sometimes caused, or at least worsened, social abuse when thousands of factory workers were packed into insanitary towns lacking almost every facility for decent social living. On the other hand the wealth of industrialism made it possible for a richer society to afford social improvement, while technological advance increased men's confidence that improvement was possible.

The pressure for such improvement came from many sources. Some of it was religious; if man is truly made in the image of God, it was asked, how can that image be defaced by such wretched living conditions. Some of it was applied by secular reformers of many schools. Much of the drive for better conditions was preventive or disciplinary, as men argued that the poor must be educated into disciplined and regular habits if social chaos was to be avoided and economic stability preserved. Different men propounded different remedies, and disagreed among themselves about what was best to be done. They all agreed, however, on one thing—the size of the problem. The Benthamite *Westminster Review* puts the point very clearly in an article on Sadler's Factory Bill (1833):

> Our poor laws stimulate the increase of an uneducated, toil-worn and ignorant working class. We have a vindictive criminal code, which is so abhorrent to common sense that juries modify their verdicts to elude its vengeance . . . . In the provinces there is no preventive police . . . . Our gaols, though improved, are still schools of vice, where the novice is initiated in the more subtle secrets of chicanery and fraud . . . . Add to all this that there is no system of national education for the people.[4]

Thomas Carlyle, ten years later (1843), spoke of the 'condition of England question'. The country was strong, wealthy and rich. Its fifteen million workers were acknowledged to be the strongest and most willing in the world. Yet over this wealthy and powerful land had been cast an evil spell. Of these fifteen millions two millions were maintained by the Poor Law, twelve hundred thousand of them in workhouses . . . 'their cunning right-hand lamed, lying idle in their sorrowful bosom; their hopes, outlooks, share of this fair world, shut in by narrow walls. They sit there, pent up, as in a kind of horrid enchantment; glad to be imprisoned and enchanted, that they may not perish starved.'[5]

Carlyle's presentation seems to us rhetorical, over-strained, but the problem of poverty in the midst of wealth had bitten deeply into the conscience of the age. In the later Victorian age the great social investigators like Charles Booth in London and Seebohm Rowntree in York threw new light upon it. The Charity Organization Society, founded in 1869, tried to combat the evils of indiscriminate charity and by their emphasis on case-work laid the foundation of much of the social investigation of the twentieth century. The Society was convinced of the virtue of self-help and cradled in an individualism which saw pauperism as the fault of the individual pauper. To the young Beatrice Potter, learning her craft as a social investigator in the London of the 1880's, their creed soon proved unsatisfactory. Ultimately it was not the poor man who was at fault, but the whole economic system which needed to be changed through closer public control.[6] With Beatrice Potter and her husband, Sidney Webb, we reach the social gospels of the twentieth century. The problems remain much the same: what alters is men's way of dealing with them.

The condition of England question was a social question, but social questions operate within the firm and regulative structure of politics, economics and administration. An attempt must soon be made to define the scope of social reform, but before that is attempted something must be said about disciplines which controlled the social life of nineteenth-century Britain. Society is like a great building upheld by the steel girders of politics, economics and administration. The men of the day were very conscious that all around them old buildings were being torn down and newer and yet newer structures were constantly being erected. It was a despondent Conservative who wrote in 1873:

The old ways of living, many of which were just as bad in their time as any of our devices can be in ours, are breaking down all over Europe, and are floating this way and that like haycocks in a flood. Nor do I see why any wise man should extend much thought or trouble on trying to save their wrecks. The waters are out and no human force can turn them back, but I do not see why as we go with the stream we need sing alleluja to the river god.[7]

To many Liberals and Radicals the changes were as welcome as to J.F. Stephen they were abhorrent, but all alike, whatever their views, shared the sense that 'the waters are out and no human force can turn them back'.

The most controversial changes had been political. The Reform Act of

1832 broke the straitjacket of tradition and began the long series of political changes which were to turn Britain into a democracy. The Act of 1867 created a working-class electorate in the towns, and was followed by the growth of the modern party organizations. Administrative change accompanied political. Two of the major achievements of the first Reform era were the New Poor Law of 1834 and the Municipal Reform Act of 1835. Changes in some ways were very slow but gradually and after many setbacks an effective administrative machine was created, and the state equipped itself for a new role in directing the affairs of a complex society. Not the least important landmark on the road was the institution of competitive examinations for the Civil Service. Sometimes too much is claimed for these examinations. The development of the central government machine began long before they were instituted, and they did not work wonders in themselves. However they did supply the public service with better-educated and more efficient servants at a time when more was being demanded of those servants. Though competitive examinations were much criticized, no one showed any desire to go back to the more easy-going systems which had preceded them, and that fact is some evidence of their success.

Political and administrative changes were often controversial, and men had sharply different views about what was to be done. Economic questions were controversial too, the most obvious example being the long struggle over the Repeal of the Corn Laws. Yet throughout the century economic policy was moving in a single direction towards the establishment of a completely free market. David Ricardo's view sums up what was to be the orthodoxy of the Victorian age:

> Under a system of perfectly free commerce, each country naturally devotes its capital and labour to such employments as are most beneficial to each. This pursuit of individual advantage is admirably connected with the universal good of the whole. By stimulating industry, by rewarding ingenuity, and by using most efficaciously the peculiar powers bestowed by nature, it distributes labour most effectively and most economically: while, by increasing the general mass of production, it diffuses general benefit, and binds together by one common tie of interest and intercourse, the universal society of nations throughout the civilized world.[8]

Until the 'seventies and 'eighties it was in the interest of British business men to try and sell in a free market because their position was so strong that they had no real competition to fear.

The economic developments of the century are a subject so complex that they can only be touched on very briefly here. Two points may perhaps be isolated. The first is the growth of industry as celebrated in Dr. Andrew Ure's *The Philosphy of Manufactures, or an exposition of the scientific, moral and commercial economy of the factory system of Great Britain,* originally published in 1835. The second is the transformation in communications produced by the steamship and the railway, which was beginning at about the same time. Within half a century the world was to become a single market. Within Britain itself local loyalties were to break down, and the problems and issues of the day acquired a new national dimension.

The two economic developments which have been selected in the last paragraph have both very clear social implications. Technological change brought with it the growth of factories, the growth of towns and the enormous sanitary and environmental problems of a new urban environment. Easier communications facilitated emigration, a much recommended cure for poverty and over-population. They made it easier to feed thronging urban populations. They made the transmission of news and opinions both easier and quicker than it had been in earlier days. In Britain the institution of the penny post (1840) comes just after the completion of the London and Birmingham Railway, the first major trunk route (1838).

Clearly all political and economic changes have social implications. They make society different from what it was before, while the condition of that society regulates the political and economic changes which are possible within it. Any society has a tolerance point, a point of strain beyond which changes cannot be effected without shattering the framework of society itself. Nineteenth-century Britain never passed its tolerance point; unlike eighteenth-century France or twentieth-century Russia it accommodated change without revolution. The changes of the nineteenth century in Britain were social as well as political and economic, and some of the most fundamental of the political and economic changes have already been outlined.

The social changes themselves are difficult to define because the whole concept of social reform is an imprecise one. Political reforms relate to the distribution of political power, to the franchise, to the structure of government. Economic reforms relate to systems of taxation, to aggregate national wealth, to new industrial and technological structures. In this book the term 'social reform' relates to changes in the everyday conditions of life of human beings, both as individuals and as the members of communities. It is primarily concerned with human relationships in their more informal and less official aspects. It deals with those relationships considered as a system of welfare, sometimes more and sometimes less highly articulated, and creating, or failing to create, a fruitful and congenial environment for the people who live under them. If social change be looked at from this point of view, the key concept is that of welfare as opposed to power, which is characteristic of the political, or wealth which is characteristic of the economic domain.

Naturally the different areas overlap, and it may help the argument to give some illustrations of what is meant. As we shall see, early nineteenth-century discussions about social reform were dominated by the problem of poverty. The Poor Laws were in one sense a political question because the assurance to the poor of a basic subsistence was thought to be one of the basic pre-requisites of maintaining peace and public order. From that point of view it was argued in the 1820's that it would not be possible to abolish the existing poor law system. The expectations which that system had raised were such that, politically speaking, changes could be brought about only very gradually. From an economic point of view the poor rates formed a heavy charge on land, and for that reason affected the whole structure of rents and profits. Another major area of social concern was education. Politically speaking education involved all through the nineteenth century bitter religious rivalries, and such rivalries could be very dangerous to the stability of governments. In 1839 the proposal for a state normal school came near to bringing down Melbourne's administration, and the increase to £30,000 of the annual grant to education was carried by a majority of only two votes. From the point of view of economics the growth in that grant throughout the century made the size of the educational budget a matter of serious concern. The Revised Code of 1862, which had profound effects on the working of the national system of education in the ensuing thirty years, was introduced partly to regulate an expanding educational budget.

If these are some of the political and economic implications of the Poor Law and of education, how did these issues appear to the social reformer? Poverty, from the social point of view, affected both the material conditions of men's lives—their food, clothing, housing—and the spiritual questions of man's individuality and the general quality of life among individuals and communities. If a man is unable to support his family by what he earns and his wages have to be made up out of the poor rates, what effect, it was asked, is this likely to have upon his habits of industry, his personal self-reliance, his sense of obligation to maintain his children and other members of his family? Can a pauperized working class possess the incentives to improve its own condition, and by improving its condition increase the total national wealth? Can pauperism be staved off by the aid of savings banks and friendly societies, which were regarded as agencies as much moral as economic because of the stimulus which they gave to men's desire to depend solely on their own efforts? Many more such questions were being asked in the last days of the old Poor Law before 1834, and these, it is submitted, are the questions of the social reformer, as opposed to the politician or the economist. Naturally enough most people who were concerned with these matters at all were something of all three, but it is possible to distinguish a distinctive social reformer's point of view.

There was a similar social reformer's point of view on education. The basic twentieth-century argument for popular education, as seen in the developing countries, is economic; that only an educated work-force can meet the demands of a technological society. On the whole this argument is not important in the first two-thirds of the nineteenth century in Britain, though the comparison between English conditions and German conditions—to the great advantage of the latter—was certainly made much of in the debates on Forster's Education Bill of 1870. In the first half of the century popular education was urged both on religious grounds—that Christian men and women must be able to read their Bibles—and because it would train the poor in habits of virtue and industry. Such habits would lead them away from the taint of pauperism and school them in habits of independence and self reliance. The acquisition of such habits loomed much larger in the minds of early nineteenth-century philanthropists than the acquisition of the skills of reading and writing. Sir Thomas Bernard (1750-1818), one of the founders of the Society for Bettering the Condition and Increasing the Comforts of the Poor (1796), defined the benefits to which the poor were entitled, as 'The Prevention of Vice and Contagion; the Promotion of Virtue and Industry; and the general diffusion of moral and religious education'.[9] Once again the collocation of ideas is significant.

Bernard was a sincere and warm-hearted philanthropist, but his published works do not suggest any depth of social analysis. But the same kind of approach to the education of the people persists in the ideas of men who had delved much more deeply than he. Dr. J.P. Kay, later as Sir James Kay-Shuttleworth to be the effective founder of the English state system of popular education, wrote at the end of his pamphlet on the moral and physical condition of the working classes of Manchester in 1832 that it would be folly to neglect the 'operative population':

> If the higher classes are unwilling to diffuse intelligence among the lower, those exist who are ever ready to take advantage of their ignorance; if they will not seek their confidence, others will excite their distrust; if they will not endeavour to promote domestic comfort, virtue, and knowledge among them, their misery, vice and prejudice will prove volcanic elements, by whose explosive violence the structure of society may be destroyed.[10]

To paraphrase the argument, education teaches man the true nature of social relationships. Because it does that, it both improves the condition of the individual and makes the society in which that individual lives a more stable and harmonious place.

By this stage in the argument a concept of social reform should be emerging if the two examples of the Poor Law and of education have made their point. Social reforms might be defined as second-order reforms. Political changes alter political and legal systems; economic changes control the way in which wealth is made and spent. Social changes result when political and economic forces impinge upon the lives of individuals and communities. Social change is faster or slower at different epochs; it is always half-hidden, half-unconscious, partly unexpected because it regulates those parts of human life which are not entirely rational and which respond to intuition rather than to deliberate decisions. Here a distinction should be drawn between social change and social reform. The former is primarily instinctive and non-rational. The latter is quite definitely planned and organized by individuals working according to a programme. Social change goes on constantly, but social reforms take place because social reformers will them to do so and persuade society that they are necessary.

ii) Poverty, public health and disease

The social reformers began with the problem of poverty and with the poor law, the legal structure ·through which the state dealt with that problem. From the problem of poverty every other social concern branched out, because every other social evil seemed to the men of the time to be either the cause or the result of it, and sometimes both cause and effect at once. It was both a rural and an urban problem, and in the towns, overcrowded and insanitary as they were, it was linked very closely with the problems of public health and epidemic disease. When at the end of the eighteenth century cotton mills made heavy demands for labour to work the machines, the demand was first met by pauper apprentices. The conditions of these pauper children in cotton mills was regulated by the first Factory Act of 1802, and protection was extended to all children in such mills by the Act of 1819. These early acts were not effectively administered, but the whole later edifice of the Factory Acts grew out of concern about the treatment of children. The problems of the pauper apprentices were tackled first, partly because their condition was the most wretched and partly perhaps because they were a group for whom organized society had a direct responsibility. The moral aspect which has already been stressed was important too. In 1836 J.C. Franks, the vicar of Huddersfield, 'persuaded 34 Yorkshire clergymen to petition that, to promote education and religion,

> it was indispensably necessary that the labour and occupation of the young, especially, should be so arranged and regulated as to allow of proper time and opportunity to attend to those important objects, upon the weekday, as well as upon the Lord's Day'.[11]

It is characteristic that shorter hours were advocated, not so much because they would allow additional leisure but because they would facilitate religious and moral improvement. It is important to realize that the nineteenth century concept of welfare was by no means the same as that of the twentieth-century, enshrined in the phrase 'The Welfare State'. To the men of the 1970's the word 'welfare' contains within it a strong element of personal choice. One aspect of better housing, more leisure, better education is that these advantages should enable individuals to choose more freely for themselves how they wish to spend their time and their money, and so to enlarge the choices open to them.

Something of this is present in the thought of nineteenth-century reformers, but they put much less emphasis on the free choice of the individual and much more stress on the direction of that individual from above—by the people who were assumed to know what was best for him. All the reformers of the century shared a fear and dislike of working-class traditions. It would be difficult to think of any reformer of the day who does not wish to break with the working-class past and to impose upon the workers a new set of habits and values which are declared to be better and more moral than their own. Thus factory work is praised because it is regular and disciplined, unlike the old traditions of domestic industry where the workman was free on 'St. Monday', and slaved very hard towards the end of the week to make up lost time. It is important not to sound sentimental, and a good deal of working-class life must have been debased and cruel. Moreover the condition of the pauperized labourers of the southern counties and of the newly recruited labour-force of the north did not provide, in 1815 or 1830, the solid foundations on which to build a better order.

Yet even if that be allowed, the note of discipline and compulsion is very marked. Reformers of all schools were strong authoritarians however devoted they were to improving the condition of the working classes. Thus Joseph Townsend, whose views on population preceded those of T.R. Malthus, wrote in 1786 that the poor law must be strictly enforced:

> It will be necessary for magistrates to pay more than common attention to the police, till industry and subordination shall be once more restored. The reins have been held with a loose hand, at a time when the idleness and extravagance, the drunkenness and dissipation, with the consequent crimes and vices of the lower classes of the people called for the most strenuous exertions of the magistrate, and the most strict execution of the laws.[12]

Once again the collocation 'industry and subordination' is to be noted. Hard work is equated with obedience. It leads not to independence but to submission, which is perhaps why it did not always appeal very strongly to the working man.

The same note is heard strongly in the Nottinghamshire poor law reformers of the 1820's, J.T. Becher and George Nicholls, who will be discussed in a later chapter.[13] It is very clear among the early education inspectors,[14] who frequently seem to regard the schools as places whose primary purpose is to save the children from the harm done to them by their parents. The task of the social reformer was to redeem the people from their own environment. The means adopted were paternalistic in purpose and authoritarian in method.

Joseph Townsend, in the passage from his pamphlet of 1786 which has already been quoted, urged the magistrates to pay great attention to 'the police'. He does not, of course, by that word mean the police force, which did not exist in any modern sense when he was writing, but rather the general coercive and restraining forces in society which prevent disorder and maintain the public peace. Social reforms in any society are inevitably in some degree coercive. One very obvious example might be the suppression of brutal amusement like cock fighting or bear baiting. These undoubtedly gave very great pleasure to the spectators, but there were other and very valid reasons for suppressing them, even though they were popular. On the whole individuals benefit from better sanitation and improved public health because epidemic disease is reduced. Yet many individuals probably suffered in their pockets when they were forbidden to keep a valuable dung-heap in the yard of their house or in a court of crowded cottages. In 1853 an act was passed requiring all infants to be vaccinated within three months of birth. This act was after a time steadily enforced and by the 1880's over 85% of all children were being vaccinated.[15] The enforcement of the law had a considerable effect in reducing epidemic smallpox, which was a great public benefit, but to many people it seemed a grave infringement of individual liberty, rather as, at a less serious level, the fluoridation of water does today.

A reformed society is necessarily a more closely regulated society. To some extent this change sprang, it has been suggested, from the reformer's distrust of working-class traditions and their desire to impose new patterns of behaviour on working people. To some extent this tendency was, I believe, defensive. Social reforms began in Britain in the age of the French Revolution when the governing classes had a deep-rooted fear of social upheaval. The question whether there was any serious danger of a revolutionary upheaval in the British situation will be discussed later, but the fear was certainly active in men's minds up to about 1850. Even if revolution itself did not occur, there was a continued fear of social disturbance, not unconnected with the fact that the country had no efficient police (in the modern sense of the word) and that any serious disorder had to be put down by the army or the yeomanry.

There were probably reasons other than the desire for moral improvement which led reformers to urge that shorter hours would give young operatives the chance to receive better schooling. They had to counter the argument that Satan finds some mischief still for idle hands to do. The factory system itself was quoted as an important agent for social discipline because it took the workers away from their homes and confined them to work regular hours. Witnesses examined for the Children's Employment Commission commented on the immorality of the young people of Sheffield and attributed this to the absence of factories in the town. The superintendent of police, Mr. Raynor, pointed out the prevalence of drinking, vagrancy, theft, gambling and prostitution among young people. 'Witness is confident that the morals of children are not as bad in Manchester and Leeds, because the factory system prevents their running wild in the same manner'. Mr. Carr, a surgeon in the town, thought that the great cause of mortality was intemperance . . . 'believes it to be greater here than in Leeds or Manchester, where the steam power factories keep the men continually at work; they don't know what St. Monday or Tuesday means; but here, where trade is good, the men don't work more than four days a week'.[16]

The town populations were a dark and unknown mass, and respectable men feared what might be seething below the surface. Society was, however, exposed to more serious dangers than the moral delinquencies of the Sheffield cutlers. National and local leaders of early nineteenth-century England believed in a divinely sanctioned order in which every man had his place and where any displacement might be fatal to the stability of the whole. In that same generation many of those leaders came to believe that the poor must be educated. The question arose; could this be done without upsetting the stability of society, in which it was ordained that the poor should be hewers of wood and drawers of water? Hannah More (1745-1833) in the isolated villages of the Mendips was one of the pioneers of popular education, and she had to tread a delicate path between the forces of ignorance on the one side and the fear of social disturbances on the other.[17]

'Schools of Jacobinical politics abound in this country', said Bishop Horsley of Rochester in his charge to the clergy of his diocese in 1800, 'In them the minds of many of the lowest orders are taught to despise religion and the laws of subordination.'[18] The problem became even more urgent ten years later with the creation by the Quaker Joseph Lancaster of a system of undenominational schools in which religious instruction was based solely on the Bible. Loyal supporters of the Establishment rallied round the rival system of Dr. Andrew Bell. His supporters created the National Society (1811) which was soon in keen rivalry with the British Society, founded by the supporters of Lancaster. The conflict is usually depicted as a denominational one and so in a sense it was, but the denominational question is not really the centre of the argument. The central point is this. It could be assumed, as the result of the greatly increased interest in the education of the poor in the first decade of the century, that the number of schools for the poor was going to increase. If this was accepted, could those schools be left in the hands of private individuals owning no special loyalty to the institutions of the country, of which the Church of England was one of the most important. To put the matter in another way, could society be secure if popular education were not in the hands of the Church, since the religious and the secular institutions of the country essentially formed a single whole. As Sir Charles Oakeley wrote to Bell on 2 December 1809;

It were to be wished that this powerful engine of instruction, recommended as it is by a fair experiment, had been earlier and more actively employed, with a view to the public establishments in church and state. The education of youth in general, is an object of too much national importance to be left to the speculative and floating opinions of individuals. What is called a free mode of instruction where no particular tenets are inculcated, seems likely to produce almost as many opinions as there are scholars, and to give birth to the most latitudinarian principles, both in religion and government.[19]

As the century went on attitudes became more liberal than they had been in the crisis years of the Napoleonic wars, but all through the century something of the same atmosphere lingered. Reforms were something which were all too often imposed from above, rather than growing out of any experience shared between the reformer and the people whom he designed to benefit. There was for a long time very little sense that the workers could cooperate in altering their own destinies. Indeed in many ways working people were conservative and resistant to change. They first began to claim a share in controlling their own destinies in the 'twenties and 'thirties, and naturally enough in areas which touched on their own working and living conditions—trades unions, the shortening of factory hours, cooperative societies. Their early efforts were naturally hesitant and often unsuccessful, as the chequered history of Chartism shows very well. Yet with the coming of working-class self-help the story of social reform gains a new dimension, as working people claimed a greater social and political role in the control of their own destinies. Even so, their own leaders tended to be men who had accepted the philosophy of the upper and middle-class reformers, with their authoritarian attitudes towards social improvement. Consequently, the growth of working-class self-help after the middle of the century changed the general direction of social reforms very little.

Social reform, as conceived by this study, covers a number of areas. A good deal has already been said about the poor laws and about education. Before 1830 more attention was given to the poor laws than to any other subject of social concern, and the New Poor Law of 1834 was the most controversial piece of legislation in the 'thirties. After that, although poor law legislation always remained important, it became comparatively less prominent than it had been in the first third of the century. Education is a very interesting and important topic because the welfare of children was always a major problem. They were the most helpless section of the population who could be expected to do very little for themselves. The point has already been stressed that better education was regarded as a cure for pauperism. Education was advocated too as a means of weaning the young away from criminal habits and was thus closely connected with the whole theme of prisons and punishment. An important figure here was Mary Carpenter (1807-1877), who first founded a ragged school in one of the poorest parts of Bristol, and then, in 1852, opened a school at Kingswood for the reformation of young criminals.

Education and personal rehabilitation were closely connected with prisons and methods of punishment. Prison conditions were a constant subject of interest. It was agreed that they should be made more humane than they had been in the eighteenth century, but there were wide differences of opinion about the respective place of deterrence and of reformation in punishment.[20] Education was closely related too to factory legislation, which gained an increasing share of public attention after 1830. Factory Acts, beginning with Graham's Act of 1844, provided that children, their hours of labour having been regulated, should attend school during the free part of the day. Thus began the 'half-time system', which had a long history. It was not abolished until H.A.L. Fisher's Education Act of 1918.

Public Health is a major topic which has hardly been touched on so far. As later chapters will show, public health problems were tackled first of all as local problems. The pioneers were the many bodies of local Improvement Commissioners which, after about 1750, undertook the uphill task of paving the streets of the towns and providing effective sewage systems and water supplies. In the early days the Commissioners were not always very efficient, but their powers and their competence alike grew steadily. It is difficult to over-estimate their importance in laying the foundations of civilized town living.

Hospitals were another important example of local benevolence. During the French Wars much attention was given to hospitals for infectious diseases. Sir Thomas Bernard of the Bettering Society[21] helped to found a Fever Institution in London in 1801 on the plan of a similar institution in Manchester.[22] In the same year a motion was carried in the parish vestry at Liverpool for the establishment of a fever hospital for the poor.[23] The power of medicine to relieve the sick was, of course, still very limited because doctors had an imperfect knowledge of the causes of disease. But those who were concerned with the hospitals felt proud of what they had done. In 1840 the Governors of the London Hospital launched a centenary appeal. Since 1740 their hospital had, they claimed, relieved 'no less than 753,972 poor persons labouring under the heavy visitation of disease or accident'. As London grew, so grew the claims upon the hospital which 'administers medical and surgical relief to a population pre-eminently exposed by its density to disease and by the peculiar nature of its employment to appalling and fearful accidents'. At the centenary dinner over £11,000 was subscribed to the hospital in one evening.[24]

Improvement Commissions and hospitals worked purely on the local scene. The public health question was raised to the status of a national issue by Edwin Chadwick in his great sanitary report of 1842. Enquiries, both national and local, followed, and many controversies too. Chadwick was always a controversial figure, and public health was a matter which inspired argument because whatever was done touched people's pockets. The General Board of Health, set up in 1848, came to an end, and Chadwick himself retired in 1854, but that did not stop the progress of reform. During the ensuing two decades a very important role was played by John Simon, who became medical officer to the reconstituted Board of Health in 1855, and who brought to its problems medical and scientific knowledge of a far more expert kind than Chadwick had possessed.[25]

Finally, there was a wide and indeterminate area of social activity where men felt that they had to act in order to put right an obvious abuse which resulted in cruelty or injustice to helpless people. One example is the demand for more humane treatment of the insane, another is the agitation on behalf of boy chimney sweeps, a third is the problem of regulating the abuses of the immigrant trade. Such subjects lent themselves naturally to publicity; the press was growing in importance and the Victorians rushed quickly into print. W.L. Burn made the point that the mid-Victorians loved a scandal: 'the public washing of dirty linen was one of the most popular of national recreations'.[26] Sometimes such scandals could have a considerable effect on national policy. An example from the history of poor law administration is the Andover Workhouse scandal of 1845 when it was discovered that the paupers were so starved that they fought among themselves for the rotting bones which they had to crush for manure.[27]

Poor Law, Education, Prisons and Punishment, the Factory Acts, Public Health: the field is enormous, and no book could attempt within a reasonable compass to give a factual coverage of the whole. Certainly no such attempt will be made here. The purpose of this study is not primarily to record facts and events, but rather to consider motives and causes. Its purpose is to examine the roots of social change in the century between 1780 and 1880.

iii) Pressures for change in society

At this point the question must be asked why, after the closing decades of the eighteenth century, pressure steadily builds up to bring about social reforms. Social reform is not inevitable; it happens because it is desired and planned by influential people who exercise control over opinion. It should not be thought that, because a society contains within itself great inequalities and injustices, this necessarily means that those inequalities and injustices will be remedied. They have in fact been characteristic of all human societies since time began, and it is only the Western European societies of the last two hundred years which have seriously tried to tackle them. In fact, it is social reform not social passivity or acquiescence which needs explanation because the latter is far the more typical of the human condition. There are two questions which need to be answered. The first is, why in the period under review, was social reform seriously attempted in Britain? The second is, why, it having been attempted, was it generally successful, because once again success in this field is not something that can be taken for granted?

The reformers fell very broadly into three schools; those who were dominated by religious motives; those who were motivated by some goal of secular improvement, the most important school being the Utilitarians; those who were not men of theory but who wanted to deal in a practical way with the pressures of society. All three groups—and naturally many individuals had affinities with more than one—were strongly committed to practical social action. Eighteenth-century religion had a strong connection with practical philanthropy. One example, which goes back into the seventeenth century, is the charity school movement. Another is the agitation against slavery. A third is the long succession of societies for the Reformation of Manners, which also have a pedigree going back to the end of the seventeenth century. A succession of pious writers preached to the rich of the rewards to be enjoyed as the result of benevolence to the poor. Thus Sir Thomas Bernard:

> Where, indeed the object of association between man and man is not merely mutual defence—not a barter of convenience, nor a compact of amusement,—but—to instruct the ignorant, to relieve the wretched, and to protect the weak and defenceless *who can never make a return* . . . the sentiment becomes virtue, and the reward is of the highest and most elevated kind.[28]

All this, and Heaven too, in fact. Much of this kind of argument seems to the modern mind intolerably paternalistic and in many ways so it was. But at least it made the powerful religious interest very conscious of the importance of social conditions and of the plight of the poor.

The contribution of Utilitarianism to social change will be discussed more fully later on, but it is worth making the point here that it is as foolish to ignore its influence as to exaggerate it. Utilitarianism was a reforming creed. Halévy argues that politically speaking it was a creed of central direction. It was the task of the legislator to harmonize and to control the interests of individuals according to the legislator's perception of the general interest. Though the Utilitarians believed in popular sovereignty, they also believed in strong administrative power.[29] In his last major work, the Constitutional Code, Bentham outlined a system of ministries for the social services—an Indigence Relief Minister, an Education Minister, a Health Minister, with wide powers of inspection over both public and private establishments.[30]

Finally the great mass of educated men—squires, clergymen, doctors—who had to grapple with the problems of a changing society were not theorists at all. They became steadily more conscious of the fact that something had to be done to meet social problems which were becoming steadily more difficult. Here the greatest single pressure point was rising population and, in particular, the growth of the towns. There is no need to go into the arguments which divide historians about the reasons for the great rise in population. The fact is incontestable. In 1751 there were perhaps 7¼ million people in Great Britain. At the first census in 1801 there were 10,943,000, a total which in 1831 had grown to 16,359,000. In Ireland in 1821 there were 6,803,000 and in 1831 nearly a million more. The actual addition to the population of towns of over 20,000 inhabitants was 1,100,000 between 1821 and 1831, and 1,800,000 between 1841 and 1851.[31] The fact of population growth provided the basis for the penetrating analysis of Malthus' *Essay on Population*, one of the most influential books of its day. It accentuated problems of poor relief, sanitation and education. It weakened the whole basis of a stable and self-regulating rural order, because population grew as rapidly in the country districts as in the towns. In many of the towns a very large number of the overflowing mass of people were newcomers with all the problems of transition to an urban way of living which this involved. They were packed into tenements or cellars in which epidemic disease spread easily and quickly. The cholera, which broke out for the first time in England in 1831, killed over 16,000 people on its first visitation.[32] There were plenty of native diseases—tuberculosis, smallpox, typhus and typhoid—which were cumulatively even more deadly. Facts such as these could not be ignored. Improvements had to be brought about, and slowly, hesitantly, with many false starts, brought about they were. Individuals, charitable associations, the state itself were all forced to adopt positive policies of social improvement.

The preceding paragraphs attempt to answer the question why social reforms were attempted. The second question—why these reforms were on the whole successful—remains to be answered. It may be instructive here to consider the case of Ireland. In 1831 there were nearly half as many people in Ireland as in Great Britain. On the whole the larger island was able to find employment for its population and became, especially after the middle of the century, steadily richer, while the smaller island suffered from the great famines of the late 'forties and lost a large proportion of its population through emigration. There were two million fewer people in Ireland in 1851 than there had been in 1841.[33] Moreover the country was confronted all through the century with political, religious and agrarian problems of the gravest kind.

The sheer size and intractability of Irish problems led, in the first half of the century, to extensive governmental efforts to deal with them. There was a high degree of central control by the administration in Dublin Castle. The Report of the Royal Commission on Irish Railways (1838) emphasized the need for direct state intervention in society. Public works were financed on a large scale. In 1831 a National Board of Education was created which set up a system of non-sectarian primary schools and in 1845 three university colleges were built and endowed by the government. In all these ways state activity advanced into areas with which at the time the government of Great Britain did not directly concern itself. The Irish situation was in a sense a colonial situation in which administrators were providing institutions which private individuals and associations could not provide for themselves. Ireland and India— and the comparison between the two was often drawn—were social laboratories for nineteenth-century Englishmen.[34]

Perhaps Irish conditions would have been even worse if these measures had not been taken, but clearly an interventionist policy in many fields of social administration did not of itself ensure the happiness and prosperity of Irish society. The point is, of course, obvious that these reforming measures either did not tackle fundamental problems or, like the policy of mixed education, provided solutions which were not acceptable to majority Catholic opinion, however desirable they may have been in themselves. In England there were deep social divisions, but nothing comparable to the terrible gulf between ruler and ruled in Ireland. Gladstone, though he was no social reformer, is perhaps a crucial figure here. His political appeal spanned an enormous gulf between the aristocracy at the one end and the artisans at the other. He was the first English statesman who made an appeal right across the spread of the democratic electorate created in 1867. Even if the wretchedness of the very poor be remembered, Britain was a more unified society when the Queen died than it had been when she came to the throne, and for that reason social improvements were both more effective and easier to carry out.

Behind this easing of social tensions, and to a very large extent responsible for it, lay, of course, the steady advance of economic prosperity. Ireland's economy was stagnant while Britain, though towards the end of the century her advance comparatively speaking slowed down, grew steadily richer. Between 1873 and 1896 prices were falling and real wage-rates rose between 35 and 40 per cent. In 1875 the gross amounts brought under review for Income Tax under Schedule D. (mainly profits) were £267,000,000. By 1896 the total had reached £352,000,000.[35] Economic improvement had been very widely distributed. A society which had become so much richer could afford to enjoy easier relationships and to make a success of reforming policies of many kinds.

An attempt has been made in the last few pages to explain why social reforms were undertaken. One main theme of the book will be to examine the ways in which these reforms were carried out and the motives of those who promoted them. The first point to make is that men of widely differing beliefs often aimed at the same practical objectives. There was a strong dose among both Christians and Secularists of what may be called Environmentalism, or the control of policy by the demands of the practical situation. In the case of the Utilitarians this followed directly from their psychology. They rejected the idea of natural law and argued that knowledge is derived from sense-experience. Causation arises from the association of ideas. James Mill, argued W.H. Burston, 'felt that, in the association principle, he had found something like the fundamental laws of physical science—a single all-pervading principle of explanation'.[36] Furthermore this principle was one of egoism. Men choose what is pleasurable and avoid what is painful. There is no standard of judgment other than that involved in this assessment.

Apart from the Utilitarians, the other major secularist thinker of the early nineteenth century was Robert Owen, whose environmentalism was as complete as theirs. He argued that human character was completely plastic. Those who control the affairs of men can make of them what they will. The first duty of the state is to direct its attention to the formation of character: hence the primary importance of a good educational system. Such a system indeed could not fail because poverty, crime and idleness were simply the results of ignorance. If people are rationally trained, Owen argued, they will behave rationally and will choose honest and useful work rather than employment which is harmful and dishonest. The end of the government, he wrote,

> is to make the governed and the governors happy. That government is then the best, which in practice produces the greatest happiness to the greatest number; including those who govern and those who obey.[37]

It seems at first difficult to apply the environmentalist argument to the many Christians who promoted social improvement, and there are, of course, obvious differences between them and the secularists. No Christian can believe in unlimited social improvement as Owen did, nor find his goal purely in terms of an earthly commonwealth, but, as we have seen, nineteenth-century British Christianity inherited a strong tradition of social action, and was widely committed to policies of social betterment. This point of view was most strongly represented in the early Victorian period by F.D. Maurice and his circle, who preached a doctrine of cooperation not of competition. They felt that the Church must speak to working men in both their spiritual and temporal condition, and they influenced the growth both of the cooperative movement and of adult education. Similar conclusions were forced upon the parish clergy who tried to preach the gospel in the towns. W.F. Hook, the great vicar of Leeds, wrote to Samuel Wilberforce in 1843 that the people in agricultural districts were indifferent to the Church, but that in the manufacturing districts she was detested by the working classes because 'they consider the Church to belong to the party of their oppressors'.[38] Hook's long and selfless labours in Leeds, his practical benevolence and his support for the Ten Hours Bill may have done something to change that opinion in one large town. So may the courage of Charles Lowder, vicar of St. Peter's-in-the-east and of the All Saints' Sisters during the cholera outbreak of 1866 in East London. Lowder, as one of the pioneer Anglo-Catholic slum priests, had faced many difficulties, but, his biographer was told by one of the sisters, 'we never had any trouble after the cholera'.[39]

Another major theme of this book will therefore be to examine the ways in which social theories related to practical reforms. Many reformers were not theorists at all but practical men trying to improve situations which they felt to be intolerable. All alike shared the conviction that the individual had the primary responsibility for his own welfare. Much of men's thinking on these matters was dominated, as we shall see, by the creed of self-help and the practice of philanthropy. The first of these insisted that the individual should improve his condition through his own efforts, the second that he had a duty to help those less fortunate than himself. As the nineteenth century went on, it became increasingly clear that private initiatives, however generous and devoted, could achieve only limited results, and that it would be necessary for the state to intervene more and more. Traditionally—and pre-eminently by A.V. Dicey—the process of legislative change has been seen as a progress from individual responsibility to collective control. There is truth in the argument, but the contrast can be overdone. In many ways it would be more accurate to think of three areas of activity which shade into one another, and all of which co-exist at the same time. The first sphere is that of individual action, expressed most characteristically in the achievements of the great industrialists like Richard Arkwright and Benjamin Gott. The second is that of the group, forming charitable societies and starting agitations. The third is that of the state working through the machinery of central and local government.

Much attention will therefore be given to this curious and subtle relationship between individual, group and state activity, which cooperated at least as often as they clashed. Self-help and philanthropy, as has already been argued, were individualistic doctrines. Yet many of the methods of self-help, adopted by cooperative and friendly societies in the interests of their own members, aimed at purposes which the state desired to promote for the benefit of all citizens. Even the trades unions, which were so harshly criticized by mid-Victorian advocates of free enterprise, were aiming at goals similar to those which the state was trying to achieve through the factory acts. There was a parallel relationship too between private philanthropy and state activity. The development by the Charity Organization Society of systematic enquiry based on case-work created methods of control which the twentieth-century state was able to use. In becoming more efficient, philanthropy became less personal and more regularized. Though its exponents were devoted individualists, their methods prepared the way for state management. The following chapters will be much concerned with these interactions between individualism and collectivism, between self-help, philanthropy and state power. It is more accurate to speak of interactions than of conflicts because there was so much common ground between all these forces. The story begins about 1780 with the dawn of the industrial age. By 1880 the relationships between the individual and the collective, the local and the national, were changing so much that a new period of social history began.

PART I

THE AGE OF PREPARATION 1780-1830

II. The Pioneers of social reform

i) The Background of eighteenth-century England

The general tendency among historians has been to begin the story of nineteenth-century social reform in the 1830's with the enquiries into the Poor Law, the factories and the municipal corporations initiated by the reformed Parliament. These enquiries did not, in fact, arise spontaneously out of the minds of the politicians and administrators of that time. They came when they did partly as the result of the reform of Parliament itself, but they had been prepared for by half a century of planning and discussion, much of it undertaken by local communities, wrestling with their own problems without much aid from the central government. Halévy pointed out long ago that the ancien régime in England was not 'a solid block which did not begin to crumble till about 1832. In reality a great reform movement began about 1780, and although this movement undoubtedly died down during the anti-Jacobin reaction, during the last years of the war it was once more in full swing'.[1] Halévy is talking here about political change, but the same is equally true of social change.

The great reforms of the 1830's have to be traced back to their antecedents in the 1780's and indeed to even earlier decades. The story is a complex one and the threads are not easy to disentangle. The development of social reform was deeply affected by the characteristics of the society in which those reforms were planned. Georgian England was not the sluggish society hit off in the *Vicar of Bray*, 'When George in pudding time came o'er'.

Rather the Georgian age was one of remarkable individuals and of deep-rooted change. From our point of view its crucial theme lies in the contrast between individual initiative and corporate passivity. It was not an age in which institutions flourished. Local municipal institutions were, as we shall see, usually ineffective and frequently corrupt. County government was more efficient, but it was narrow in scope and confined in its personnel to a limited social class. Yet in town and countryside alike merchants and industrialists were, as private individuals, planning the boldest enterprises and laying the foundations of a new industrial age. The English universities were in decay, though they contained in their colleges learned and hard-working men. Organized Christianity was in many ways at a low ebb, yet the century produced one of the greatest of English religious geniuses in John Wesley and a great deal of practical piety in ordinary people.

The contrast between individual achievement and collective inertia was one of the major legacies which the nineteenth century inherited from the eighteenth. This contrast may have been further emphasized by the growing political and economic importance of the Protestant Dissenters who played a very important role in the industrial changes and who achieved equality in the Reform Age. Their religion itself was highly individualistic in tone. More than that, they had been, for a hundred and fifty years or more, excluded from any participation in the national institutions. Organized government to them was an enemy. They had, for generations, been accustomed to depending entirely on their own exertions. In consequence, as they grew in economic and political power, they had very little concept of the role of corporate activity in the life of their society. It took a long time before their inherent individualism was overcome.

For this, and for many other reasons, the nineteenth century inherited from the eighteenth a legacy of administrative weakness. It was easy to believe in 1800 or in 1830 that the private individual, in pursuit of his own interest, served both that interest and the interest of society as a whole. In comparison public and corporate activities all too often lacked both dignity and honesty. A very apposite example comes from the report of the Municipal Corporations Commissioners on the borough of Cambridge. Mr. Starmer, giving evidence about the leasing of the Corporation property, testified

that about the time of the sales to himself and Mr. Alderman Butcher, several members of the Corporation got very good bargains. That Butcher's was the best bargain, but that there were several as good as his [Mr. Starmer's].[2]

There were too many Alderman Butchers and Mr. Starmers in English towns for their contemporaries to be able to appreciate what local government would achieve for the common good.

The story of administrative weakness and of the means adopted to remedy it was worked out by Sidney and Beatrice Webb in their massive series of volumes on *English Local Government from the Revolution to the Municipal Corporation Act*. In one sense, their story is one of administrative failure. The borough corporations had, they argued, lost any sense of public obligation for the effective administration of the town.[3] Even where, as in Liverpool, this was not the case, the small closely-knit Tory group which tended to dominate Corporation affairs became increasingly unpopular with Whigs and Dissenters demanding a greater measure of popular control.[4] Difficulties were at their greatest in London, growing rapidly in size and without any unified administrative system. The City Corporation did little for sanitation, for prisons, and, in striking contrast with the Corporation of Liverpool, nothing to improve the port.[5]

In the Middlesex parishes outside the narrow limits of the City the problems were even greater. In the absence of any competent group of salaried officials, accounts became more and more confused and corruption grew. Many among the Justices of the Peace were corrupted by the same influences as affected the parish officers. In an urbanized society the forces of public opinion and of social pressure which maintained the generally high standards of the rural magistracy had ceased to operate. One particularly serious problem in a great city was the sanitary work carried out by the various Commissions of Sewers. By the beginning of the nineteenth century these Commissions, in places like Westminster, Holborn and Finsbury, had gone much the same way as the parish officers and the Middlesex magistracy. The Metropolitan area had, the Webbs claim,

> become the happy-hunting ground of similar, if not identical gangs of self-seeking building speculators, architects, surveyors and others who could make a profit out of them, whilst the agents of the great estates, keen only on getting for their owners the maximum benefit from the sewers and contributing as little as possible to their cost, had every motive for not making themselves objectionable to the other Commissioners by resenting their minor partialities and corrupt bargains.[6]

London's problems were unique in scale—not in kind. On a smaller scale the same kind of thing was happening in a great urbanized parish like Manchester. Yet it would be a great mistake to underestimate the meliorative influences in late eighteenth and early nineteenth-century society. Long before the central government intervened to decree changes from the centre, the local communities were—slowly, hesitantly, but with increasing assurance and confidence—trying to improve their own ways of doing business. The parishes tried to organize their vestry procedures more effectively, and to find ways of controlling the parish officers. They laid down policy instructions over matters like the letting of contracts and they appointed Standing Committees.[7]

Even more important than these attempts to reform the ancient organs of local government was the creation of new administrative bodies to meet new needs. Many of the measures which are generally regarded as characteristic of the New Poor Law of 1834—the more efficient management of the workhouses, the union of parishes, the employment of salaried officials—had all been attempted in the eighteenth century by the Incorporated Guardians of the Poor which had been established in many areas.[8] The Turnpike Trusts, though often in early days badly managed, were beginning in the early nineteenth century to create an efficient administration. Many of them, in their search for greater efficiency, consulted the great surveyor John Loudon McAdam, who became surveyor of the Bristol district trust in 1815.[9] His son James became surveyor in 1826 of a new body of commissioners incorporating fourteen trusts in the London area north of the Thames.[10]

These reforming ventures very often reflected a combination of local and of central initiatives. Prison reform for example had been a subject of constant debate since the beginning of John Howard's enquiries in the 1770's. During and after the French wars the Home Office had undertaken a steadily more continuous supervision of the Justices of the Peace, of police and of prisons. In 1823 the Prisons Act was passed, the first measure of general prison reform, though it achieved comparatively little. No inspectors were appointed, no sanctions imposed, and very few of the borough prisons were affected.[11] Yet it marked an important step towards closer central control as the national government came to take an ever-increasing share in the regulation of institutions, both of social welfare and of social discipline. The work of successive royal commissions, the creation of central administrative agencies, the increased reliance on detailed statistical information will all be discussed in later chapters. Slowly a new type of directive administrative machine was being created, though there were to be many false dawns and blind alleys along the way. The existence of the necessary machinery on paper did not always mean that it operated successfully in practice. It has been shown, for instance, that there was much more continuity than contrast in the operation of the Old and of the New Poor Laws in Lancashire.[12] It was a particularly difficult task to find competent men to administer the new laws, difficult enough at the level of central authority and even more difficult at the local level of the relieving officers, the workhouse masters, the surveyors of highways, who were immediately responsible for operating the system.

In the case of both the Poor Law and of popular education national policies developed out of local initiatives. The first founders of schools had been pious individuals or parish communities.[13] As the scale of operations grew, the nationally-based society becomes more important, and, in the early nineteenth century, Church and Dissenting interests supported the National Society (1811) and the British Society (1814) respectively. The *Quarterly Review* published an article in 1812 on the occasion of the National Society's first annual report. The bulk of this article is a straightforward defence of the society and of education according to church principles, but stress is also laid on the close inter-dependence of local and of central activity. Unless the local societies and the schools constantly keep in mind 'the necessity of *Union with the parent institution*', they will be left without a head to direct their exertions. The functions of this central body are defined as follows:

> To correspond and to cooperate with its affiliated institutions throughout the kingdom; to hold them together in a bond of general union; to promote uniformity both of principle and of conduct; to provide them with masters from the central institution; and to provide pecuniary assistance as far as its means will permit.[14]

Once again, as in the case of the Poor Law, the thread runs from the local leader, the enthusiastic parish clergyman keen to found a school, through the local society to the national body. In this case the national body is a voluntary organization and not a state department, but it is still a national institution. In some cases, and Education is pre-eminent among them, the great voluntary societies pre-figured the activities of the government departments which were largely to supersede them.

The roots of all these social improvements lie in the philanthropic activities of the eighteenth century. The first of these in time, stretching back indeed into the Restoration period, was the Charity School Movement, based both on local activities and on the work of a national body, the Society for the Promotion of Christian Knowledge, founded in 1698. Its objective had been both spiritual, to save children's souls, and temporal, to improve their condition by enabling them to earn an honest living. The Sunday School Movement, whose first hero is Robert Raikes, aimed later in the eighteenth century to achieve the same goals. Since its schools operated only on one day of the week, its objectives were more limited than those of the charity schools, but on the other hand it influenced a far greater number of children. In a quite different field the century was a time of advances in medical science and of the foundation of hospitals.[15] The London Hospital, founded in 1740, was mentioned in the last chapter.[16] At Birmingham a leading local physician Dr. John Ash suggested the foundation of a General Hospital in 1765. Initially progress was very slow and the building, with about a hundred beds and an outpatients' department, was not opened until 1779. In 1792 a Dispensary was established. Its staff during the War years consisted, in addition to the visiting medical man, of an apothecary, a midwife and a dispenser.[17] Similar institutions were founded in many other towns. For the first time an attempt was being made to use medical knowledge in the service of the great mass of the people. In addition such institutions provided a mass of clinical material for the training of the doctors themselves and for the future elimination of disease.

From the point of view of the social historian, however, much the most important of these eighteenth-century movements for social amelioration is the Campaign against the Slave Trade and Slavery, which began about 1770 and reached its climax with the abolition of slavery in the British Empire in 1833. Traditionally the whole campaign has always been treated by historians as one of the few wholly disinterested acts in the history of the nations, as a campaign directed solely by the demands of an over-riding moral law that men should not be held in subjection by other men. More recently it has been argued that British capitalists destroyed West Indian slavery when the West Indies were no longer economically important to them, and they found the West Indian monopoly a nuisance.[18] From our point of view it is immaterial which view is correct because of the instrinsic interest of the campaigns themselves. Firstly they were the clearest example of a policy of social amelioration motivated by religious impulses. Secondly they illustrate the strength in executing such campaigns of personal and family connections. Thirdly they were the first such movement which systematically made use of publicity and con-stitutional agitation to achieve its ends.

The issues of religious motivation and personal connections will be taken up again later, but something more must be said about the publicity campaign waged by the anti-slavery men, since it pre-figured many later movements during the nineteenth century. Halévy makes the point that they were the first to make systematic use of the right to petition King and Parliament which had been affirmed in the Bill of Rights of 1688.[19] The right to petition formed only one part of what were highly-organized publicity campaigns. In 1792, when Wilberforce attacked the slave-trade in the Commons, 312 petitions were presented from England and 187 from Scotland. These had been preceded by the work of Corresponding Committees throughout the country in close contact with the London Committee, and by organizing tours undertaken by Thomas Clarkson in England and Dr. Dickson in Scotland. It was natural enough to circulate pamphlets and reprints of parliamentary debates. It was more adven-turous to circulate thousands of copies of a poem by William Cowper, *The Negro's Complaint* which had been set to music, while the great potter Josiah Wedgwood designed a cameo depicting a negro in an attitude of entreaty, which was widely used to decorate snuff-boxes, bracelets and hairpins.[20]

By the 1820's the target was the abolition of slavery itself, since the trade in slaves had been forbidden in 1807. Once again the petitions appear—225 of them in 1823, nearly 600 in 1824. In May 1823 Wilberforce published a substantial pamphlet, and in 1824 James Stephen the elder a substantial two-volume work, *The Slavery of the British West*

India Colonies Delineated. What was new was the use of the periodical press. In 1823 the *Anti-Slavery Monthly Reporter* began to appear, to be edited after 1825 by Zachary Macaulay. By that time the press was becoming a serious power, and the *Reporter* was influential, not only because it kept the issue before the public but because it was universally accepted that what it printed was accurate.[21]

The anti-slavery movement, by making use both of parliamentary petitioning and of a monthly periodical, combined the methods of the seventeenth century with those of the nineteenth. It was one of the few major philanthropic campaigns which spanned the years of the great war. Because of its religious background and of the social and political eminence of its proponents, it did not fall a victim to the anti-Jacobin reaction, and for that reason it forms a remarkable link between the philantropy of the eighteenth century in which it originated and the movements of the Reform Era in which its aims were finally achieved.

ii) Foreign war and domestic disturbance

The war years (1793-1815) divide the years of preparation (1780-1830) almost exactly in half. They were years of political repression which put back the changes, which had seemed so near at hand in the 1780's, for a generation. While Britain fought the French Revolution abroad, she experienced the full force of the industrial and agricultural revolutions at home. New disciplines, new habits of life had to be created for the industrial workers, while out-workers like the weavers, who had at first profited from the growth of machine-spinning, sank into a long decline. Their living standards steadily fell as their trade grew more and more overcrowded. It was a harsh age in which great fortunes were made—and as easily lost. All alike, from worker to industrialist, were exposed to ruthless competitive forces which contemporaries understood very imperfectly.

Historians have keenly debated the effect of all these changes on the living standards of the people in the crucial half-century from 1790 to 1840. It seems to be agreed that initially the rich and well-to-do classes benefited most from the changes. H.J. Perkin, attempting to sum up the argument, concluded that industrial changes affected the living standards of different sectors of the population in different ways. Among working men the first group to benefit were the craftsmen, people like printers, joiners, cabinet-makers and the like, followed by the cotton operatives and the factory workers. On the other hand the handicraftsmen like the handloom weavers and the framework knitters steadily lost ground, and the poorest of all were the farm workers whose condition in the South of England did not improve at all until after 1870. Though the long-term trend was towards a higher standard of living overall, this was achieved through the advance of some groups and the suffering and ultimate disappearance of others.[22] Even after 1850 when standards did rise all round the enquiries of Booth and Rowntree at the end of the century showed the wide extent of poverty and misery which still existed in the nation. For the earlier period (1790-1840) E.J. Hobsbawn rejected the view that general living standards were rising and considered it to be at least possible that during this time these standards declined, though it is impossible on the basis of the evidence available to reach a conclusive judgment.[23] Working men remained very near subsistence level while their betters were clearly advancing very rapidly. As E. P. Thompson wrote, the workers were 'surrounded by the evidence of the increase of national wealth, much of it transparently the product of [their] own labour and passing, by equally transparent means, into the hands of [their] employers'.[24]

Hobsbawm makes the point that the widespread popular discontent of the early nineteenth century is very difficult to explain on the basis of an optimistic explanation of economic change whereas 'on a gloomy interpretation, the popular discontent . . . makes sense'.[25] The war years were certainly a time of tension and crisis when the upper classes feared, on occasions at least, that they might share the fate of their fellows across the channel. One particular time of stress occurred during the Luddite riots of 1812. An event like the Luddite attack on William Cartwright's mill at Rawfolds in the Spen Valley of the West Riding survived in men's memories to re-appear as the attack on Gérard Moore's mill in Charlotte Bronte's *Shirley*, published in 1849.[26] As the towns grew in size, political agitation also grew among the working people, and the government feared the spread of political activities which might easily cross over the line into political conspiracy. Twenty years before the attack on Rawfolds the Deputy Adjutant General had described the association formed by the Sheffield mechanics. 'Here they read the most violent publications, and comment on them, as well as on their correspondence not only with the dependent Societies in the towns and villages in the vicinity, but with those established in other parts of the Kingdom.'[27]

How significant, in wider terms, was an event like the attack on Rawfolds? Was there any serious danger in the war years and immediately afterwards that the discontent which undoubtedly existed among the working masses would spill over into revolution? The general tendency among historians has been to argue that, though there was a good deal of disorder from time to time, much of it connected with the absence of a proper police force and the need to call in the military to keep order, the line of development was towards an orderly and peaceful solution of social and political problems as exemplified in the career of a working-class Radical like Francis Place.[28] Halévy explained the stability of English institutions by the strong influence of Methodist and Evangelical ideas on the leaders of the working class, who had, he argued, 'been imbued by the Evangelical movement with a spirit from which the established order had nothing to fear.[29] A historian of our own day, Professor McCord, in a study of the North-East, has written of the strength of the conciliatory forces in English central government and local society. When, he argues, it is considered how great were the strains to which early nineteenth-century society was submitted it is remarkable how little social conflict, violence and bloodshed accompanied them.[30]

The major opponent of what may be called the 'conciliatory' view is E.P. Thompson. In his book *The Making of the English Working Class* (1963) he argued that there was an active revolutionary tradition working underground throughout the period 1790-1830. He is particularly interesting on Luddism, the movement against machinery in the Midlands and the North during the last years of the war. The Luddites had, he considers, a hidden revolutionary fringe, very difficult to trace because of the suppression of evidence by the interested parties. They were not merely ignorant hand-workers blindly striking out against machinery. Theirs was, he argued, 'a *quasi-insurrectionary movement*, which continually trembled on the edge of ulterior revolutionary objectives'.[31] Nor did the tradition end with the riots of 1812. The leader of the Pentridge rising of 1817 in Derbyshire, Jeremiah Brandreth, was by persistent tradition a Luddite, even perhaps a Luddite 'captain'.[32]

Thompson himself argues that after 1817 the constitutionalists dominated working-class agitation, as the danger of armed conspiracy receded.[33] There can be no doubt that the fear of a revolutionary uprising had, from time to time, a considerable influence both on the policy of the government and on the general attitudes of the well-to-do classes. Several modern writers have noted that during the war years charity took on a harsher and more repressive tone. More emphasis was placed on the need to discriminate and to limit aid exclusively to the deserving. Writers like Patrick Colquhoun, of whom more will be said later, [34] showed little optimism about what private benevolence had been able to achieve. Indeed it seemed to them that 'a prodigious outlay for charity had produced only trivial benefits'.[35] There could have been many reasons for this feeling, not least of them the fear of ever-rising population . Yet another factor may have been the fear of violence, among a pauperized population which had lost the habit of relying on its own exertions and was very ready to demand as a right what had first been given to it as a charitable concession.

By 1830 some experienced observers certainly believed that the condition of the people had improved, whatever may be the views of modern economists and historians. Perhaps this helps to explain the weakening of the revolutionary impulse in the post-war years. Edwin Chadwick published his first article in *The Westminster Review* in 1828 on 'Life Assurances'. In considering the whole subject of protection against illness and mortality he argued that there was a pressing need for more statistical information, not only about the expectation of life itself, but about related subjects like wages, food prices, the age of marriage and the fruitfulness of women. He pointed out the great differences in mortality which existed between different classes, and the deleterious effects on the poor of poverty and bad diet. Yet he also argued that the mode of living among all classes, including the workers, had improved. Artisans, for example, 'are more cleanly and regular, their houses are better constructed, they have acquired some notion that fresh air is conducive to health, and the streets where they reside are less filthy and pestilential than formerly'.[36]

A very similar picture is given by Francis Place, who had grown up among London tradesmen and who had established himself successfully in business as a tailor. He makes it clear in his autobiography that in his view there had been great moral and social improvements since his childhood in the 1770's. The people among whom he had grown up were, he thought, dirty, drunken, obscene and depraved in their habits, and many of them had come to financial ruin in consequence. He explained this great change as arising from a variety of reasons. Among them a were a better regulated police and magistracy, better health and greater cleanliness, the rapid increase in trade and wealth after the American War, the breakdown of traditional notions by the French Revolution, the promotion of an active interest in politics among working men by the political societies, and the spread of education.[37] A somewhat mixed bag perhaps, but the very diversity of the causes given makes it clear that Place believed there had been progress along a very wide front.[38]

Both Chadwick and Place were, in the passages which have been quoted, recording their own impressions and such impressions are not verifiable by any objective test. Both were however intelligent and thoughtful observers, and their testimony about an improvement in social conditions cannot be discounted. It is worth pointing out that Chadwick specifically mentioned the artisans and Place seemed to be thinking principally of skilled workmen and tradesmen. Perhaps these people were the favoured group of craftsmen, the labour aristocracy who, H.J. Perkin argues, were the first among the workers to benefit from the changes of the new industrial era. It was a long time before the great mass of working men were as fortunate as they. By 1830 improvement had hardly begun. The worlds of the poor and of the well-to-do were divided by a gulf so deep that it was difficult for sympathy and human understanding to bridge it. Many observers bemoaned the deep cleavages between the classes and the heedlessness of the rich about the sufferings of the poor. Many would have echoed the sentiments expressed by J.C. Symons, one of the early H.M.I.s, who compared the situation in England with that of other countries:

... I have lived among some of the older nations of Continental Europe, where I have seen family prestige and the distinctive privileges of lineage upholden even more tenaciously than in England, and never have I elsewhere witnessed the same alien spirit or class antagonism, especially between the labourer and his employer, as have so often riven asunder and deadened social sympathies in England.[39]

That judgement, made in the 'fifties, is as true of the period before 1830 as of the decades after that date.

To Symons and many like him social reform was a secular crusade which inspired a missionary spirit in its devotees. This spirit grew steadily in intensity as men appreciated more and more clearly the scope of the problems and the enormous tasks which lay before them if adequate solutions were to be achieved. The reformers themselves did not form a single school and they advocated many different solutions. All of them, however, whatever their individual opinions, shared four basic characteristics. The first of them was a serious reflective temper which measured individual lives by the standard of broad ideals and principles and which was combined with a crusading passion for human betterment. Such a temper may correctly be described as religious, though many of the reformers were not themselves orthodox Christians. Secondly, these men were, by birth or by their own achievement, members of the upper and upper middle classes, and they had close links with the small and coherent ruling group. Without such a background the reformers would have lacked either the leisure or the education to participate in schemes of improvement, nor could they have gained an audience among the people who mattered.

Thirdly, they believed in self-help, individualism and hard work. Their creed of improvement laid even more stress upon deterring the idle and the improvident than upon encouraging the industrious and the thrifty. They certainly wanted to improve the lot of the poor but their prescriptions were often harsh, even punitive in their nature, and they seem to us sometimes to be lacking in ordinary human sympathy. The reformers of all schools were strongly authoritarian. They combined with their individualism, in a way which was more deeply felt than logically argued, a strong paternalism. They believed that they could see the directions in which the poor man ought to walk, and that it was for him to follow obediently in the paths which they had laid down. Many, though not all of them, came in consequence to believe more and more strongly in the benevolent activity of the state and desired to extend its authority.

These four themes—the religious temper, the upper-class background, the individualism, the paternalism—were exemplified in many individuals who formed part of the very small group enjoying political, social and economic power in early nineteenth-century England. Among this group, because it was small, personal ties were naturally very close. It is to those ties and to a more detailed study of the reformers' motives that attention must now be given. The patterns, alike of motive and of personal friendship, reflect the characteristics of the Age of Preparation which have been surveyed in this chapter.

III. Reformers and their ideals

i) Relationships between men of different schools

Some of the reformers, like Jeremy Bentham and Henry Brougham, are still very familiar figures in the history books. The people we now remember were, on the whole, men who lived and worked in London, and who were thus in a position to influence national opinion through their access to Parliament, the law courts and the press. Yet it is a great mistake to think of social reform exclusively in centralist or national terms. London was, as it had been for centuries, much the greatest of cities, but it did not represent the whole of Britain. Society in the early nineteenth century was still intensely localized. The great landowners, in their estates and their great mansions, had local power-bases on which their influence at Court or in Parliament depended. They were, of course, a rural aristocracy, deeply imbued with country habits and interests, but the source of their wealth did not derive entirely from the land. The dichotomies, traditional to the history books, between town and country or industry and agriculture are in many ways over-simplified. The Duke of Bedford had great rural estates in the South Midlands and in the West, but much of his wealth came from the London properties in Bloomsbury and Covent Garden. Lord Fitzwilliam was a great West Riding landowner, but that very fact made him a participant in the growing wealth of the area round his palace at Wentworth Woodhouse, when the coal seams were developed in South Yorkshire. At lower levels too there was a constant interchange between landed and commercial wealth. Sir George Onesiphorus Paul (1746-1820) was a Gloucestershire magistrate who is remembered as a prison reformer. The family wealth had been made in the manufacture of fine woollen cloth at Woodchester in the same county.

The society of the early nineteenth century was centred on the county towns and on the major centres of commerce and industry. The influences radiating from London were certainly very important, but they were crossed and inter-penetrated by other influences emanating from scores of provincial towns and great houses. The giants like Bedford or Fitzwilliam were very much divided in their interests between London and the areas in which they held estates. The substantial gentry and the richer beneficed clergy, who made up the County Commissions of the Peace, were much more strongly localized. In an age when the power of the central government was weak, the local nobility and gentry controlled the government of the counties far more completely than in any other period of modern English history. County society threw up local leaders who worked to regulate the condition of the poor, to improve roads and bridges and to clean up the prisons. Their local activities often influenced national policy. The standard of efficiency of the county Commissions of the Peace was rising in the early nineteenth century. At the same time they were becoming more socially exclusive, a fact which did not endear them to the Radicals and Dissenters who became more powerful when the Age of Reform began. The Webbs made the point that almost every statute passed about 1830 which altered the law of local government took away some power from the county magistracy. What is remarkable, however, is not how much authority the justices lost but how much they retained. No-one wanted to replace them by stipendiary magistrates, and there was no real possibility of an elected county board, which would take their place.[1] It was not until 1888 that the counties acquired an elected system of local government.

Like the counties, the towns had their own leaders. The contrast which has already been drawn between individual enterprise and corporate passivity[2] can be traced in them in its most marked form. The municipal corporations were at best inactive, at worst corrupt, but the towns also contained, alongside their official rulers, many intelligent, forward-looking, public-spirited men who gave an unofficial leadership to their fellow citizens. It is a mistake to think of the towns merely as gloomy collections of disease-ridden hovels, fouled by effluent and darkened by industrial smoke. The wealth brought by commerce and industry gave some men leisure for intellectual interests or for improving the condition of their fellows. It provided a livelihood for professional men, such as doctors, whose concerns often extended beyond their own patients to the foundation of hospitals or the removal of nuisances which bred disease.[3]

The growth of the new industrial towns strengthened the role of these provincial centres of wealth, culture and new ideas. London in 1750 had been overwhelmingly the most important city in England, in a different class entirely from the old provincial capitals like York, Norwich or Exeter. By 1850 the growth of Manchester and Birmingham, of Liverpool, Leeds and Sheffield, had done something to reduce that disparity. One particularly interesting development is the growth of societies in the major provincial centres which stimulated intellectual and scientific discussion among their members. Among the pioneers was the Lunar Society in Birmingham which included among its members Matthew Boulton and James Watt, Joseph Priestley and Erasmus Darwin. Its recent historian dates the first meeting of the society to the New Year of 1775-6[4] but the members of the circle which created it had been in touch with one another for a number of years before that. The Manchester Literary and Philosophical Society was founded in 1781, and these pioneer bodies were followed by similar institutions in many of the larger centres. The merchants, industrialists and business men who founded them also created reading rooms and subscription libraries.

Their zeal for information, their desire to exchange idea commercial interests produced an increasingly active provincial press. In one sense the new industrial age strengthened the unifying forces in Britain because it helped to make the whole country a single economic unit. On the other hand, industrial and mercantile profits, by creating new and more widely diffused centres of wealth, strengthened and enriched the life of the provinces, and made the major towns places of creative activity in a wide variety of fields.

Two men may be taken as exemplars of the townsmen who were trying to find solutions for the problems of their age. Thomas Percival of Manchester (1740-1804) and James Currie of Liverpool (1756-1805) were both medical men. Percival had been a pupil at the Dissenting Academy at Warrington.[5] After studying medicine both at Edinburgh and at Leiden, he settled at Manchester in 1767. In his early years there he drew up a scheme for establishing accurate bills of mortality, a subject on which he corresponded with Benjamin Franklin. His study of comparative death rates led him to point out the much greater unhealthiness of the town of Manchester in comparison with the surrounding rural districts, and he emphasised the very high death rate of children in the great towns.[6] This tendency to demand accurate statistics is fundamental to the development of any effective social policy. In 1796 Percival was active in establishing a Board of Health in Manchester which aimed to put down fever and epidemic disease by providing hospital treatment for the sufferers as well as better sanitation and greater cleanliness in the districts inhabited by the poor.[7] Percival's activities were by no means limited to preventive medicine and public health. He was an early supporter of the abolition of the slave trade. He was deeply interested in providing better educational and cultural opportunities in Manchester. The Literary and Philosophical Society began with meetings in his house. He helped to promote the Manchester Academy which was intended to educate both dissenting ministers and young men going into commerce. He supported the College of Arts and Sciences, an institution for public lectures in mathematics, science, the fine arts, commerce and manufactures. The College lasted only a very short time, and the Academy closed in 1802. Nevertheless both institutions illustrate the way in which a new and thrusting community was trying to meet its needs for new and for more widely disseminated knowledge.

Percival was one of the most wide-ranging and versatile of these town leaders, though James Currie of Liverpool runs him close.[8] In 1786 he was made one of the physicians of the Liverpool Infirmary. He was interested in the treatment of the insane and he took a leading part in creating a lunatic asylum in connection with the Infirmary. After a good deal of effort he persuaded the parish vestry of Liverpool to establish a hospital for contagious diseases. Nor were his interests limited to medical matters. In 1800 he published his life of Robert Burns. He took part in the foundation of the Athenaeum Library and Newsroom, writing to his son that hitherto the town had had nothing better than 'a common circulating library' but that it was proposed to establish 'a library of valuable books'.[9] Like Percival he was an opponent of the slave trade and he corresponded with him on that topic, about political matters like the Repeal of the Test and Corporation Acts, and about the establishment of a House of Recovery for the sick at Manchester. One of Currie's letters to Percival on the last subject echoes the perpetual cry of the reformer:

> Yet, when I consider by what irrefragable as well as by what important considerations it was supported, how vehemently it was opposed, and, if I mistake not, how narrowly it escaped being overthrown, I confess to you my satisfaction is mingled with wonder and sorrow, and I reflect with a sigh on this new proof, how little man is rational![10]

Hard the task of the reformer might be, but by 1800 the work of social improvement was becoming increasingly popular among men of position in both town and countryside. In an age where the large landowners dominated society many of the local leaders were naturally drawn from the ranks of the aristocracy and the commercial men who had become assimilated with it. Some of them, like John Howard and Sir George Onesiphorus Paul the prison reformers, concentrated their attentions on a single class of evils. Many, like Thomas Butterworth Bayley (1743-1802), perpetual chairman of Lancashire Quarter Sessions, extended their concerns very widely. He was actively involved in the erection of a new gaol in Manchester and with the improvement of the County Gaol in Lancaster Castle. He was interested in workhouses, and was in favour of the public control of conditions of work in factories. He was consulted by Robert Peel over the bill for regulating the conditions of parish apprentices which became the first Factory Act of 1802, though he considered that the Act did not go far enough. He was interested in education. He encouraged Sunday Schools and was involved both with the Manchester Literary and Philosophical Society and with the College of Arts and Sciences. He was active in promoting the abolition of the slave trade, and was the first person who signed the petition against it in Manchester.[11]

Men like Bayley might be called 'cross-fertilizers', because they represented so many interests. They were not ideologues but men of good will who struggled to set evils right wherever they found them. The three great dogmatic forces which impelled men towards social change in the early part of the nineteenth century were religious conviction, political economy and Utilitarianism. Since they were predominant in the intellectual atmosphere of the day they affected everyone, whether consciously or unconsciously, but the local leaders were not directly inspired by such theoretical considerations. They saw the world around them full of problems and difficulties. Faced with situations which often seemed intolerable, they did what they could to deal with those situations in the light of such knowledge as they had. Their own common sense and warmth of feeling directed their efforts far more than any political or social theory.

This cast of mind was to be found not only in the countryside but among many of the leading men in London. In the country it was characteristic of the other two social groups who, together with the squirearchy, took the principal role, the parsons and the doctors. The clergy played an active part in the local government of parish and county. It was a country incumbent, Richard Burn, vicar of Orton in Westmorland, who wrote the standard treatise on the duties of the Justice of the Peace, and many of the Justices who took a leading part in the affairs of the County Commission and in the management of the Poor Law were clerics. The same width of interest that we have already noted in T.B. Bayley can be seen in the career of the clerical poor law reformer, J.T. Becher of Southwell. Like Bayley he was a chairman of Quarter Sessions. He rebuilt the House of Correction at Southwell and was particularly interested in finding the inmates work and in rehabilitating them by rewarding them according to their exertions.[12] He gave evidence on the subject to a House of Commons Select Committee in 1811, in the course of which he criticized Bentham's proposed scheme for a national penitentiary.[13] A few years later he was examined, by another Select Committee, on the better regulation of madhouses, since he was a governor of the Nottingham Asylum which had been set up a few years previously on the humane lines pioneered by the Quakers in the Retreat at York.[14] As side issues from his major interest in the poor law he wrote on book-keeping methods for Savings Banks, on Friendly Societies, and on 'a system of endowments for the Provident classes in every station of life'.[15]

The medical men were figures of the town rather than of the country. J.P. Kay (-Shuttleworth), one of the most famous of them, had been a pupil in Edinburgh of W.P. Alison whose work among the poor convinced him of the connection between destitution and epidemic disease and who fought for a more uniform and regular system of poor relief in Scotland.[16] Kay worked in his early years of professional life as a medical man in Manchester, but later on he moved into public service, passing through the poor law into education, and thus came to London. It should be noted how many of the practical reformers in the years after 1830 were doctors. Thomas Wakley of the *Lancet* (1795-1862) campaigned on many issues from mismanagement by the Royal College of Surgeons to the adulteration of food. Thomas Southwood Smith (1788-1861) was a friend of Jeremy Bentham, wrote on medical matters for the *Westminster Review*, and served on official enquiries into factory conditions and children's employment. William Farr (1807-83) did important statistical work in the Registrar-General's office and as a census commissioner. Sir John Simon (1816-1904) was a pioneer of modern public health services.

The contribution of the medical profession to social improvement all through the nineteenth century was certainly very remarkable. Despite the serious limitations of their medical knowledge, the doctors were the only applied scientists with a regular professional training, who had learned to observe and to record in a systematic way. Their activities increasingly spanned the whole country, through government service, medical journalism, the hospitals and private practice. One aspect of their work which is worth noting is the foundation, through the efforts of the medical men themselves, of local medical schools. For the first time a general medical qualification was made available to provincial practitioners when an act of 1815 authorized the Society of Apothecaries to hold examinations and grant licences to practice. In the West Riding, for example, a group of Leeds doctors opened a medical school in 1831.[17] In Sheffield the Medical Institution had been opened in 1829.[18]

One of the leading promoters of the Sheffield medical school was Dr. A.J. Knight. An Edinburgh graduate like Kay and physician to the Sheffield Infirmary, he was also the first president of the Sheffield Literary and Philosophical Society and one of the founders both of the Public Dispensary and of the Mechanics' Institute.[19] Knight, to use the term already introduced, was another of the 'cross-fertilizers'. In an age when specialism had not developed and when the educated group was small, such men took an active share in all the concerns of their area. This is understandable enough in a remote provincial town like Sheffield, where the educated group was small indeed, but it is also true to a considerable extent of London itself. Here too those who were interested in social improvement formed quite a small circle, and the ties between them were close.

The relationships of Bentham and his circle are of particular interest from this point of view. The spread of Utilitarian ideas can be related very closely with personal contacts, first of all those made by Bentham himself and subsequently those made by his disciples. Nor were these connections confined to people who shared a common philosophy, because the lines of personal contact and common concern ran across ideological barriers in a very remarkable way. Men who began from very different viewpoints often combined to achieve common ends. In the Bentham circle James Mill occupied a special place. Bentham met Mill, who was to become one of his most active disciples, in 1808. Four years later Mill introduced to him Francis Place, the radical tailor who was a very effective propagandist and election manager. Later Place went to stay with Bentham at Forde Abbey in Dorset, and, after Mill's appointment to the India Office in 1819, Bentham relied more on Place for companionship.[20] It was through James Mill too that Bentham met David Ricardo, Robert Owen, and Joseph Lancaster.[21] The concern for popular education and the interest in the mutual system of instruction, which

Lancaster had pioneered, were shared by Bentham and his disciples, who were free-thinkers in religious matters, and by the Quakers and other Nonconformists who were prominent in the British and Foreign School Society. Mill and Place worked together in 1813-14 in the West London Lancasterian Association, though eventually Place withdrew from the movement, partly because he did not see eye to eye with its Non-conformist supporters.[22]

Throughout Bentham's life law reform was one of his major pre-occupations. As early as 1784 he had made the acquaintance of Samuel Romilly (1757-1818), who was the first campaigner in Parliament for a more humane penal code, and, four years later, through Lord Lansdowne, Bentham again met Romilly and made the acquaintance of Romilly's friend, the Swiss Dumont, who did more than anyone else, as the editor and reviser of Bentham's works, to disseminate the master's ideas.[23] Apart from his interest in legal reform, which gave him a link with Bentham, Romilly was also an opponent of the slave trade, and, though himself a deist in religion, a friend of the devout Evangelical William Wilberforce.

Slavery, like prison reform and popular education, was a subject which interested reformers of all shades of opinion. Romilly himself was in some ways one of the 'cross-fertilizers'. A much better example of a reformer who had links with people of widely differing views was the Whig politician and law-reformer, Henry Brougham. Brougham is a key figure in the reforming movements of the time, and a man who, in his heyday in the 1820's, enjoyed a very wide personal influence in the country. He was the only one of the major leaders of the campaign against the slave trade and slavery itself who was not an Evangelical.[24] In 1811 he carried through the Act which made the carrying of slaves a felony. In 1823 he was an early supporter of the movement for the total abolition of slavery, leading an attack on the treatment of the missionary John Smith, who had died in prison, having been sentenced to death after a slave rising in Demerara.

He was deeply interested in popular education. He played an active part in the foundation in 1811 of the Royal Lancasterian Institution, later the British and Foreign School Society, and was a friend of the Quaker William Allen who had worked with Lancaster. He played a leading part in the enquiry of 1816 into the education of the London poor and the enquiry of 1818 into charities. In 1820 he introduced an Education Bill which would have enabled the government to set up schools. He was an active promoter of Mechanics' Institutes, and he initiated the Society for the Diffusion of Useful Knowledge, because he was particularly interested in making good reading material available to working people. At much the same time as he was advocating better education for the poor, he was one of the main initiators of the scheme for a University in London. In 1828 he made an important speech in the Commons in favour of law reform, which resulted in the appointment of commissions to investigate the

Common Law and the law of real property. Most of the reforms which he had proposed were adopted in the ensuing ten years.[25]

Brougham had connections with all shades of opinion and, as an active writer in the *Edinburgh Review*, he used the new engine of the press to appeal to a wide audience. Though he was not a Benthamite, he was in personal contact with Bentham and he was for a long time a friend of James Mill. Through his interest in education, he had contacts both with the Quakers and with Robert Owen, who shared with him a keen interest in infant schools. In 1830 Brougham became Lord Chancellor in Grey's Whig government. During the previous twenty years there had been few movements to improve the condition of the people which he had not actively promoted. Like the local leaders who have already been described, he was neither an ideologue nor a theoretician, but a practical man who struggled to set right the abuses which he saw around him. To achieve that objective he was ready to work with all men who shared that common purpose.

ii) The Religious impulse

It has already been suggested that the three great ideological forces behind social change were religious conviction, political economy and Utilitarianism, and that the Antislavery Movement is the clearest example of a policy of social amelioration directed by religious impulses. Among the leaders of the antislavery crusade the so-called Clapham Sect, closely linked both by personal relationships and by Evangelical faith, were men of social and political weight. William Wilberforce was their best known political spokesman, but the banker Henry Thornton and the lawyer James Stephen, the proponent of the Orders-in-Council against maritime trade with France, were also important parliamentarians during the war years. Lord Teignmouth had been Governor-General of the British territories in India, and Charles Grant controlled the affairs of those territories at India House. Zachary Macaulay had put the infant Sierra Leone colony, founded in 1787, for freed slaves, onto its feet, and he later became an effective propagandist in the antislavery cause. Nor was that cause the only philanthropic work fostered by the Evangelicals. Among the other activities which they actively promoted were the foundation of the Church Missionary Society in 1799 and of the British and Foreign Bible Society in 1804.

The philanthropic work of the Evangelicals of that time is of great importance. Some forty years later the younger James Stephen painted a very vivid and attractive picture of Wilberforce and the Clapham circle in the *Edinburgh Review*.[26] T.B. Macaulay, himself like Stephen the son of one of the Clapham leaders, commented in a letter to one of his sisters:

I think Stephen's article on the Clapham Sect the best thing he ever did. I do not think with you that the Claphamites were men too obscure for such delineation. The truth is that from that little knot of men emanated all the Bible Societies, and about all the Missionary Societies in the world. The whole organisation of the Evangelical party was their work. The share which they had in providing means for the education of the people was great. They were really the destroyers of the slave-trade, and of slavery. Many of these whom Stephen describes were public men of the greatest weight.[27]

It can be argued that religious men often planned a better future for the poor and oppressed in the next world rather than in this, and on many practical issues like factory reform men with equally strong religious motives often took opposite sides. The sheer total weight of religious influence was very great, even though it did not always bear in a single direction. One interesting example is the growth in the publication of religious literature. Within its first half-century (1804-54) the British and Foreign Bible Society 'distributed about sixteen million English Bibles and Testaments. In 1804 the Religious Tract Society printed 314,000 copies of tracts; by 1861 its annual output was in the neighbourhood of twenty million tracts, in addition to thirteen million copies of periodicals. The S.P.C.K., meanwhile, raised its yearly production from 1,500,000 in 1827 to over eight million in 1867'.[28] Very many of these books and tracts must have remained unread, but the total influence of such a barrage of print cannot have been negligible, whether it provoked acceptance or revulsion among those who read it. The obvious parallel in our own day is the social effect of television.

Many of those who worked for better social conditions were deeply religious people. Among the prison reformers John Howard and Elizabeth Fry are obvious examples. Among the factory reformers of the post-1830 generation Lord Shaftesbury is another. Much of the information given to the Select Committee of 1816 on children's employment in factories by those who wished to reduce the hours worked was derived from the Sunday Schools. These schools were probably the only places, outside the factories themselves, where it was possible to talk to and to observe the factory children, while it was also possible there to compare the appearance of the children who worked in factories and those who did not. If the children worked shorter hours, it was argued, they would have more opportunity, to gain instruction and might be able to attend the National Schools.[29] The connection between factory conditions, religious belief and education in the reformers' minds is very apparent.

Sir Thomas Bernard (1750-1818), who has already been mentioned in the first chapter, [30] is a very interesting example of a philanthropist whose objectives were strongly influenced by religious ideas. Like so many men of his kind he had ties with Wilberforce and was an opponent of the slave trade. He was very interested in hospitals, doing a good deal both to reform the Foundling and to create Fever and Cancer Hospitals in

London. He was a strong advocate of better education for the poor, because he saw it as one of the principal ways by which hard work and regular habits of life might be promoted among them. Like Dr. Andrew Bell and the founders of the National Society, he argued that 'a system of moral and religious instruction, *connecting the rising generation with our civil and ecclesiastical establishment*, is not only the first and most beneficial act of charity, but the wisest and most politic measure of the state'.[31] A relative and the diocesan chancellor of the philanthropic Bishop Barrington of Durham, he wrote an account of the Barrington School at Bishop Auckland which had been founded, on Bell's system, both to educate children and to train teachers.[32]

Bernard's philanthropic ideas are most clearly set out in the prefaces which he wrote to the Reports of the Bettering Society, which he had founded in 1796.[33] Much of what he wrote about the condition of the poor and the poor laws is conventional enough in the terms of the great debate on poverty during the war years. He wanted to reduce parochial expenses, he feared the extravagance which prevailed in the workhouses, he opposed attempts to fix the rate of labour according to the price of bread. Yet his ideas are much more positive than those of many of his contemporaries. He saw that exhortation was not enough and that the poor must be helped in a practical way to help themselves. He wanted to provide good cottages for them, to see that they had gardens and were able to rent a small piece of land so that they might keep a cow. He wanted to ensure adequate supplies of fuel, to provide a village shop in which they might make their purchases, a mill and an oven in which they might grind their corn and cook their food. The true social policy was, he argued, to build up the poor man's life around his cottage and his domestic attachments. 'The cottager, unused to change of place or condition, centres all his desires to the spot where he was born, and the family to which he has given birth.'[34]

There is a warmth and natural sympathy with the poor in Bernard's writing which was not always characteristic of the philanthropists of his day. Yet he too shared the strong belief of his contemporaries in social discipline. If the poor were to learn the advantages of steady and industrious habits, they must be kept clear from the contagion of idleness and vice. Among the dangers which Bernard pointed out were breaches of the Sabbath, the prevalence of spirit drinking, the evil done by lotteries and by 'profane and immoral representations on the stage'.[35] In 1787 the King had issued a proclamation condemning Sabbath-breaking, drunkenness and immoral amusements, and an active society, later re-named the Society for the Suppression of Vice, maintained an active warfare against such moral evils, and against Sabbath-breaking in particular.[36] Moral crusades of this kind took up, all through the nineteenth century, a very large part of the time, the interest and the money of the Churches and the religious societies.

The religious interest was united in its general views about the obligations upon individuals of the moral law, but it was sometimes sharply divided over the application of moral principles to practical politics. One particular bone of contention all through the century was the development of popular education, because the creation of new educational institutions was seen to have important political con- sequences. The Church of England claimed that the church of the nation should control the schools of the nation. The Nonconformists, gradually throwing off the shackles of political and social inferiority, were not willing to grant to the Church in the schools what they had rejected in political and religious terms ever since the seventeenth century. The contest which began in the first decades of the nineteenth century between the supporters of Andrew Bell and of Joseph Lancaster flared up for the last time in the conflicts over the Education Act of 1902. The conflict held up the development of a national educational system and even threatened the stability of governments. All the major issues of social reform created controversy at one time or another, but education alone provided a major political issue over a long period of time. In a society with deep religious divisions it was inevitable that this should have been the case. There was no other social issue over which opinion polarized in the same way.

iii) The Political economists

Political economy was the second major ideological force in effecting change and here we move into very different areas of concern. The political economists were not philanthropists like the churchmen. Rather they influenced social reforms because they were analysts. Their objective was not to relieve suffering in its obvious manifestations, but to search out the roots of the problems which caused it, and to suggest ways in which society might so order its affairs that those basic evils might be removed. Their methods form part of the movement towards the quantitative examination of social questions which is one of the major characteristics of the new industrial age. Indeed the very existence of political economy itself was a part of that new age, both a cause and an effect of the rapid changes transforming society in the century after 1750. The new society knew much greater and more widely distributed wealth than the old, but the transitions between wealth and poverty were much more rapid and more intense. More and more, men's livelihood lay at the mercy of international movements, of booms and slumps which had no direct relationship with the economic life of the region affected by them. The political economists, beginning with Adam Smith, provided a key to the problem based very broadly on the idea that the wisest course was to encourage individual enterprise and to remove the barriers imposed on economic life by governmental restrictions.

We in the later twentieth century err if we think of the political economy of the early nineteenth century as the 'dismal science'. To the men of that day it was not dismal, but hopeful, at least in the sense that, if it uncovered very serious problems, it offered constructive suggestions for dealing with them. In a bewildering world of rapid change, desperately complicated in the early years of the century by a major war, the teachings of political economy seemed to offer a way to create a society more successful than the old because it had, for the first time, uncovered the springs of an effective economic policy. Because they offered this hope to men who were struggling with problems which often seemed insoluble, the political economists were the great educators of the age. Lytton Bulwer wrote in 1833 about the dominance of the science:

> We as yet are under the dominance of the philosophy of Adam Smith. The minds that formerly would have devoted themselves to metaphysical and moral research, are given up to inquiries into a more material study. Political economy replaces ethics; and we have treatises on the theory of rents, instead of essays on the theory of motives.[37]

The doctrines of individualism and of self-help, preached in those treatises, seemed to many to bear hardly on the poor, who found it so difficult to stand on their own feet. Yet Francis Place, who had himself been a working man, argued that the political economists were in fact the best friends of the workers. They had obtained the modification of the Navigation Acts and the repeal of the Combination Acts. They had promoted knowledge about a secure currency and tried to increase the knowledge of the working classes in every way possible. The political economists were, Place argued, 'the great enlighteners of the people'.[38]

For the purpose of this study, three very different men will be taken as representing the influence of political economy in early nineteenth-century England. David Ricardo (1772-1823) was the author of a major systematic work, *On the Principles of Political Economy and Taxation*, published in 1817, which brought out the clash of interest between the capitalist and the landowner. Ricardo's friend, T.R. Malthus (1776-1834), the first edition of whose *Essay on the Principle of Population* had appeared in 1798, made a great contribution, immediately to the debate on poverty and the Poor Laws, and, at longer range, to the wider problems of the relationships between population, subsistence, and the harmony of human societies. The third name is Robert Owen (1771-1858), the manufacturer who built up a great enterprise at New Lanark in the early days of industrialism and who wished to remodel society, through education and through association, on cooperative instead of on capitalist lines.

Malthus is always remembered as the author of the principle of population which he expounds in the following words in the first edition of the *Essay*:

Assuming then my postulate as granted, I say, that the power of population is definitely greater than the power in the earth to produce subsistence for man.

Population, when unchecked, increases in a geometrical ratio. Subsistence increases only in an arithmetical ratio. A slight acquaintance with numbers will show the immensity of the first power in comparison of the second.[39]

Malthus never abandoned the broad concept of the pressure of population upon the means of subsistence, but the principle, as he developed it through his writings, is far from being the barren fatalistic denial of the possibility of all social improvement which it is sometimes made to appear.

The key to understanding the development of Malthus' thought on this critical issue lies in appreciating that the first edition and the second and subsequent editions of the *Essay on the Principle of Population* are in many ways different books.[40] The first is a brilliant polemic; the second and later editions are detailed sociological treatises. In the first edition Malthus attacked Condorcet's belief that human society is perfectible and that human life would be indefinitely prolonged. Nor does he show any more sympathy for Godwin's view that equality and anarchy should be the fundamental social principles, since the force of circumstances would impose on men the institutions of property, of marriage, and the inequality of conditions. The growth of population was checked, Malthus argued, by two major forces; the preventive, the check of caution which led men not to marry when they could not support a family, and the positive check, enforced upon the poor by hunger, unemployment, poor housing and high infant mortality. To these might be added 'vicious customs with respect to women, great cities, unwholesome manufactures, luxury, pestilence, and war', all of which checks 'may be fairly resolved into misery and vice'.[41]

Population had certainly, he argued, advanced very rapidly in new countries with unlimited virgin land like the United States and, even in old settled countries, it recovered very quickly after war and pestilence. Yet the checks of misery and vice soon began to operate and to limit human increase. This existence, Malthus argued, in the first edition of the *Essay*, worked against

any very marked and striking change for the better, in the form and structure of general society; by which I mean any great and decided amelioration of the condition of the lower classes of mankind, the most numerous, and, consequently, in a general view of the subject, the most important part of the human race.[42]

In England, though there had been an increase in wealth in recent years, this had not increased the happiness of the poor because the increased employment had been in manufactures and not in making agriculture more productive of food for men.[43]

The argument of the second and subsequent editions of the *Essay* and of his other works shows a marked change of emphasis, because in them Malthus puts a far greater emphasis on the operation of the preventive check. This form of control, he argued, was characteristic of modern societies whereas, in more primitive ages, the positive checks imposed by hunger, pestilence and war were predominant. The vital contrast which must be appreciated here is that the positive checks are arbitrary and outside human control, whereas the preventive checks operate as the result of deliberate human choice. In that sense the preventive checks express man's free will, and the more effectively they operate, the more they increase man's control over his environment. In a developed society, according to the revised form of Malthus' argument, the principle of population expresses a concept of human choice not of blind submission to an ineluctable fate. The very fact that man appreciates the terrible force of his own reproductive powers gives him a new opportunity to use those powers to achieve better social conditions. Freedom is to be achieved by the very acceptance of constraint. Governments and human institutions, he wrote in 1830, can have a great effect 'in directing these checks (to population) in such a way as to be the least prejudicial to the virtue and happiness of society'.[44]

The principal check which operated in civilized contemporary societies was that of prudential restraint on marriage. In the later editions of the *Essay* Malthus used the situation in France after the Revolution to establish his point. It was clear, he thought, that there had been a very marked improvement in the condition of the lower classes. Between 1802 and 1813 the population had increased, but it had increased slowly, the improvement in the conditions of the people being reflected in a smaller proportion of births, deaths and marriages.[45] The effect of this diminished proportion of births had been to give the labouring classes a great share of the national produce and to maintain the advantage they had gained by the sale of the church lands and national domains.

> The effect of the revolution in France has been, to make every person depend more upon himself and less upon others. The labouring classes are therefore become more industrious, more saving and more prudent in marriage than formerly; and it is quite certain that without these effects the revolution would have done nothing for them. An improved government has, no doubt, a natural tendency to produce these effects, and thus to improve the condition of the poor.[46]

Thus, Malthus argued, civil and political liberty are desirable because they give man the opportunity to improve his situation. Only the individual himself can raise his own standard of living through his own efforts, and governments are powerless to remove the basic causes of want and unhappiness. However they can certainly provide the conditions which make it easier for the individual to achieve his goals. One such form of assistance on which great stress is laid is the provision of a system of parochial education on the lines already suggested by Adam Smith. It was a disgrace that nothing beyond a few Sunday Schools had been provided for the education of the poor. No government was doing what it might to raise the standards of the labouring people unless it provided a general system of education for them.[47]

The changes between the principle of population, in its original form of 1798, and the later development of the idea in Malthus' later thinking is certainly very striking. Unfortunately Malthus' ideas are usually quoted in that first formulation, not in the much more sophisticated shape which they later assumed. In the late 'twenties Malthus seems to have agreed with Nassau Senior's argument that the principle of population was not a blind assumption that change and improvement were impossible.[48] Malthus' later view was to emphasize the need for individual improvement, for better education, for the need for intelligent self-discipline which was stressed by the social reformers of all schools. As man learns to understand the forces which control his destiny, he can use them to achieve a more prosperous future for himself and for his descendants.

Malthus' emphasis on individual self-restraint and personal independence made him, throughout his career, an opponent of the poor laws, because in his view their existence weakened those qualities in the poor which he valued so highly. The knowledge that parish relief was available encouraged imprudent marriages and thus helped to increase population without increasing the food available for its support. Since therefore provisions were distributed to everyone in smaller proportions because population was increasing, it became increasingly difficult for those who were at work to purchase an adequate supply, and they in turn were forced to seek relief. If men knew that they could depend on parish assistance, they had no incentive to save against seasons of sickness and unemployment.[49] The practice, commonly adopted during the war, of making up wages out of the parish rates had helped to increase pauperism. The remedy, he argued, was the gradual abolition of the poor laws, because they lowered the wages of the workers and therefore made their condition worse than it would have been, had they never existed. In the country the poor did receive some compensation for their low wages because their children were supported by the parish. In London and the great towns, on the other hand, very little assistance was given while wages were lowered by the country folk, their numbers increased by the influence of the poor rates, who flocked into them.[50]

In Scotland, on the other hand, poor relief was much less generously given and was regarded as a great stigma. 'The consequence of this is', Malthus wrote, 'that the common people make very considerable exertions to avoid the necessity of applying for such a scanty and precarious relief'.[51] The contrast between the virtuous independence of the Scottish poor and the pauperized dependence of the English poor was made over and over again in the great debate on poverty in the years after the war. To Malthus and the many who thought like him the key to the whole problem was personal independence. If that was lost, nothing could be gained. Only the individual could redress his own situation. Government and society might be very anxious to help but essentially they were powerless to do so. 'Whatever attempts they may make . . . they are really and truly unable to execute what they benevolently wish, but unjustly promise.'[52]

The same appeal to individual initiative and self-reliance is a major aspect of the work of David Ricardo. If commerce is left entirely free, he argued, each country will concentrate on those products for which it is the best suited and all countries will profit from the resultant free exchange. The natural price of labour varies in different countries, and, like all others, labour contracts should be left to the free competition of the market. The tendency of the poor laws is to counteract these principles by absorbing a great proportion of the net revenue of the country.[53] Ricardo accepted the Malthusian doctrines of population, and argued, like Malthus, that the only way to encourage prudence and restraint was gradually to abolish the poor laws and to teach the poor to depend for their livelihood on their own exertions. It was an absurd policy to regulate money wages by the price of food because the effect of doing so was to raise still further the price of corn to the labourer. If the supply of corn, as a result of bad seasons, was deficient, the distress of the labourer was unavoidable and no legislation would provide a remedy.[54]

Both Ricardo and Malthus, in their different ways, were apostles of freedom, though, especially in Ricardo's view, the freedom allowed to the labourer was severely limited by the economic forces which pressed him towards a bare level of subsistence. Ricardo's economic doctrine was not a creed of social harmony, because he taught that there was a permanent clash of interest between the landlord on the one hand and the manufacturers and consumers on the other. It was always in the landlord's interest that corn prices should be high, while it was in the interest of everyone else that corn should be low in relation to money and commodities.[55] *The Principles of Political Economy* teaches that, within a society directed by the search for economic freedom, there are serious conflicts between the particular freedoms claimed by different groups.

A strongly contrasted interpretation of social relationships was provided by the great industrialist Robert Owen, who made his fortune and worked out his ideas at the mills of New Lanark. Both Malthus and Ricardo saw grave problems in the path of all human advancement, but they found the way forward in individual effort pursued through discipline and self-denial. Thus, Ricardo argued, pauperism would cease when the poor had learned the value of independence and had appreciated that 'prudence and forethought are neither unnecessary nor unprofitable virtues'.[56] Owen would have echoed many of the same conclusions, but he would have reached them from a different starting point. He denied that man formed his own character. Rather that character was formed for him by society and particularly by the directing group within it. Owenism was an environmentalist creed. Any character, Owen argued, may be given to any community, even to the world at large, 'by the application of proper means'.[57] The first of these means is the provision of a general system of education, and the desire to make such a system possible made Owen one of the early advocates of a reduction in children's working hours.[58] A well-organized system of education was the basis of his prescription for a reformed society. Education was not limited to childhood, for adults too were to learn the proper ways to bring up their children and to protect themselves against future want. If men have been rationally educated, Owen thought, they will be anxious to promote the happiness of all irrespective of party or creed. They will become healthy and vigorous in body because proper attention will be given to recreation. They will avoid vicious habits and become temperate and industrious. Since there will be no idleness, there will be no poverty. Such are the gains to be obtained by 'a national system for the formation of character', but governments are not to stop there. Their next aim is to prepare 'a reserve of employment for the surplus working classes, when the general demand for labour throughout the country is not equal to the full occupation of the whole: that employment to be on useful national objects, from which the public may derive advantage equal to the expense which those works may require'.[59]

iv) Jeremy Bentham and the Utilitarians

William Lovett the Chartist, looking back in his old age on his early days in London in the 1820's, wrote that, although he differed from many of Owen's views, he had 'the highest respect for [his] warm benevolence and generous intentions'.[60] Lovett, as he reflected on Owen's teachings, thought that great benefits were to be expected from cooperation in the production of wealth, but that community of property was a chimaera because it would remove from men the opportunity of freedom of choice and the spur towards self-improvement. Though much might be expected from an improved system of education, there would always be a need to enforce obedience to the laws and to preserve the general welfare from those who wished to harm it. The problem which Lovett outlined is closely related to the central dilemma of Utilitarianism. If, as Utilitarians believed, happiness is to be the main goal of human societies, how far is that aim to be achieved through the actions of individuals pursuing their own interest and how far is it to be planned by the central directing organs of society itself?

Jeremy Bentham and his followers were the most important group of political and social thinkers in nineteenth-century England, and many of their ideas had passed, by the middle of the century, into the general currency of discussion so that, in many cases, what they preached had become commonplace. The governing principle of Bentham's teaching was utility, achieved through the pursuit of self-interest. Men seek pleasure and avoid pain. Therefore the aim of legislation is to achieve the greatest good of the greatest number, while man is in general the best judge of his own interest. Bentham reacted sharply against the doctrines of natural law which had dominated political speculation when he was a young man, and he erected utility as a standard capable of practical verification. To decide whether something was or was not useful appeared simple enough. Yet, in itself, the principle of utility was as abstract and as absolute as the doctrine of natural right had been, and as little capable of empirical proof or disproof. Moreover to define happiness proved to be an extremely difficult task. One of the major problems lay in reconciling the happiness of the individual with the happiness of the group. The question which must inevitably arise is whether the coincidence is automatic or whether it is something which has to be achieved by the conscious decision of the legislator. Such a decision, in turn, implies a choice which may appear to advance the interests of some people at the expense of others. The 'laissez faire' economists, who became increasingly linked with the Utilitarians, tended to argue that the harmony of interests between the individual and the group was automatic, though, as we have seen, Ricardo's teachings threw considerable doubt on this comforting doctrine. Nevertheless, so Halévy argued, the economists generally believed that economic freedom would resolve all problems and advance the general interest on all points.[61]

In an age when Britain was the only capitalist power of the modern kind, there may have been sound practical grounds for such economic arguments. Bentham was a lawyer and a jurist, not an economist, and the clashes of interest within the British legal and political system were too striking to be brushed aside. Though Utilitarianism spoke of individual happiness and of freedom from restriction, it accepted that the interests of individuals and of groups did not automatically coincide, and that it was the task of the legislator, working in the light of what is rationally known to him to be 'useful', to bring about harmony between them. In other words, Utilitarianism, as a juridical and political creed, is a creed not of liberty but of strong government. The role of the Utilitarian legislator is clearly expressed by Bentham in these words:

> But ought the legislator to be a slave to the fancies of those whom he governs? No. Between an imprudent opposition and a servile compliance there is a middle path, honourable and safe. It is to

combat these fancies with the only ones that can conquer them— example and instruction. He must enlighten the people, he must address himself to the public reason; he must give time for error to be unmasked.[62]

To the Utilitarians individuals are not able to achieve happiness merely by following their own desires. Rather happiness is found through the observance of rules decreed by those who are more intelligent and better informed than the majority. Like all the creeds of the time Utilitarianism is a creed not of liberty, but of social discipline.

Bentham himself was an arranger of ideas rather than a philosopher. It was his disciple and friend, James Mill, who attempted to base the teachings of the school on a systematic psychology which rejected general ideas and rested everything on sense-impressions and on the association of ideas derived from them. Mill's psychology was highly atomistic. Man experiences separate sensations and gradually shapes out of them continuous images of the universe. Yet the creed, though it is based on individual sense-impression, is extremely abstract. Once the simple sensations have been experienced and the basic principles established, the whole development of the ideas is deductive and rationalist rather than inductive and empirical. The model by which Mill and his fellow-thinkers were trying to shape the social sciences was that of the exact sciences like geometry. They placed great emphasis on units of individual egotism because these appeared to be the most precisely comparable and the most exactly measurable of human motives. The whole process, in psychology, as in legislation and in economics, is as deductive and rationalist as it can be made.

Yet the Utilitarians have a great reputation as empirical thinkers who had a major influence in achieving practical reforms. What, then, is the relationship between these two different aspects of their ideas? Clearly both Bentham and James Mill had active practical concerns. The Panopticon and the Chrestomathic School are obvious examples. Mill's article in the *Encyclopaedia Britannica* on prisons and prison discipline is highly practical in tone.[63] Some writers have interpreted Bentham's work very largely in terms of its presumed practical consequences. C.M. Atkinson, writing in 1905, argued that 'the real end and aim of all his labours was *practical legislation*', and quoted Leslie Stephen's opinion that his writings 'may be regarded as so much raw material for Acts of Parliament'.[64] Graham Wallas, in an essay originally published in 1923, called the Constitutional Code 'the mine from which a new system of English administration and a new relation between English central and local government were extracted in the years that followed the Reform Bill of 1832'. From the code, Wallas argued, Chadwick took the details of the Poor Law of 1834 and Parkes and Place the details of the Municipal Corporations Act of 1835.[65]

On the other hand a more recent writer, D.J. Manning, draws a distinction between Bentham as a political theorist and as a man of designs, or what might be called a political engineer. As a theorist, Manning claims, Bentham was arguing from philosophical principles which were not directly related to practical issues. As an engineer, he expressed a view about the inadequacies of the social arrangements of his own day which was independent of, but related to, the ideas expressed by his contemporaries because he and they alike were confronted in their daily experience by much the same difficulties.[66]

Manning's distinction between Bentham the theorist and Bentham the engineer is helpful in understanding the difficult relationship between the theoretical and the practical in Bentham's ideas. Reference has already been made to the very abstract character of the principle of utility itself. That principle, once put in motion, operated with little reference to empirical verification, as little indeed as in the case of the natural rights of which Bentham was so scornful. To make this distinction between theory and practice is not, of course, to deny that Bentham's analysis of practical problems was more far-reaching than that of his contemporaries. He thought more clearly and argued more forcibly than most of them. But his approach and theirs perhaps differed in kind less than has commonly been argued. He saw more deeply, but he saw the same problems, and the fact that the legislation of the 'thirties and 'forties reflected many of his solutions does not necessarily mean that those solutions would not have been arrived at had Bentham written nothing at all. He and his contemporaries were often confronting the same problems with very similar weapons.

Bentham and the Utilitarians, on the one hand, and the reformers who were not Benthamites, on the other, should be thought of as moving on parallel lines. If the matter is considered from this point of view, some light may be thrown upon the argument, so strongly contested during the last decade, whether the social and political reforms of the 'thirties and 'forties took place under the direct influence of Utilitarian teaching or whether those reforms were the reaction of practical men to intolerable conditions, a reaction which would have occurred had Bentham never written a line.

The traditional view, represented by A.V. Dicey, made Benthamism the primary force in the great reforms of the period between 1825 and 1870. Recent scholars like Oliver MacDonagh have suggested a different chain of causation by which reforms took place when the situation had become intolerable and something had to be done. The way to improvement, MacDonagh has argued, lay first through spasmodic efforts to achieve reforms to the subsequent creation of a coherent governmental machine which created a new standard of public administration.[67] The emphasis, according to this interpretation, lies not on political and economic theories as the prime movers of change, but on the efforts of practical men trying to deal with pressing problems in a practical way.

Much of what has been written here has shown that, between 1780 and 1830, many reforms had been brought about in the way MacDonagh suggested. One very strong argument in favour of reform was the statement that existing conditions were intolerable. Many men of good-will must have associated themselves with the kind of argument employed by the *Edinburgh Review* in writing about the sufferings of child sweeps:

> We should have been loath to believe that such deep-seated and disgusting immorality existed in these days; but the notice of it is forced upon us. Nor must we pass over a set of marvellously weak gentlemen, who discover democracy and revolution in every attempt to improve the condition of the lower orders, and to take off a little of the misery from those points where it struck the hardest.[68]

This kind of reaction to obvious abuses is an important factor in social change, but to say that is not to affirm that reform was in every case the result of pragmatic reaction to current problems.

Bentham and his ideas provided a programme. Lytton Bulwer, writing in 1833, said that Bentham 'acted upon the destinies of his race by influencing the thoughts of a minute fraction of the few who think'.[69] The Utilitarians defined principles and standards according to which practical measures could be assessed. They gave a solid shape to ideas and aspirations which might otherwise have remained inchoate, and, because inchoate, ineffective.[70] They formed a very influential pressure group, devoted to the manipulation of public opinion and to the steering of royal commissions along what was seen as the right lines. S.E. Finer has defined the methods by which they worked as three-fold: irradiation, suscitation, permeation. The first was the process by which the committed attracted other people and introduced them to Bentham's ideas. The second was the process of stimulating public interest and creating a favourable climate in the country at large. The third was the process of securing public employment for the faithful, who then influenced new friends and set the whole process going once again.[71] Though Finer is careful to point out that not all reforming administrators were Benthamites, and that not all plans came to fruition in the way their protagonists intended, he concludes:

> . . . in respect to India and the colonies, to penology and to health, education, and the protection of paupers and factory workers, to financial administration, fiscal policy and the machinery of central administration; in respect to them, it seems to me, Bentham's thoughts and attitudes played a predominant role.[72]

It is particularly interesting to consider the Constitutional Code, the last major achievement of Bentham's career, and written with the help of Chadwick and of Southwood Smith. The Code envisaged a complete series of ministries to cover all aspects of government, including many with which the state had not previously concerned itself. In addition to the traditional areas of trade, finance and the armed forces, there were to be ministers for the social services: a Preventive Service Minister, an Interior Communications Minister, an Indigence Relief Minister, an Education Minister, and a Health Minister. These ministries were to have extensive powers of inspection over institutions such as poor-houses, schools, dispensaries and hospitals. They were to control an efficient system of statistics, of registration and of the publication of information.

Their duties were defined in great detail. The Preventive Service Minister was to prevent calamities resulting from inundation, or earthquake, or fire, from disease and mortality arising from unhealthy situations and employments, from contagious disease and famine. The duties of the Interior Communications, Indigence Relief and Education Ministries are clearly enough defined by their titles. The Education Minister was to take special care to safeguard freedom of opinion, and in particular 'to avoid giving offence to any persons concerned, in respect of the opinions respectively professed by them on the subject of religion'.[73] The Health Minister was to execute all the laws aiming at the preservation of the national health. He was to inspect prisons, madhouses and buildings controlled by other ministries. He was to supervise the sale of drugs and surgical instruments, to control the water supply of towns when the Prime Minister declared this necessary, and to supervise mines, drains, theatres, and factories giving off exhalations dangerous to health. He was to record bills of mortality and registers of the weather, to regulate and examine medical practitioners, and to give to all his functions the utmost publicity.

Government officials were to be appointed by competitive examination, 'the location system' as Bentham christened it.[74] The candidates were to be examined by 'the examination judicatory' which was to include among its members the candidates' instructors, with the Education Minister presiding at the examinations.[75] Those who showed the greatest aptitude and who had provided testimonials of good character were to be selected to serve the public. It was a very Benthamic touch to argue that, among them, those should finally be chosen who were prepared to offer their services on the lowest terms! Finally the candidates had to serve a long period of probation before their appointments were confirmed.

Nor did the Code limit itself to central government. Bentham appreciated the importance of local government and pointed out the chaotic state of affairs which existed in his day. In each region of the country, he thought, there should be a sub-legislature to carry out the decrees of central government, to institute public works, to raise taxes and control expenditure, to organize, where necessary, transfers of property, to collect evidence and secure publicity, and to adjudicate between subordinate districts. There should also be local functionaries to represent central government, a headman to act as a general legislative and judicial agent and a registrar to record statistics and all information dealing with population, disease, religion and economic life.[76]

There is no need to see 'the location system' as the blue-print for the Northcote-Trevelyan Report and local government developed on lines different from those which Bentham suggested. Many of his proposals never came into effect as he suggested them. Others, like the emphasis on statistics and information-collecting, were part of the general tendency of the thought of the time and are not specifically Benthamite. Yet the Constitutional Code gives a remarkably accurate forecast of the welfare-based state which was to grow up in the century after Bentham's death. To say that is to argue, neither that without the Constitutional Code the welfare state would never have come about, nor that the Code had no effect at all on what actually happened. A clearer historical judgment would be to regard Bentham as moving further and farther than contemporaries often wanted to move, but yet moving, in a broad sense at least, in very much the same direction as social and administrative reformers had already been moving all over the country. The Code set out in a coherent form many of the improvements towards which reformers in all parts of the country had long been fumbling.

The relationship of the Constitutional Code towards the development of the Victorian administrative state has been the subject of a good deal of discussion.[77] It has been claimed that it was Bentham's purpose to give supreme control of the state machine to the legislative arm, and, by so doing, to limit the discretion of the administrators. According to this interpretation the Benthamite state would be a static society dominated by legal codes in which the executive would have little opportunity to develop new powers to meet new situations. The Constitutional Code does not read like that. Certainly the legislature is regarded as supreme, but it was expected to make full use of its discretion, within which the administrators were permitted a wide initiative. Certainly the relationship between legislative control and administrative discretion is a difficult problem in any society, and in early nineteenth-century England it presented particular problems because the whole tradition of an effective state machine had been gravely weakened in the eighteenth century. The programme outlined in the Code prefigured many of the measures adopted by public men under the pressure of practical problems. Among those who made a major contribution to the solution to those problems was Edwin Chadwick, who had helped to draw up the Code itself.

Benthamism is best understood if it be regarded, not as an exclusive creed, the *primum mobile* of political and administrative change, but rather as a set of ideas which affected different men in different degrees, and which worked together with other creeds and with the demands created by particular situations to bring about a political and social revolution. Religious faith, political economy and Utilitarianism were the three great ideological forces of the day. However great the theoretical differences between them, they often reached very similar practical conclusions.

IV. Policies and achievements in social reform, 1780-1830

i) Poverty and the Poor Law

As has been said many times, the overmastering concern in men's minds between 1780 and 1830 was the problem of poverty, which men saw as the nerve centre of the whole social question. The fact of pauperism was inescapable. Public expenditure on poor relief was a steadily rising burden during the period from 1780 to 1830, and the men of the day were very conscious of the liability, though it is difficult to relate the sums expended either to the growing population or to the increasing wealth of the country. The Poor Law Returns of 1786, based on the outgoings of the years 1783 to 1785, showed an annual expenditure of just over two millions. By 1803 this had risen to some four and a quarter millions and by 1818 to little short of eight millions. The figure fell during the 'twenties, but in 1832 had again risen to seven millions.[1] The greatest strain had come during the war years as a result of the rising prices which the war brought with it. One of the remedies adopted was the grant by the justices of relief in aid of wages from the rates, the expedient usually known as 'the Speenhamland system' after the decision of the Berkshire justices in May 1795 to make up wages according to a scale related to the price of bread. In fact the Speenhamland scale was not the first such scale adopted nor was it to be unique.[2] In 1796 an act of parliament enabled the guardians of an incorporated poor law district to regulate the wage assessments according to the price of wheat, and another act explicitly allowed outdoor relief.[3]

The system of making grants in aid of wages remained a matter of controversy up to the Act of 1834, though it appears to have become less common after 1815, and it never applied to the whole country. Traditionally the system has always been said to have contributed to over-population and unemployment, to have depressed rents and helped to destroy the small landowners. This interpretation has recently been criticized by Mark Blaug who claims that the system may actually have increased productivity by supplementing the low wages paid in the agricultural sector of the economy.[4]

Contemporary observers were generally critical of the idea of supplementing wages because, in their view, it depressed real earnings and lessened the independence of poor people. The judgment of Sir Frederic Morton Eden, in his large-scale enquiry into the state of the poor, published in 1797, is typical: 'The Poor should not be deceived; the best relief they can receive must come from themselves. Were the Rates once limited, the price of labour would necessarily advance.'[5] The existence of a legal provision for the relief of the poor, Eden argued, checked the need that a man should depend on his own efforts, though Eden did not think it likely that the system could be abolished after it had existed for two hundred years. The existence of a 'poor's fund' actually tended to increase the number of those demanding such relief. The poor rate pressed on different kinds of property in a very inequitable way. It reduced the dependence which ought to be placed for the relief of distress on personal and family ties, and, since it made available the distribution of large sums of public money, it was bound to encourage peculation and other forms of dishonesty. Poor law assessments should be limited and the balance of obligation left to private charity, since it was not the responsibility of the nation to act as a general agent of benevolence to those in need of it.

In 1795 and in 1800 Samuel Whitbread proposed legislation to allow magistrates to fix a minimum wage, though nothing came of this, nor of a bill introduced by the Prime Minister, William Pitt, in 1796. Pitt's bill was criticized by Bentham, who in 1797 produced his own scheme for a uniform national system under a board of management. Among his proposals was a plan for 'Frugality Banks' or savings banks, a favourite scheme among those who wished to encourage self-reliance among the poor.[6] Some of the most interesting ideas put forward during the war years were contained in a book by Bentham's friend, Patrick Colquhoun, published in 1806.[7] A Treatise on Indigence is a very comprehensive study which looks right across the whole range of social problems. Colquhoun began by drawing a distinction between poverty, which is the general condition of most human beings, and indigence, which may be either innocent or criminal, when people are unable to maintain themselves by their own exertions.[8] He saw a close connection between indigence and criminality, estimating that, out of a population of nine millions, 1,320,716, were on poor relief, or were beggars, vagrants, prostitutes or criminals.[9] Indigence and crime were, Colquhoun argued, 'so linked together, that it will be found impracticable to ameliorate the condition of the poor without taking more effectual measures at the same time for the prevention of criminal offences.'[10]

Colquhoun was himself a magistrate who had earlier produced a substantial study of the London criminal class with suggestions for re-organizing the police of the city.[11] In both these books Colquhoun put great emphasis on the importance of effective organization and on the collection of statistics. The London police should be placed under 'a superintending agency, composed of able, intelligent and indefatigable men.'[12] Similarly the Poor Law should be administered by a Board under the control of the Home Secretary. The duties of this board were to be largely to collect information and keep statistics, though they were also to make suggestions about necessary reforms. They were to grant licences to people in certain occupations and to regulate alehouses. They should publish a police gazette, both explaining the law on criminal matters and enforcing religious and moral lessons, which should be sent, among other places, to be posted up in taverns. They were to keep a central register of 'all idle, suspicious and criminal persons.'[13] If this kind of organization could be established, Colquhoun argued, the number of paupers would be reduced, vagrancy lessened, and moral and criminal offences diminished. Like many other critics of his time, Colquhoun was convinced of the tendency of workhouses to corrupt the poor and to take away their self-respect. To avoid these dangers, he suggested that workhouses should be divided into three distinct classes: for the young, for the aged, and for the vicious and depraved. The greatest remedy of all for the moral degradation to which the poor were exposed would be to put the system of relief on a national rather than a local basis, and thus to equalize the burden over the country as a whole. 'The poor', Colquhoun wrote, 'thus emancipated, would naturally resort to those districts where labour was most abundant, and where it was likely to be permanent.'[14]

In all Colquhoun's work there is a heavy emphasis on the deterrent and punitive aspects of the management of the poor. However, his ideas went much further than that. Though he feared that friendly societies might be used as a cloak for political subversion, he thought that government should encourage providence among the poor by creating a national Deposit Bank which local societies might join. If this national bank were publicized through the suggested Police Gazette, he thought that at least two million people would enrol in the first year.[15] There should be a national system of education for the children of the poor. The bishops and some laymen should form a central board of education, controlling schools to be established in each parish or district, supervised by local managers and conducted on the mutual system of instruction. The buildings should be paid for out of the poor rates, and parents who refused to send their children to school should be refused poor relief. One of the responsibilities of the Board of Education should be to supervise apprenticeship, since the poor could not launch their children into productive life successfully without the help of the state. Full records should be kept, both for the benefit of parents and employers and in order to afford to the statesman 'a fund of information, explanatory of the strength and resources of the country which would be invaluable'.[16]

Colquhoun had been, in earlier life, a Glasgow business man and had been Lord Provost of that city. Later he removed to London. He had connections with Bentham, but he was a practical man rather than a theorist. Yet his writings contain many of the ideas which are generally called Benthamite and which were put into practice by the reformers of the 1830's. Like Bentham he put considerable emphasis on publicizing the activities of government. His writings certainly bring out many of the ideas of centralized control and developed administrative techniques which are often considered to have been the distinctive doctrine of the

Utilitarians. Ideas similar to Colquhoun's appeared in many of the other writers of the war years, though no one else developed such a coherent programme of practical action. Malthus urged that the state was not doing its duty to help the poor achieve personal independence unless it instituted a national system of parochial schools on the lines proposed by Adam Smith.[17] He prefigured the doctrine of 'less eligibility', preached by the poor law reformers of the 'thirties, when he argued that the idle and improvident might be relieved, but that they must 'on no account be enabled to command so much of the necessaries of life as can be obtained by the wages of common labour'.[18]

The same creed of thrift and self-improvement was preached in the Reports of the Bettering Society. In one of his prefatory letters Sir Thomas Bernard attacked the practice of subsidizing wages according to the price of bread. The result of this would be that the manufacturer could no longer afford to employ his workmen. Corn would remain uncultivated because of the high price of labour, and the result would be pauperism, scarcity and famine. It was not, Bernard argued, 'within the supremacy of human power, to provide a regular supply of occupation for the poor, to be paid for in proportion to the price of bread'.[19] To him as to Colquhoun, workhouses corrupted the poor and degraded their characters. Moreover, their inmates enjoyed better conditions than the industrious poor could provide for themselves by their own efforts. The result was that workhouses spread 'THE INFECTION OF IDLENESS AND IMMORALITY throughout the land'.[20]

Both Bernard and Colquhoun were supporters of friendly societies, which had been legalized by an act of 1793, as a means of encouraging the poor to save.[21] Another active supporter was the Cumberland colliery owner, J.C. Curwen. Curwen saw the societies as offering to the poor 'the basis of an independent and adequate support, solely arising from their own industry, and productive of the happiest and most extensive consequences to the community at large'.[22] He thought that the societies might be financed by a partnership between the workers and their employers, who would eventually gain through lower contributions to the poor rate. Though he did not favour universal compulsion to subscribe, he thought that some of the well-paid industrial workers and their employers might be required to contribute. If he argued, men drew relief from a fund which they regarded as belonging to themselves and their associates, they would regard it as dishonourable to claim unless the need were real. If the societies were aided from the rates, an individual would be able to transfer to another society if he moved to another parish, a provision which would overcome the problems resulting from the law of settlement. In his paper Curwen gave details of the collections made by, and of his own contributions to, the various societies in and around Workington. The societies had, from both sources, raised more than the cost of maintaining the sick and aged poor in the town of Workington, and much more could have been raised had other employers assisted.[23]

Some membership figures for 1813 for the friendly societies in another county of the North-West, Lancashire, show that there was roughly one friendly society member for every family in the county as enumerated in the 1811 census. Most of the members were in the industrial south, with concentrations in Colne, Burnley and Blackburn, which were calico-weaving towns. In the agricultural north of the county most of the members were to be found in the towns and market villages while most of the rural township had no members at all.[24] Another institution advocated by philanthropists as an important means of self-help was the Savings Bank. The Savings Bank Acts of 1817-18 provided a system of legal regulation for them. By 1833 there were 408 such banks in England and Wales with over 400,000 depositors and balances of over £14 million.[25]

The links between idleness, indigence and criminality, which had been so strongly emphasized by Colquhoun, were to be stressed even more forcibly in the years after 1815. Halévy pointed out the increase at that time of Malthusian literature.[26] Townsend's treatise of 1786, which had preceded the *Essay on Population* in its teachings about the pressure of population on food-supply, was republished in 1817 as a contribution to the debate on the poor law problem.[27] A different, but equally compelling note was struck by the Scottish divine, Thomas Chalmers, with the argument that Christian almsgiving was a far preferable alternative to compulsory poor relief. Basing his arguments upon his practical experience as minister of St. John's parish in Glasgow and upon the traditional Scottish system of voluntary relief through the church collections, Chalmers wanted to depend for the removal of want on private charity administered through what he called 'a Christian parochial economy'.[28] He claimed that the public provision of relief destroyed frugality, that it quenched the kindness of relatives, that it shut up the sympathy felt by the wealthy for the poor and removed the sympathy which the poor felt for one another.[29] He appreciated that in England the change from a coercive to a voluntary system could not be made overnight though he argued that alterations might be made, parish by parish, where there was a strong feeling in favour of it. The rights of existing permanent paupers should, in such cases, be preserved, but the justices should lose the power of ordering relief to be given to new paupers who would have to depend on the money raised by voluntary collections. The new system would demand, Chalmers argued, very close supervision. The parish vestry would be required to act, like a Scottish kirk-session, 'in the spirit of a moral and ecclesiastical court'.[30] The parish should be sub-divided, and each area put under the care of an individual vestryman. The money given for the poor might be used to assist the blind and insane, or to help finance the village school.[31] On one subject Chalmers differed from English poor law reformers. He did not want to make the workhouses more severe and deterrent; he did not wish workhouses to exist at all.[32] His teachings reinforced the belief held by some reformers in the superior qualities of the Scottish system of relief.[33]

Public concern with the problem of poverty led to the establishment of several Select Committees of the House of Commons during these years. Their reports reflected the judgments which have already been expressed, though they found it much easier to analyze the problems than to find remedies for them. The Select Committee of 1817 keenly admired 'the admirable practice of Scotland'.[34] They expressed the fear that the poor law assessments would grow until they absorbed the whole of profits earned by property. They condemned grants in aid of wages which, they thought, had both pauperized the labourers and swollen the assessments. It was not possible to provide work for all who required it because by interfering with the laws of supply and demand, the system of grants in aid reduced the wages of free labour and heavily burdened the occupier of the land who had to pay the rates. If wages were left to adjust themselves they would rise. The provision of work for the able-bodied should be either withdrawn or limited and where it was necessary to provide it care should be taken to avoid any idleness. Emphasis was also laid on the more efficient administration of the workhouses.

The Report also made suggestions for improving the administration of the system because in many areas, and particularly in the towns, the old system of control by the parish officers had broken down. This problem had been exercising men's minds for a generation. Gilbert's Act of 1782 had permitted the establishment of unions of parishes for poor law purposes with salaried guardians of the poor. Comparatively few Gilbert unions were established, however, and their administration was not more effective than the traditional method.[35] Other attempts at a more effective system were made, particularly in the growing towns, where amateur management had become unworkable. By 1808 Manchester was employing a number of permanent overseers, and was developing a formalized system of professional administration.[36]

The Select Committee of 1817 pointed out the difficulty of administering the law through overseers appointed annually. They were anxious that parishes should be enabled to appoint paid overseers, and to set up select vestries to control the granting of relief. If such measures were to be effective, they argued, those who were most interested in the welfare of a parish must take an active share in administering its concerns. Their recommendations were put into effect by Sturges Bourne's Act of 1819 which gave to those parishes who wished to do so the power to establish select vestries and appoint paid overseers.[37] In many cases the new system worked well. The sums spent on poor relief were reduced, and parish business was more efficiently conducted by paid overseers than it had been in the past. There was the danger, however, that the small group controlling the close vestries might become too dominated by their own personal interests. Nor did they commend themselves, particularly in the London parishes, to the growing demands for more democratic control which produced Hobhouse's Act of 1831 for the establishment of elected vestries, on a permissive basis, with a high voting qualification.[38]

The Select Committees of 1824 and 1828 concentrated on grants in aid of wages, condemning the practice on the now familiar lines that it reduced the wages of free labour and encouraged improvidence among the poor. What is interesting about these reports is not so much the practical proposals they make, but rather the value-judgments they express, because these lead on directly to the reforms of 1834. The Report of 1824 argued that, if the poor be found employment, 'the parish should, if it be possible, provide them with labour less acceptable in its nature than ordinary labour, and at lower wages than the average rate of the neighbourhood'.[39] The Report of 1828 urged the adoption of 'a well-regulated system of workhouse industry, where a full measure of labour may be constantly exacted, proportioned to the labour of each individual, and where such proper regulations may be observed as experience proves to be necessary'.[40] The first report proclaims the principle of less eligibility, the second foreshadows the deterrent workhouse.

It is not particularly important whether the judgments thus expressed were valid. What is important is that more and more people in positions of influence had come to think in this way. The solution seemed to be in more stringent management. Once again remedies were applied in the local communities before they were taken up as national policy, and the work of the Nottinghamshire reformers, particularly of J.T. Becher and George Nicholls at Southwell, is of particular interest. Indeed Becher's 'strict, frugal and judicious administration of the Poor Laws'[41] had considerable influence on subsequent national policies.

Becher had long been active in public work in Nottinghamshire, and has already been cited as one of those public-spirited clergymen who did so much to improve local administration and, according to their own lights, to bring about better social conditions.[42] Nicholls had been a captain in the East India Company's merchant marine who had settled in Nottinghamshire and who undertook the post of overseer of the poor at Southwell in 1821. He remained in Nottinghamshire for a few years only, but he had a distinguished later career in poor law administration as one of the commissioners under the Act of 1834 and the founder of the poor law system in Ireland.[43] At the same time that Becher and Nicholls were introducing reforms at Southwell, another clerical reformer, Robert Lowe, Rector of Bingham, was practising similar policies independently in another part of the country, though he and Nicholls subsequently became friends.

Both Nicholls and Becher described what they had done in pamphlets written during the 1820's,[44] and Nicholls returned to the subject long afterwards in his history of the English poor law, published in 1854. Their objective was to reduce the poor rates by preventing waste and extravagance and by compelling the able-bodied poor to depend on their own exertions instead of on relief. Nicholls, according to his own account, became overseer at Southwell on Lady Day 1821. Relief expenditure, which had been £2,069 in a parish of 3,051 souls in 1820-1 had fallen to £515-14 by 1822-3.[45] In 1823 49 surrounding parishes founded the Thurgarton Incorporation to provide a common workhouse which was occupied in December 1824. In Nicholls' view this measure did not reduce the rates, but it did prevent them from growing.[46].

The central object of their policy was to grant relief in the workhouse solely to the aged, the infirm and the impotent and to ensure that conditions there were so severe that the able-bodied were under no temptation to remain. Becher claimed in 1828 that, neither in the Southwell workhouse nor in the workhouse of the Thurgarton Incorporation, was there a single able-bodied male adult.[47]. Within the workhouse itself men, women and children were to be separated from one another, and 'wholesome restraint' exercised 'upon the idle, the profligate and the refractory'.[48] Both Becher and Nicholls laid a very similar emphasis on the sanctions imposed by strict rules. Becher wrote of 'a system of secluded restraint and salutary discipline, which, together with our simple yet sufficient Dietary, prove so repugnant to their dissolute habits that they very soon apply for their discharge, and devise means of self-support, which nothing short of compulsion could urge them to explore'.[49] Nicholls urged that the inhabitants of poor-houses ought not to be placed in a better position than the poor outside. 'The living, the clothing and the comforts provided . . . should be of such a description, as not to excite a desire for partaking of them among others.'[50]

Nor were the conditions outside the workhouse to be any gentler than those within the walls. No grants were to be made in aid of wages, no money to be paid towards house-rent. The provision of employment by the parish was, as far as possible, to be discouraged. The parish was, in Nicholls' view, to be 'the hardest Taskmaster, the closest Paymaster, and the most harsh and unkind friend that they can apply to'.[51] Any work provided, such as quarrying or stone-breaking, Becher argued, should be rewarded by a wage 'not more than one-half or three-fourths, of the sum yielded in the District by Voluntary Labour'. Becher was anxious that the labourer should be paid a just wage from which he might be able to maintain himself and his family. On the other hand he must make no claim to relief after a short period without work. 'The poor must learn to subsist', Becher argued, 'not upon their Daily Wages, but upon their Annual Average Earnings. Neither the fluctuations of Trade, nor human casualties, will allow any workman to labour regularly six days in the week.'[52]

The remainder of their policies followed much the same lines. Becher recommended that proper records should be kept and accounts published. All tenements, except parish cottages provided for the aged and infirm, should be assessed to the poor rates. Cases of bastardy should be severely dealt with and alehouses carefully controlled. A paid overseer and a surgeon should be appointed, and the overseers should be properly supported by the magistrates, who must not make grants in aid of wages.

In the second edition of the *Antipauper System* published in 1834 Becher gave many examples of the way in which the Southwell system had spread to other areas. It had been taken up by reformers like T.F. Lloyd Baker of Uley in Gloucestershire and the Rev. Thomas Whately of Cookham, who told Becher in July 1830 that in his parish the rates had been reduced from 12s. to 2s. in the pound, 'while the comforts of the poor, late paupers, are increased in exactly the same ratio'.[53] One modern writer has argued that Becher, through his long experience of the Nottinghamshire countryside, had the more constructive attitude to the problem of poverty, while Nicholls was both more repressive and more doctrinaire.[54] The Nottinghamshire reformers had a good deal of influence on the new poor law, because they offered a model which, it appeared, had achieved practical success in controlling pauperism and which was capable of being extended to other areas. Nicholls wrote long afterwards that the examples of Bingham and Southwell had been of great value to the Poor Law Commissioners and he picked out 'workhouse relief, or the workhouse principle' as the foundation of everything which had been done there.[55] The deterrent programme of the new poor law can be seen taking shape in the Nottinghamshire countryside during the 1820's. It is typical of the age that national policy was so much influenced by local reforms initiated by parish clergymen and a former sea-captain.

ii) The Welfare of the young: education and factory reform

By 1830 many schools for the poor had been established by the National and British Societies, and the Utilitarians had also shown an active interest in the movement for better education. The rivalries between the advocates and the opponents of denominational schools had produced much controversy, but it is possible that, under the conditions of the day, such conflicts had increased general interest in popular education rather than held back progress. Many of the thinkers and publicists whom we have studied, Malthus, Colquhoun and Robert Owen among them, had advocated a system of national education, as Adam Smith had done long before.[56] Those who favoured such a system believed that it could not be established without some help from the state, though there were wide differences of opinion about the extent to which government should be involved. F.M. Eden, for example, writing in 1797, argued that there should be a school in every parish paid for by the public.

> To be able to read, write, and cast accounts are acquisitions worth paying something for. If they contribute at all, as no doubt they do in a very great degree, to encourage an artisan, or a labourer, either to exert more ingenuity, or to practise more integrity, the Public, heavily as they are already laden with such burthens, should not begrudge it.[57]

James Mill concluded, though reluctantly, that state assistance would have to be given 'as far at least as to the erection of schoolhouses, and to the appointment of such small salaries as should be sufficient, and not more than sufficient, to secure the residence of a teacher'.[58] The state was, he thought, more likely to give aid to the Lancasterian or non-denominational schools than to the church schools with their divisive system. Mill's friend, Henry Brougham, in a Commons' speech of 8 May 1818, argued that government should provide aid only where nothing could be done without it. He stressed that it was dangerous to legislate too much, that confidence should be placed in the desire of individuals to better themselves, and that government interference might produce a dangerous tyranny over the expression of ideas. Even so, Brougham was, like Mill, ready for public funds to be used to erect schoolhouses, the form in fact taken by the first government subsidy for education in 1833.[59]

Bulwer, writing in that same year, introduced another argument—the need to follow the lead of other countries where public education was already far advanced. He suggested a national system of popular education under the control of a Minister of Public Instruction with the schools managed by local committees. Both intellectual and industrial instruction should be provided, and religious teaching should be given according to the wishes of the parents. They would pay fees, the benevolent would make donations, and money would be available from charitable bequests. The system would therefore be self-supporting except that the state would maintain teacher-training schools. The model for the plan was the state system already at work in Prussia, which was, Bulwer argued, both comprehensive in scope and excellent in standard.[60]

To the men of the time the advance of popular education presented certain dangers. It appeared to many to threaten public order by raising the lower classes above their proper station. The fear of social disturbance had been, as we have seen, one of the problems confronting Hannah More in her schools in the Mendips.[61] An enquiry into the state of the poor, instituted by order of Hampshire Quarter Sessions (?1795) considered that Sunday schools and other schools were valuable only in so far as they helped children to attend and to understand divine service. 'As far as they [the schools] have any tendency to raise an *idea* of scholarship, to make those who attend them *conceive* they are scholars, and hence to place them in their *own conceit* above common labour, they become prejudicial instead of serviceable to the community.'[62] These examples come, of course, from the early years of the Age of Preparation. By the 1820's opinion seems to have been moving towards the point of view which was to be expressed by Kay-Shuttleworth, that education acted to prevent disorder by civilizing the poor and making them understand the bases on which the institutions of society were founded.[63] Thus in the late 'twenties the *Edinburgh Review*, in attacking those who opposed the extension of education to the workers, argued that better education had helped to prevent the return, in the depression of 1825, of the disorders of 1817-19.[64] The older view was still echoed by the *Quarterly*, which pointed out the danger that the Mechanics' Institutes might promote both sedition and infidelity. Even so, the *Quarterly* was prepared to accept that some benefits would ensue from the movement.[65] Twenty years before, Tory opinion would hardly have passed a judgment as favourable as that upon institutions created to advance the education of working men.

Another problem which raised difficulties was the relationship between education and pauperism. It was widely argued that education offered a cure for pauperism because it helped the poor to become more independent. Yet there was also a reverse argument. Education was itself a charity and, as such, incurred the suspicion of those reformers who believed that charity, however well-intentioned in its origin, did harm rather than good because it removed the motive for self-reliance. There was a widespread fear of the effects of almsgiving, whether indiscriminate or organized. The *Westminster Review*, for instance, while arguing in favour of more schools for both children and adults maintained that it would be a mistake to maintain children while they were at school because this would encourage the growth of population and enable more children to be reared.[66] The same evil effects might be expected from lying-in hospitals and the dispensing of free medicine. The same fear of almsgiving and of charity in general extended to a highly critical view of endowments, and education, in one form or another, had for centuries been a major recipient of such gifts. It was widely believed that charities to educate and apprentice children and to pay out portions on marriage had become, in the towns and villages which enjoyed them, temptations to indolence and vice.[67] There is an interesting reference to this point of view in a pamphlet written by Henry Brougham in 1825 to promote the education of adults. One of the most important developments of the decade was the creation of the Mechanics' Institutes and of the Society for the Diffusion of Useful Knowledge to promote better educational facilities and more plentiful reading material for working men. Supported by the Utilitarians, publicized by the *Edinburgh Review*,[68] the movement had Brougham as its great publicist.[69] In his pamphlet[70] he advocated the issue of cheap publications, on politics as well as on other subjects, because these were the primary method of encouraging knowledge among the poor. Book clubs should be encouraged and elementary treatises written suitable in standard for working-class readers. Public lectures should be arranged, and the workers should themselves have the chief control over the institutions.

Money might be found for all this by diverting charitable gifts from purposes which were actually harmful to the recipients. Doles and pensions, in Brougham's view, encouraged idleness and poverty and the provision of clothing and other maintenance for children promoted improvident marriages and thus increased the population.[71] The familiar dangers of pauperism, as the men of the time saw them, might attend every gift. Everyone who subscribed to such purposes had a duty to consider whether he was spending his money wisely, and whether it might not be a wiser objective to help adult workers who were able and anxious to help themselves.

Brougham's interest in charitable endowments had already produced the great enquiry into charities which he had suggested in 1818. His concern as a lawyer to improve the effectiveness of trusts combined with his interest in education to launch his campaign to put endowments, many of which were misappropriated, to effective use. His plans met with opposition from the many people who were concerned to maintain the existing system.[72] The enquiry's terms of reference were more restricted than Brougham had wished, but gradually it got under way, and by 1830 the commissioners had issued 24 reports covering charities with a total income of over £500,000.[73] Their work was by no means completed by that date, and the establishment of an effective system of charity administration lay still a long way ahead. Nevertheless Brougham's initiative had launched a very important reform. For the first time, dependable information about charitable endowments was available, which was in itself a major step forward towards more effective administration. Moreover, the charities enquiry provided a model for the investigations which were to be launched into so many national institutions during the ensuing decade. As the tide of reform rose, it brought with it the demand for much more complete information as the necessary foundation of effective policy-making.

Another social problem relating to young people to which increasing attention was being given was that of child labour in factories. Factory reform did not became a major national issue until the very end of the period under discussion; Oastler's Ten Hours agitation began in 1830. Child labour was nothing new, for children had worked with their parents or with their masters on the land or at the loom ever since the beginning of history. The growth of factories had put the matter in a different perspective. In them were concentrated large numbers of workers, many of them children and young people, necessarily controlled by discipline more rigid than that of the domestic workshop. Opportunities for cruelty and brutality were greatly increased, more particularly because many of the early factory workers were parish apprentices with little protection against employers trying to expand their business in a fiercely competitive market.

The need for some control of the situation was apparent before the nineteenth century began. Thomas Percival and F. M. Eden had both recommended the control of children's labour, but effective action against child labour in factories was long in coming. It has been argued that the humanitarian conscience was quiescent during the war and post-war years, and that men did not become fully aware of the evils they saw around them until the 1830's.[74] Peel's Factory Acts of 1802 and 1819 made a beginning, but they were not very effective. W.D. Evans, the Manchester stipendiary magistrate, told the select committee of 1816 that the act of 1802, regulating the labour of parish apprentices, had not been put into operation in Cheshire and Lancashire. He had not himself read it until the day before he gave evidence to the committee. There were, he observed, many acts of parliament which were not put into effect![75]

The evidence given to this select committee of 1816 on the state of children employed in manufactories provides valuable information on the whole problem. The manufacturers rebutted their critics with three main arguments. First of all they claimed that, from the economic and financial viewpoint, it would be inexpedient to interfere with freedom of contract. If children's hours of labour were to be limited, this would put British manufacturers at a disadvantage in relation to their foreign competitors. Since family incomes would be reduced, poor rates would have to be increased to make up the deficiency. Harm would also be done to parents who depended on their children's labour to help maintain the family. 'I conceive', said the potter Josiah Wedgwood, 'that the only safe way of securing the comfort of any people, is to leave them at liberty to make the best use of their time, and to allow them to appropriate their earnings in such way as they think fit.'[76] Regulation of children's hours of work would, therefore, be in the interest of neither employers nor labourers.

Secondly they claimed that hard work was favourable to good morals, and that the long hours and strict discipline of the factories were essential instruments of control. If factory workers had more free time, they would only use it badly. G.A. Lee, of Philips and Lee, Manchester, was asked whether the morals of factory workers were better than those of workers in 'fluctuating and uncertain occupations'. He replied: 'Nothing is more favourable to morals than habits of early subordination, industry and regularity. I never knew a single instance of any immorality between the sexes in the mills.' To allow people to stop work earlier would, Lee thought, both harm their morals and the tranquillity of the town.[77] This is, of course, another form of the now familiar argument in favour of strict social disciplines for the lower classes. Finally the manufacturers denied that the hours worked in factories harmed the children's health or stunted their growth. Thus Henry Hollins, cotton spinner, produced certificates, some of them from medical men, witnessing to the good health of children in the Nottinghamshire mills.[78] Joseph Creswell, manager of a mill belonging to the Leeds industrialist Benjamin Gott, testified that children were less fatigued by their work than were grown-up people.[79]

Inevitably those who wanted restriction produced evidence which ran directly counter to that offered by the manufacturers. They argued that children who worked in factories had lower moral standards than those who did not. They claimed that factory children were weak and debilitated in appearance, though the evidence on which they relied was no more than that of common observation. Mr. Thomas Oldmeadow Gill, a Manchester merchant, testified, for example, that he with two other gentlemen had recently visited most of the Sunday schools in Manchester and Salford. The number of scholars present in them was 1,381, of whom 255 were very young and were asked no questions. '133 appeared to us to look very sickly, which induced us to ask what was their employment in the week-day, and 95 out of that 133 answered that they worked in factories, leaving 38 only in all other employments; and it is to be observed, that not one-third of the Sunday school scholars work in factories.'[80] Finally the reformers countered the argument that more free time would lead to immorality and disorder by claiming that it would enable young people to receive more schooling and better religious instruction.

The most considerable figure who gave evidence in favour of the limitation of children's hours was Robert Owen. He testified that he did not himself employ children younger than 10 years old, and he thought that it would be better not to emply them for full-time work until they were 12, though those between 10 and 12 might work half-time. Shorter hours, he argued, would lead to better health, better instruction, and lower poor rates. In his own factory the reduction in the hours of work had increased the number of those attending schools. Moreover the amount of work done in the factory had increased as a result of the strong feelings of gratitude felt by those who had benefited from the changes.[81]

Two other aspects of the testimony are important for the development of social reform as a whole; the evidence given by the medical men and the evidence about conditions among the pauper apprentices at Back-barrow. Medical opinion was quoted on both sides of the argument, but the many medical men who gave evidence to the select committee were in general opposed to the existing hours of child labour, and pointed out the dangers to health of close confinement for long hours without proper breaks for meals.[82] The medical profession was, as we have seen, an active agent in procuring social change.[83] It was of some importance that the doctors examined, many of them men of high standing in the profession, were so critical of the long hours which children had to work.

Most of the information about Backbarrow comes from the evidence of John Moss, who had been master of the apprentices there in 1814-15 and who was at the time of giving his evidence governor of the Preston workhouse. The children at Backbarrow had all been parish apprentices. They worked 15 hours a day, of which one hour was allowed for meals. On Sundays they worked for six hours cleaning the machinery, and sometimes on Saturdays they worked until midnight. Frequently at night they were so tired that they lay down on the mill-floor and fell asleep there. Their behaviour was very bad, and they learned so little that very often they could not get work after their apprenticeship was finished. Moss was unwilling to state that the long hours worked resulted in a general injury to the children's health, but he agreed that the hours—12 to 15 per day for children between the ages of 7 and 10—were too long. Their health was damaged by the high temperature in the rooms, and some of them had become deformed. When asked whether he would send children of his own to work in a cotton mill, Moss replied: 'Not if I could provide for them in any other way'.[84]

Peel's Act of 1819 was but a modest step towards reform, and improvements in factory conditions took a long time to achieve. In an age so devoted to individual enterprise there was a deeply felt reluctance to prevent a man from running his own business in the ways which seemed best to him. However, when reforms came, they were often achieved as much through a sense of revulsion against intolerable conditions as through logical argument. For that reason such accounts as those of life among the Backbarrow apprentices had their effect in changing public opinion about child labour in factories.

iii) Prisons and punishment

Prisons, even more than factories, were places set apart where the denizens might be subjected to intolerable conditions. If there were conflicts between the health and well-being of child workers and the pressures on employers to increase profits, there were tensions too between the determination of the state to punish crime and to deter the criminal and the hope of the reformer that the criminal might be reclaimed. The period 1780-1830 began with John Howard's campaigns to improve the prisons and ended with Peel's reforms of the criminal law. Howard advocated the building of secure and sanitary prisons, where the fear of gaol fever, endemic under the old conditions, would be removed. He campaigned to abolish the fees levied by gaolers and to make them the paid servants of the maintaining authority. He wanted to introduce regular work, to restrain debauchery and immorality, and to prevent the sale of liquor. He urged that prisons should be regularly inspected by the magistrates or by persons appointed by Parliament.[85]

Parliament acted for decades in a slow and piecemeal fashion, and once again progress was made by local reformers rather than by the efforts of central government. The best known and most interesting of these local figures was the Gloucestershire baronet, Sir George Onesiphorus Paul. In 1783, in a speech as chairman of the county grand jury, he paid tribute to Howard's work and suggested the creation of a three-fold system. There should be a gaol for debtors and for those committed for trial by jury, a penitentiary for prisoners convicted of serious crimes and for felons sentenced to death whose sentences had been commuted to imprisonment, and a house of correction for minor offenders. Paul was successful in persuading his county to adopt his policies. The new prison at Gloucester, opened in 1791, represented the most advanced interpretation of Howard's ideas. Four new houses of correction were built with facilities for dividing offenders into four classes, each with its appropriate discipline. The prison officers all received salaries, and magistrates periodically visited the prisons and checked their journals. An adequate dietary was provided, and careful attention given to cleanliness, warmth and ventilation. Paul was not simply a Gloucestershire celebrity. His ideas about prison discipline had a national influence, as did his ideas about the treatment of the insane, a field in which he was much guided by the Quakers who had started the Retreat at York in 1792.[86]

Prison reforms were carried out in several other counties. In Dorsetshire, for example, a new gaol was occupied in December 1793. According to an account by William Morton Pitt, manufactures had already been introduced in 1791, and convicts and debtors were allowed to keep part of their earnings. Most of the money was held for them until they were discharged, so that some men had left prison with £8 or £10 in their pockets. The prison, Pitt thought, had been very successful in reforming offenders 'so as to restore them to Society in an improved state and encourage them to persevere in a course of industry and virtue'.[87] Similar ideas were expressed by J.T. Becher, whose numerous interests included prison management.[88] He had rebuilt the house of correction at Southwell, and was particularly interested in providing work for prisoners. Part of what they earned they were allowed to keep for themselves, and, although they had to pay for part of their own maintenance, they were also allowed to remit money to their families. The scheme tended, Becher believed, to reform men who had been convicted and to teach them to get their own livings after they had left prison.[89]

During the second decade of the century national interest quickened in the problems of prison conditions and penal reform. Bentham produced the Panopticon scheme, which was given up by the government after the report of the select committee on prisons (1811) under the chairmanship of George Peter Holford. Instead of Bentham's scheme a prison at Millbank was begun in 1812 and finished in 1821, though it had a long record of ill-health and disease among the inmates.[90] In 1812 James Neild (1744-1814) produced his *State of the Prisons in England and Wales,* a survey on lines similar to Howard's, and in 1816 Elizabeth Fry began her work in Newgate.[91]

Attempts to improve prison conditions were likely to enjoy only limited success unless the cruel and archaic criminal law was also reformed. The pioneer efforts of Sir Samuel Romilly appeared to have met with no success when he committed suicide in 1818. Yet Romilly had drawn the national attention to the issues. 'To his followers', writes Professor Radzinowicz, 'he bequeathed a programme to fight for and an example to follow.'[92] In the decade after his death Robert Peel carried through the abolition of a number of capital offences and a reduction in the scale of punishments for lesser offences against property, though Radzinowicz has argued that Peel's policy actually lagged behind the public pressure for changes in the criminal law.[93]

At a time when more and more attention was being given to penal reform, it seems likely that crime was increasing as towns expanded, traditional social patterns were broken up, and population grew.[94] The connections between pauperism and delinquency had already been traced by Patrick Colquhoun.[95] His demand for an effective police force in London was met by Peel's creation of the Metropolitan Police in 1829. In the previous year the *Quarterly* had examined the great increase in crime in the country and the especial weaknesses of the police system of the capital. The primary cause, the review argued, of the majority of the criminal acts committed was the want of an organized deterrent body, of 'a regular police force—characterized in its movements by activity and unity, its members by respectability, and its superintendence by increasing vigilance'.[96] Such a force did not leap into existence in 1829. It took the Metropolitan Police a decade to establish itself, and the rural police came even later. From the beginning, however, the establishment of the Metropolitan Police had been regarded as merely the first stage in the more effective policing of the whole country,[97] and its foundation marked the beginning of an important new instrument of administrative control.

While, in one branch of criminal administration, the executive gained a new weapon through the new police forces, in another the central government took new powers over the prisons. The Prisons Act of 1823 was, according to the Webbs, the first measure of general prison reform to be enacted on the responsibility of the national executive.[98] The justices were required to organize their prisons on a prescribed plan, and to make quarterly reports to the Home Secretary about their administration. The act, however, laid down no sanctions for non-compliance, and made no arrangements about appointing inspectors, while it applied to very few of the borough gaols. Another act of 1835 authorized the Home Secretary to make administrative regulations and provided for supervision by salaried inspectors whose reports were to be submitted to Parliament.[99] In the prison service, as in so many other areas of administration, both executive efficiency and humanitarian sentiment led towards ever-growing central direction.

The internal management of prisons also caused controversy. There was constant debate about the use of the tread-wheel, a simple form of which had been invented by Sir William Cubitt about 1818.[100] There were differences of opinion about the kind of work which should be given to prisoners, and particularly whether they should be allowed to profit directly from their efforts. Work schemes usually involved bringing men together in groups, and this was thought to lead to dangers of moral contamination of the less hardened criminals by others. This in turn led to the question of whether prisoners should be associated in groups at all or rather be confined separately. There was conflict between the view that prisoners must be given some incentive to reform and the fears of those who thought that prisons might become altogether too comfortable.

The Utilitarian viewpoint, descending from Bentham's Panopticon scheme, was expressed by James Mill.[101] He placed great emphasis on the importance of regular inspection, both to keep the prisoners under surveillance and to prevent abuses by the gaolers. The management of the prisons should, he argued, achieve a balance between benevolence and economy. Those who had been sentenced to be punished should not be condemned to unwholesome quarters or to unwholesome food. Solitude was recommended only for short periods and on particular occasions. The treadmill was not a desirable form of punishment because it was much more severe on some than on others, and because the degree of suffering inflicted was left to the decision of the gaoler, who ought to have no control over the punishment, as opposed to the discipline of the prison process. The best way of reforming prisoners lay through labour, and they must receive rewards for their work. If the gaolers too had a claim to share in these rewards, they would have an incentive to make the prisoners' labour profitable, though in such a case the gaolers' posts should be thrown open to competition in order to preserve the public interest.

The objects of reformatory discipline, Mill argued, were four-fold: to create habits of industry; to preserve health and impose no suffering not prescribed by the judge; to generate good dispositions by moral and religious tuition; and to attain these ends at the smallest possible expense. Provision should be made for Sunday schools and for religious services. An establishment should be set up for the employment of those who had been released. To make the prisoners productive labourers in this way would, Mill claimed, increase rather than diminish the means of employing others, for the prisoners had to be maintained, and their labour would cover the expense of such maintenance.[102]

The Utilitarian view, as Mill expressed it, placed much more emphasis on the rehabilitation of the criminal than on the punitive effect of prison discipline. A different and much more severe note was struck by John Clay, chaplain of the Preston gaol, another local reformer, who was to become by the late 'thirties a national figure in determining prison policies.[103] He had been appointed chaplain at Preston in 1823. He tried to improve cleanliness and discipline, he endeavoured to start a school, he got a matron appointed for the women prisoners. By 1827 he had reached the conclusion that the only effective form of prison discipline lay in the introduction of individual separation, and for years he plied the magistrates with arguments in favour of the change. In 1843 a corridor of 75 separate cells was built, and in his report of the same year Clay described the combination of periods of solitude and of disciplined labour which prevailed in the prison. During the day-time some of the prisoners were at the wheel; others were in the work-room, in the cookhouse or cleaning the building; some were undergoing the sentences of separate confinement which had been passed upon them. All alike were 'seldom, if ever, from under the eye of an officer'.[104]

Clay seems to have been one of the breed of philanthropists, common at the time, who combined great severity in practical matters with a genuine concern for the welfare of the disadvantaged. Once again social disciplines are emphasized in their harshest form. 'He implored the bench', his biographer wrote, 'to make the prison an object of terror, even if reformation were abandoned; to brace up the lax discipline, and make it sharp and stringent; to keep the treadmill going much longer and quicker; to flog boys, and discharge them at once, rather than keep them in prison to be trained in crime.'[105] Clay may have been influenced by the rising tide of crime in the country. He was not the only begetter of the idea of separate confinement, much of the impulse for which came from the United States. Certainly his priorities were very different from those of James Mill and the Utilitarians.

iv) Environmental questions

Pauperism and crime were closely associated with bad housing conditions, poor sanitation and overcrowding, which in turn bred epidemic disease. Once again public health and sanitary improvement was a cause taken up at the local level long before it emerged as a national issue. In almost every town of importance a body of Improvement Commissioners was set up by act of parliament with its own staff and funds and with power to levy rates. The Commissioners were primarily concerned with cleansing and lighting the streets and with providing a watch, but as time went on, their powers and their self-confidence grew. The first such act for lighting, watching and cleansing the streets was obtained by the Corporation of Liverpool in 1748,[106] but generally the commissioners and the municipal corporations were separate bodies. Indeed, in the early nineteenth century, the commissioners were far the more active of the two with a much larger annual budget, and they maintained their independence for some time after the Municipal Corporations Act of 1835.[107]

The achievements of the commissioners must not be exaggerated, and even the most active of them did not achieve a comprehensive public health policy. The best way to consider what they did achieve is to take some examples, and, for this purpose, Manchester and Birmingham, as two major industrial cities, seem appropriate. The major problems at Birmingham seem to have been concerned with the removal of obstructions in the streets and the better organization of the markets.[108] The first two Improvements Acts were passed in 1769 and 1773. Another bill was prepared in 1790, which included the financial powers to maintain a watch, but this came to nothing after the Birmingham riots of 1791. A new act was finally passed in 1801, partly as a result of the fear of disorder arising from the war situation. This act gave powers to raise higher rates to pay for a watch, to build a public office, and to make further street improvements. A watch was set up after 1801, though it patrolled the streets only in the winter months. The market tolls were leased for 21 years, and a public office was built in 1807.

In 1812 a new act made the commissioners the sole authority for the highways, increased their borrowing powers, and gave them compulsory powers to acquire land for a market for hay, animals and straw. In 1818 the central streets were lit by gas, though the commissioners had a great deal of trouble with the companies which provided it. The new Smithfield Market was built, and in 1824 the market rights were finally purchased. By that time pressure was growing for a new act, partly because of the need for further development of the markets and partly because of the demand for a new town hall for the magistrates' courts and for musical and other public occasions. This new act was obtained in 1828. In November 1834 the new Market Hall was opened, and in 1830 a site had been purchased for a new town hall, though it was to be a long time before the building was completed. The powers of the Birmingham commissioners were not taken over by the Town Council until 1851, and they remained active until the end; after 1845, for example, they began systematic sewerage of the town. In 1850 they spent more than £50,000. In 1804 their income had been a mere £2,700.[109] The difference between the two figures shows how much their duties had grown in half a century.

The story of the Manchester Police Commissioners is broadly similar, though, towards the end of the period, their work was much more affected by political rivalries than was the case at Birmingham. The Manchester and Salford Police Act of 1792 set up a body of 200 commissioners.[110] The new body became much more active after the turn of the century. In 1800 a new Committee on Nuisances was appointed. In 1801 the commissioners took over the street lighting themselves as opposed to appointing a contractor, and in 1803 they undertook the scavenging, though largely because they could not find anyone to undertake it. By 1807 they had greatly improved the main public services, and had extended their work into areas like the suppression of nuisances, the regulation of hackney coaches, and the management of fire engines. The Manchester Police Commissioners were very early supporters of municipal enterprise. In 1808-09 they failed to get control of the water supply, and they had a good deal of trouble with an inefficient waterworks company. In 1817 they decided to establish a gas works. In 1825 they obtained a new act which sanctioned the principle 'that gas establishments might be created by public funds and be conducted by public bodies for the public benefit'.[111] By the end of the 'twenties the profits from the gas department were making a considerable contribution to the costs of local administration. Two further acts followed in 1828 and 1830. The first created separate bodies of police commissioners for Manchester and for Salford. The second, the Manchester Police and Gas Act of 1830, enlarged the borrowing powers of the gas undertaking, and widened the commissioners' administrative functions; for example, they were given control over the day as well as the night police.

The achievements of the many bodies of improvement commissioners were not contemptible, and should not be forgotten. There was, however, a limit to what could be achieved by local bodies operating with comparatively narrow powers and with little expert help. The public health enquiries of the 'forties revealed how much remained to be done if the towns were to become healthy and commodious places to live in.

PART II

THE AGE OF REFORM 1830-1850

V. The Acceleration of change

i) Political and economic background.

The fall of Wellington's government in 1830 and the coming of the Whigs to power began the Age of Reform, and the ensuing two decades— from 1830 to 1850—form one of the turning points of English history. The basic point about the reforms of the 'thirties and 'forties, in relation to those of the earlier part of the century, is not so much that the topics are new, but rather that both the pace and the scale of change have been revolutionized. Many of the characteristics of an older England lingered on. Local issues and local pressures remained very strong. It was difficult for government and Parliament to plan and carry through coherent policies of social change. They tended to take important steps and then to draw back when difficulties appeared. Yet, when every account has been taken of these facts, great innovations were brought into effect very rapidly. Central government undertook important new duties in conjunction with new or reformed local agencies. The pressure of change was felt in a fashion and to an extent which had not been known before 1830. Modern scholars have tended—quite correctly—to emphasize the elements of continuity between the England of George IV and the England of Victoria. Yet this process can go too far. Certainly the country which celebrated the triumphs of the Great Exhibition of 1851 was a very different place from the England which had learned twenty-one years earlier of the fall of the Bourbons in France. These changes were the result of the great reforms which we are now to consider.

In the general history of the time the most striking events were the Reform Act of 1832 and the repeal of the Corn Laws in 1846, which split the Tory party and began twenty years of weak governments. In social administration the New Poor Law of 1834 brought to a head the great debate about pauperism and introduced far-reaching administrative changes which were to lead to another generation of controversy. In 1835 the reform of Parliament was complemented by the reform of the municipal corporations, although it was to be another forty years before the possibilities of effective local government in improving the welfare of the population were to be fully understood. In 1833 the first great campaign for social betterment attained its goal when slavery was abolished.

In the story of social reform the abolition of slavery marks the end of a chapter. The Evangelicals, who had fought so hard for the slaves in the West Indies, were often criticized because they cared more for the comfort of the black man on the plantation than for the well-being of the labouring man at home. When Richard Oastler wrote to the *Leeds Mercury* in September 1830 about the evils of factory conditions, he spoke of 'Yorkshire Slavery'. In 1833 Parliament passed the first Factory Act with some pretensions to be effective. It limited the hours of labour of children and young persons in textile mills. In the same year the first government grant of £20,000 was made towards popular education, and six years later a government department, with James Kay (-Shuttleworth) as secretary, was set up to administer the grant. In the minds of the reformers poverty and want were closely linked with crime, and the men of the day were deeply concerned about the problem of public order. The attainment of better social conditions was closely connected with the demand for a more effective police force in an age when the level of crime in the country was possibly increasing.[1] The Metropolitan Police force, set up by Peel in 1829, really established itself during the 1830's. Boroughs were empowered to create police forces by the Municipal Corporations Act of 1835, and the counties were given similar powers under a permissive act of 1839, though the requirement did not become mandatory until 1856. Although its recommendations were not fully implemented, the report of the Constabulary Force Commission of 1839 ought to rank among the major state papers of its day in the field of social policy.

By that date, there was a growing concern about the debilitating effects of dirt and disease. The pioneer enquiries of the three medical men, Neil Arnott, James Kay (-Shuttleworth), and Thomas Southwood Smith into sanitary conditions in East London were undertaken in 1838. Four years later the theme broadened out into Chadwick's great Sanitary Report of 1842. Once again the concern with public health and epidemic disease was not new; something has already been said about the foundation of hospitals and the work of the local boards of improvement commissioners.[2] Yet in the 1840's the problems of sanitary reform were taken up in a fashion which marked a fundamentally new departure in social policy making. Major enquiries were held, and legislation, both national and local, passed, the most important measure being the Public Health Act of 1848. Yet, if public health problems raised wide interest and, on the occasion of the cholera epidemics, widespread apprehension, any measures adopted to deal with them also raised particularly bitter opposition. Water supply and sewerage touched every man in his own home at a time when people believed very strongly that an Englishman's home is his castle. They affected not only the pride but the pocket of landlords and tenants, of investors in water companies, of local notabilities with vested interests in abuses which reformers wished to remove. The public health campaign, which was closely linked with the ideas of Edwin Chadwick, the ablest and more controversial of the social reformers of the time, went down in partial failure in 1854, when

Chadwick was retired and a new health department was set up. The end of Chadwick's active career marked the end of an era in social policy.

Reference has already been made to the question of the living standards of the people in the first age of industrialism.[3] It is very difficult to make with confidence broad statements about the movement of real wages or about varying levels of poverty among different groups, but it is clear enough that, until easier conditions came in for many of the workers during the 'fifties, poverty pressed very hard upon the great mass of the workers during some period of their lives. The miseries of rural poverty remained unremedied, though perhaps the farm labourer suffered less than the factory worker or the worker in domestic industry from the vagaries of boom and slump. The years after 1837 were bad years for trade and industry, culminating in the terrible years 1841 and 1842, which have been called 'probably the most serious depression ever experienced by the factory workers'.[4] The factories of the day provided work for many more women and children than for adult males, and the position of skilled men was seriously threatened by the development of automatic spinning machinery.[5] Serious as were the problems of the factory workers, the condition of the hand-loom weavers, whose economic position had been declining for a generation, was far worse. The Royal Commission on unemployed hand-loom weavers, which reported in 1841,[6] showed that their employment was very irregular and that their wages had been steadily pushed down as the competition with machinery had grown in intensity. Since the skills of hand weaving were very easily acquired, the trade was seriously over-stocked, while, the Commission argued, the power of the trades unions in other industries made it difficult for hand-loom weavers to move into other work. The hand-loom weavers, as an economic group, died a slow and painful death. It is not surprising that they were strongly represented in many of the extreme movements which aimed to bring about change by means of physical force.

John Foster has concluded that, in the three towns of Oldham, Northampton and South Shields, with their different social and economic backgrounds, the poverty was appalling, even in the fairly prosperous year 1849.

Taking the subsistence minimum used by the late nineteenth-century poor law authorities (and assuming that all occupied members of census households were in fact in full employment) one finds that the incomes of an outright majority of working families in all three towns were either already too low for them to buy all the food they needed or would be if they had to support just one extra adult member. Moreover these figures relate merely to primary poverty. The larger reality of additional (secondary) poverty caused by illness, unemployment or debt was certainly very much worse.[7]

Poverty, like child labour, was nothing new; both had always been permanent features of the lives of the great mass of the people. Yet to the factory workers and hand-loom weavers of Yorkshire and Lancashire the new industrial age brought new pressures to add to the old. Engels pointed out that the English 'proletarian' was far more insecure than the poor German peasant:

> He possesses nothing but his two hands and he consumes today what he earned yesterday. His future is at the mercy of chance. He has not the slightest guarantee that his skill will in future enable him to earn even the bare necessities of life. Every commercial crisis, every whim of his master, can throw him out of work.[8]

The Age of Reform was a period of severe pressures, political, economic and social. The tone of popular movements was often extremely violent. Chartism summed up in an inchoate and incoherent whole the strains and tensions, the miseries and the hopes of thousands of poor people. It was hardly a revolutionary movement as such, but it certainly had revolutionary undertones which looked towards a major social upheaval. As J.R. Stephens said in a famous speech, 'The question of universal suffrage is a knife and fork question, after all, a bread and cheese question'.[9] It must have seemed to many observers in the years 1839-42, when both Chartist activism and economic depression were at their height, that there might develop a genuinely revolutionary situation.

It says something for the English ruling class of the time that it kept its head and rarely adopted coercive measures. Yet the sense of tension and fear was certainly there. The Tory Robert Southey wrote in a book published in 1829 that the growth of manufactures had produced a population liable to suffer great privations from the fluctuations of the economy, people

> if not absolutely disaffected to the institutions of the country, certainly not attached to them . . . directing against the country their resentment and indignation for the evils which have been brought upon them by competition and the spirit of rivalry in trade.[10]

Nor was the danger limited to the manufacturing districts. The Whig government of 1830 took harsh measures against agrarian discontent in the southern counties, and it is noteworthy that the Poor Law Report of 1834 makes frequent reference to the connexion between pauperism and agrarian unrest. After about 1850 the sense of tension very much lessened in English society, not so much because the people understood economic circumstances any better but because these circumstances were working in favour of better conditions for a large proportion of the population. Consumption increased and unemployment declined. Both employers and workers began to come to terms with the conditions of the new industrial society, and the employers felt rich and confident enough to abandon the old concentration on long hours and low wages.[11] Large sections of the population remained in grinding poverty, as the late Victorian social investigators were to show, but for the country as a whole an easier period began. The Age of Reform changed into what W.L. Burn called the Age of Equipoise.

ii) The Pre-conditions for social change

From the point of view of the social reformers of the 'thirties and 'forties change seemed to be controlled by three main pre-conditions. The first of these may be called men's appreciation of the cumulative chain of circumstance. The second was the extent to which people were able to help themselves to lead better lives and the degree to which they needed the state to assist them. The third was the negative delaying factor imposed by the brakes set upon change by localism, by self-interest, by suspicion of governmental activity in any form. The phrase 'the cumulative chain of circumstance' is used to describe the very deeply felt sense among the reformers of the time that change was never simple, that, as soon as the equilibrium was disturbed, the consequent displacement of force produced a chain reaction which had to be dealt with as a whole if social betterment was to be achieved.

Clearly the fundamental problem was that of pauperism. Want and crime on the one hand both led to misery and were produced by misery; self-improvement and moral education were both the cause and the effect of better material and moral conditions. The upward chain of aspiration was thin and weak, and could be fractured at many points by harsh circumstance and weak human will. The forging of the chain brought in the work of industrialists, economists, moral reformers, educators and churchmen. It was a major theme binding together the activities of men of many divergent schools of thought. It deeply influenced the ideas of Edwin Chadwick from the Poor Law Report of 1834 through the Constabulary Report of 1839 to the Public Health movement of the 1840's. It can be picked up in the writings and speeches of many of the public men of the day.

There are numerous examples which drive the point home. The statistician G.R. Porter pointed out the close connection between the moral and the physical condition of the working class. Want and ignorance alike led to criminality; . . . from these considerations the minds and hearts of the ruling class have, at length, been awakened to the duty and the necessity of making provision for the education of the people'.[12] Better instruction, he argued, would keep men from crime; statistics showed that, over a period of 13 years, 90% of those committed for crimes had been 'uninstructed persons'.[13] The criminal law reformer Matthew Davenport Hill, giving evidence to a select committee in 1852, pointed out the connection between bad housing and crime and between material and moral destitution.[14] The importance of moral improvement comes out strongly in some of the local reports made for the Sanitary Enquiry of 1842. Edward Twistleton, reporting on the condition of labourers' cottages in Norfolk and Suffolk, emphasised that better living conditions do not necessarily mean better morals among the poor: '. . . no external and mechanical benefits can supply the place of good moral training; and I would say, as a corollary, that at the same time that you build first-rate cottages, you should establish first-rate schools'.[15] E.C. Tufnell argued that material improvement might actually do harm unless 'by extension of a sound education, parallel endeavours are set on foot to improve the higher and nobler parts of our natures'.[16]

If these statements are carefully considered—and many more could be added to them—they help to explain why arguments about education played such a prominent part in the social debate of the time. It is usually claimed that education was seen as an essential tool of organized religion. Men and women were to be taught to read as a means of saving their souls. There is something in this, but the core of the matter is both deeper and more complex. Education as a factor in 'moral improvement' was certainly defined in religious and moreover in denominational terms, but morality spilt over into many practical situations which were quite outside the narrowly religious context. Indeed the issues of social reform were interpreted in strongly moralistic terms.

Perhaps education was an attractive remedy for social evil because, in the sense of organized schooling for the great mass of the people, it was something which had all the charm of novelty. Despite the experiments of the eighteenth century with charity schools and Sunday schools, the attempt to educate the mass of the people through organized institutions was something which had never been attempted in England, and about which, in practical terms, not much was really known. In our age, in which education means schools and colleges rather than apprenticeship or the tutelary role of the family, this rather simple fact about early nineteenth-century society is often forgotten. The untried nature of large-scale educational ventures makes the claims of its advocates rather surprising. It is difficult sometimes to understand how they can have been quite so confident. Samuel Wilderspin the infant school pioneer told one select committee on education that 800 babies might be instructed for one year 'for what it costs the country to transport every individual, taking the expense of his first apprehension, trial and voyage'.[17] It would be an economy to have infant schools rather than policemen. Kay(-Shuttleworth) told another such committee that, if the workers were better educated, they would not fall victim to political agitators because they would understand more clearly the workings of economic laws.[18] It was believed that the best instructed workmen were the more easily controlled. A witness told the Children's Employment Commission that sometimes pressure of competition made it necessary to reduce wages. In such cases witness calls his men together and explains the circumstances to them, and inquires if they are willing to submit to execute the order upon the terms offered; on these occasions has found that the educated class is most easily convinced of the real state of the case, and therefore willing to accede to what the market requires.[19]

The chain of circumstances has acquired even more links. The upward movement through moral and material improvement makes men not only more comfortable but more submissive. In an age which put a heavy emphasis on social disciplines, submissiveness ranked high among the virtues which it was desirable for working men to possess.

The second precondition of change was a correct understanding of the extent to which individuals were able to help themselves. It is usually argued that, according to the economic doctrines of the time, men were free agents and that the state had little more to do than to hold the ring in a condition of free competition. In fact those who investigated social problems most deeply seem to have been very divided in their opinions on this subject. There were those who thought that the main hindrance to the progress of the workers was their own improvidence and profligacy. Thus E.C. Tufnell, in the Sanitary Enquiry of 1842, considered that, although the poor could do nothing about the diseases arising from undrained marshes, the harm done by those diseases had been much augmented by the 'dirty habits, neglect of ventilation, and want of foresight' of poor people.[20] Nor was it always easy to see how in practice regulations could be enforced. The great London building contractor Thomas Cubitt believed that improvements would spread most rapidly where architects and builders were left to themselves to adopt the most modern methods. He thought that, when more stringent regulations were introduced, accommodation for the very poor would simply be built just outside the limits of the area to which regulations applied.[21]

Yet informed opinion seems more and more to have come to the conclusion that the poor could not help themselves unless they were given help by the state which must create the parameters within which a system of free enterprise might operate. This demand for greater state intervention was expressed with especial force in the field of public health, because this was the area in which the poor—and especially the poor of the rapidly growing towns—were most helpless. The keenest search for moral improvement could do little to help the inhabitants of a slum with no adequate water supply or decent sanitation in which, according to the medical theories of the time, disease was spread by exhalations from heaps of garbage and stagnant sewers. The problems faced by the poor in such conditions are summed up in this passage from the report of the General Board of Health's inspector on the town of Rotherham:

I examined Scott's house, and found his wife just recovering from fever, after being ill between two and three months. I saw night-soil on the floor of the kitchen, and oozing through the wall. She said:-

We have to keep our victuals in that nasty place. I wash for hire, and we fetch water from the well 150 yards below, and from the brook for slopping. I am most in the house, and have been ill several times. I have had worse health since we lived here than before.[22]

More and more people came to believe that such conditions could not be allowed to continue in a society which claimed to be civilized and Christian, and it was only public control which could prevent them. The less fortunate members of society needed the protection of the state, even though this would mean in many cases that working men must be protected by 'peremptory enactments' against the consequences of their own profligacy and improvidence.[23] The same measures would, of course, also reduce the profits of the manufacturers and property owners who employed them and rented them living accommodation. The issue we are considering raises in one form the old paradox of freedom. If men are to be free to improve themselves and to lead happier lives, they must be restrained from actions which made the achievement of such goals almost impossible.

Since the arguments in favour of 'peremptory enactments' were so strongly expressed by many contemporaries, it seems surprising that social reform advanced so slowly and that so little practical progress was made. Public health was a burning issue in the 'forties, yet the environment of towns did not really improve until the 'seventies and 'eighties. The plea for a system of public education had been made in the 'thirties yet no effective Education Act was passed until 1870. Here we have to consider the third pre-condition of change—the negative factors, the brakes which impeded the reformers' plans. Perhaps the first point to make is that the reformers never commanded the heights of political power. They were able to get things done under circumstances of particular urgency like the crisis in poor law administration which produced the Report and the Act of 1834. To hold the interest and loyalty of parliament and government for the long-term measures required to implement a national policy in education or in public health was a very different matter, and this was something which the reformers of the period never really achieved. They were always working on the politicians from the outside, and the politicians had many other pre-occupations which, for most of the time, loomed much larger in their minds.

Cabinets were unwilling to frame coherent policies and to carry them through against opposition. Governments tended to do little unless they were forced into action by some scandal like the maltreatment of the paupers in the Andover Union workhouse which led to the creation of the new Poor Law Board in 1847.[24] When times were quieter, it was easier to leave well alone. The tradition of eighteenth-century government had been that governments should do little, and such traditions took a long time to change. There was a strong legacy of anti-government feeling which was exemplified in the campaigns of Joseph Hume for financial retrenchment and in the administrative reform movement of the 'fifties.[25] For all these reasons it was difficult to get governments to move.

Resistance to change was even stronger in the towns and counties than at Westminster, because it was linked with the power of local interests and the traditional independence of the justices of the peace. Social reforms meant closer central control, the imposition of standards dictated by experts and administrators in London. Such control was unpopular; even such a comparatively powerful body as the Poor Law Commissioners did not find it easy to manage the locally elected Guardians of the Poor. Some of the resistance was the natural reaction of people, powerful in their own communities, whose ancestors had been left for two centuries to manage their own affairs. Some of it was led by those for whom local autonomy meant a free rein for jobbery and who feared the loss of profits made at the public expense.[26] The England of that day had no experience of a centralized administrative machine exerting effective control over the affairs of its citizens. Such a machine took a long time to create, and its creators, especially when they were hasty and doctrinaire men like Edwin Chadwick, made their fair share of mistakes in managing a very sensitive public opinion. It is not surprising that, in a free society, where men of wealth and authority were accustomed to a complete control over their own affairs, changes were brought about slowly and with difficulty.

iii) The Administrators and their objectives

Modern work on the nineteenth-century revolution in government has rightly placed a strong emphasis on the role of the administrator and the expert, and their activities were certainly central to the whole process which is being studied. Yet in an important sense the early nineteenth-century governmental system never really found a place for the administrative experts. They did not occupy the seats of power themselves. They did not fit easily into a world still dominated by the two great party cousinhoods, interconnected by marriage, by education and by social habit. One reason for the downfall of Chadwick was the bitter opposition to him of his superior at the General Board of Health, Lord Seymour, later 6th Duke of Somerset. In a contest between a middle-class administrator and a Whig grandee the dice were still loaded in favour of the latter, however much or little he might know of the points at issue.

It would, of course, be an over-simplification to polarize as permanent opponents the experts on the one side and the grandees on the other.

Chadwick, if he was bitterly opposed by Seymour, worked well with Morpeth (later Earl of Carlisle) and with Shaftesbury. Yet it should be noted that some of the greatest of the administrative experts were sidetracked or pushed aside. Kay-Shuttleworth held no further official post after his illness and resignation from the secretaryship of the Committee of Council for Education in 1849, when he was only 45 years old. Chadwick was pensioned off in 1854. John Simon resigned in 1876 after he had failed to gain control of the policies of the Local Government Board, set up in 1871, which was dominated by the traditions of poor law administration. This is not the place to consider in detail the development of the new civil service in the twenty years after the Northcote-Trevelyan Report of 1853.[27] Competitive examinations were designed to test the qualities acquired in a good general education; technical skills were to be learned on the job. The late Victorian civil servant was a very indirect descendant of the social reformers like Chadwick and Kay-Shuttleworth, because he followed a much narrower and more closely delimited path than theirs. He was not an expert or a technician with special skills, but rather an educated gentleman who, it was assumed, could apply an alert intelligence disciplined by a good general education to the solution of any problems which confronted him. If there was a Victorian revolution in government, one fruit of it was an administrative system staffed by non-specialists with degrees in classics or history. Their world was a long way from the world of Bentham's Constitutional Code or even from that of Edwin Chadwick.

The pioneers of the 'thirties and 'forties were men of an heroic age who faced greater difficulties and enjoyed greater opportunities than their successors. The important figure who appears in these decades for the first time is the Inspector, that agent of central government who played such a crucial role in helping to enforce new legislation, in circulating information, and in opening the eyes of the public to scandals which would otherwise have gone unheeded. The crucial step was taken when the Factory Act of 1833 provided for the appointment of inspectors to ensure that its provisions were observed, and similar measures were taken to enforce the law in other areas. Inspectors were appointed under the New Poor Law of 1834 and under the Prisons Act of 1835. The first inspectors of schools were appointed after the establishment of the Committee of Council for Education in 1839. In the emigrant trade, which was much less central to the main concerns of governments, the executive officers built up their control at the ports over a long period of time.[28] Some of these men, like the factory inspector Leonard Horner, became influential figures in their own right. Indeed the factory inspectors were probably the most prominent group of all because of the importance and the controversial nature of their work. The regulation of child labour, the fencing of machines and the investigation of accidents aroused keen passions on both sides of industry and sometimes issues of wider national importance. The HMIs too were an important group.

Without their efforts the new system of state aid for education would hardly have got under way at all. They brought new ideas to many isolated communities, they were closely concerned with the training of teachers, they were the essential link between the power and resources of central government and the voluntary bodies which ran the schools.

It has been suggested in an earlier chapter that the social reformers had four principal characteristics: a serious and often religious temper of mind; an upper-class background; a belief in individualism and self-help; a strongly paternalistic attitude towards the poor and under-privileged.[29] The inspectors as a whole fit closely into this pattern of ideas and behaviour,[30] but, since generalizations about the whole body are difficult to make, it is more revealing to consider in some detail the career of one of them. Jelinger Cookson Symons (1809-1860) was the son and grandson of clergymen.[31] Born at West Ilsley in Berkshire, he published at the age of seventeen a pamphlet 'on the horrors of the slave trade as practised in our colonies', an act which foreshadowed his later pre-occupations. In 1827 he matriculated at Cambridge, taking his degree in 1832. He was clearly a serious minded and religious man of strongly Protestant views, who, naturally enough for a man of his background, had been intended for the ministry of the Church. However, he was not ordained, and after quite a long interval—perhaps because he spent some years abroad in early manhood—he was called to the bar of the Middle Temple in 1843. In 1848 he became an inspector of schools, concentrating on pauper children and on children who had been in trouble with the law.

No evidence has survived to explain why Symons did not take holy orders. Clearly by temperament he was a controversialist, a man who took up causes and made them his own. In later years as he wrote his annual reports on pauper schools, the sense of outrage, anger, almost despair at the meanness and short-sightedness of the guardians of the poor still burns through the sober language in which the reports are couched. Temperamentally he was a crusader, and in an age of great religious fervour, such a man might have been expected to find his place in the ministry. Yet for intelligent young men in the 1830's there were many crusades other than the purely religious, for the new gospel of secular improvement attracted much of the enthusiasm earlier channelled into Methodism or Evangelicalism. The new creed—to repeat words which have already been used—was 'the Enthusiasm of Humanity'.

Symons and many of his contemporaries were profoundly religious people. Yet the depth of their social concern tended to shift religion out of the centre of things and to replace it by a doctrine of social improvement, aiming at this-worldly rather than other-worldly objectives. The new doctrine was not as such irreligious. Plainly it had strong Christian antecedents, but the centre of gravity had profoundly shifted. Men of Symons' kind were crusaders like the Evangelical missionaries or the Anglo-Catholic slum priests of a slightly later generation, but they crusaded not to save souls, but to put down epidemic disease, to remove the root causes of pauperism, to make individuals more moral, more hard-working, more independent.

The many royal commissions of enquiry were one form taken by the social crusade. Symons was an assistant commissioner for the commission on unemployed hand-loom weavers (1839) and for the commission on children's employment (1843). His enquiries for the first of these took him abroad to France, Belgium, Switzerland, and Austria, and he published a book in 1839, called *Arts and Artisans at home and abroad*, in which he examined social and industrial conditions in the countries which he had visited. He was deeply concerned with the moral degradation in which the English poor lived. He was a compassionate man; he saw people as individual human beings and not as statistical abstractions. Like most of his contemporaries he was not prepared to leave well alone. There is in his thinking a strong desire to mould people's characters and to direct them along paths chosen for them by the reformers. He and his contemporaries felt that the times demanded drastic action. Some of this authoritarian streak may come from the clerical tradition in which he had been reared, for there is a strong authoritarian note in the teachings of all the church parties of the time. There is a similar note in the ideas of the Utilitarians, who may talk about the greatest happiness of the greatest number, but who generally assume that the Utilitarian publicist is able to detect where the greatest happiness lies and to direct people towards it.

Symons at least was no believer in exhortation for exhortation's sake. He was always strongly practical in his ideas. He saw that nothing was to be gained by urging people to be moral and hard-working unless the conditions were provided which made morality and hard work possible objectives. This common sense approach came out very clearly in his reports on the education of pauper children. The workhouses, he argued, were merely breeding grounds for more paupers, and children should be taken out of them and brought up in district schools so that they might be trained in basic learning and habits of hard work. It was folly, he claimed, to say that it was unjust to give the child of the pauper more liberal treatment than the child of the independent working man. Indeed it was only by giving pauper children such liberal treatment that they as individuals and society as a whole could be rescued from the continuing scourge of pauperism. Only an act of social generosity could break the chain of ignorance and want.

His attitude towards the poor appears, from our standpoint, rather a curious mixture of severity and generosity. He had little patience with the existing customs of working-class life which to him, as to most of the social reformers, seemed to be merely debased and degrading. On the other hand, he felt a genuine sympathy for the individuals who suffered as a result of the cruel situation in which they were placed by the existing order of society.

These attitudes towards the poor come out very clearly in his reports for the Children's Employment Commission on the young people employed in the cutlery trades of Sheffield and in the ironworks of Leeds and the West Riding. In a style reminiscent of Dickens' accounts of London, he described the lodging houses and beer shops, the penny theatres and dance halls of Leeds, and he sketched the misery and utter destitution of the very poor. His basic concern was not, however, the wretched conditions, but rather the moral dangers to which these conditions exposed the poor, and particularly their children, for whom their parents could do little, since 'they were prisoners of the same situation. Like many of his contemporaries he took a gloomy view of the position. In the Sheffield trades, he thought, boys and girls were exposed to especial danger because they became their own masters at an early age and because they worked in close proximity with older people. Immorality was rife in the town:

> Its proximate cause must be sought in the bad example of the parents, in the general neglect of religious instruction; and in the prevalence of vicious feelings and corrupting associations to which the children are peculiarly exposed by their very close intermixture with elder youths and men while at work.[32]

For Symons, as for so many of his contemporaries, the key to improvement lay in better education. He urged strongly that this should not be mere book-learning, but that it should aim very directly at fitting the child to earn its own living. The vital purpose, he argued, was to accustom children to regular labour, because idleness was the breeding ground of bad habits and the root of pauperism. Schools for the children of the workers should train both mind and body. A regular part of the day should, where possible, be set aside to agricultural work for the boys and domestic work for the girls, because these were the occupations in which the great majority of them would earn their livings. This seems to us a severe regimen for children who, if they were still at school, were likely to be very young. Children who had been before the courts were to have even more rigorous treatment in reformatory schools. The period of training should begin with solitary confinement on a limited diet before regular manual work was allowed at all. Yet Symons perceived that a better future could not arise from harsh discipline alone. Coercion, he said over and over again, was not enough. The teacher must always appeal to the hearts and consciences of the children. Symons' message is one of compassion and Christian love, though severity is there as well. There is, he wrote in 1849,

> more real Christianity in one ragged school than a score of National ones, with their comely, well-clothed Sunday-schooled children; or a whole herd of heathen missions. Our charities must descend several degrees in the scale of society if they are to rise in that of the gospel.

We must accustom our elegant humanities to contact with the real misery and rough vices of low life; nor must it recoil from its most revolting aspects or debasing incidents.[33]

The quotation forms no bad summary of Symons' ideas. He was not a major figure in his own right, but he exemplified many of the characteristics of his own day. In one sense he was a prophet of a new world more secular in tone, more centrally directed by the authority of the state. Yet in another sense he was strongly influenced by traditional ideas. There are close links between the theories of the social reformer and the beliefs of the clergymen from whom he was descended. The Age of Reform was a strange mixture of tradition and change, of old and new.

iv) The Reactions of working men

Thus far the problems of the poor have been considered from the standpoint of their social superiors. It is time now to ask how the poor themselves reacted to the harsh conditions of their lives. The traditional reaction to hardship and grievance of any serious kind was, as it had always been, rioting and violence. Eighteenth-century England had been a disorderly society and much of this tradition lingered on, though rather in the industrial districts of the north than in London which had been the centre in the previous century. The serious disturbances of the winter of 1830 took place, however, in the agricultural counties of the south. There were serious outbreaks of machine-breaking and rick-burning under the leadership of an imaginary 'Captain Swing'—like the 'Ned Lud' of an earlier time. The movement was put down by the new Whig government with great severity; three persons were executed and 457 transported.[34] During the Reform Bill agitation of the same period there were serious riots in Bristol, when the bishop's palace and much of the centre of the city were destroyed, and in Nottingham, where the castle, the property of the High Tory Duke of Newcastle, was burned out.

The agitations against the New Poor Law and in favour of the People's Charter went on against a steady background of violent talk and, very occasionally, violent action. Orators like Oastler and J.R. Stephens whipped up popular passions, and the monster meetings held on the Pennine moors quickened the fears of the manufacturers and the justices of the peace. All through the late 'thirties and early 'forties there was a close connection between this threat of violence and the poverty and wretchedness of working men hounded by economic depression and, in the case of the hand-loom weavers, seeing their traditional way of life dying around them. The only occasion when disorder and threats spilled over into armed rebellion was the attack of John Frost and the Monmouthshire Chartists on the town of Newport in November 1839.[35] David Williams, the modern biographer of Frost, thinks that the

Monmouthshire men had not acted by deliberate policy but had been pushed into a corner where they had little control over events. Theirs was perhaps a blind reaction to circumstance rather than a rising. There were however rumours of projected risings in different parts of the country at this time, and belief was widespread that some kind of conspiracy was afoot.[36] Certainly in Sheffield a rising was planned for the night of 11 January 1840. Arms were collected, and plans were made to seize local strategic points and to divert attention by firing the houses of magistrates. However the vigilance of the authorities enabled the chief constable of the town to arrest the leader, Samuel Holberry, just before the rising was due to break out.[37] He was sentenced to four years imprisonment and died in prison. Of the Monmouthshire rebels eight were sentenced to death for high treason, though the sentence was commuted to transportation, and Frost lived to return to England in 1855. After the winter of 1839-40 the threat of armed risings never loomed so large again, but there was again serious unrest in the 'Plug Plot' of 1842 when working men closed the mills in many towns in Lancashire and Yorkshire.[38]

Violent disorders of this kind were gradually cured, partly by greater economic prosperity, partly by a more effective system of police, but, quite apart from these things, the nature of working-class protest was changing as a better educated and more articulate group distilled out of the mass. The skilled workers in the London trades and in industries like cotton and engineering were beginning to form an aristocracy of labour which adapted to its own purposes the middle-class virtues of self-help and self-improvement. Among the older generation of the London men Francis Place represented these people as did William Lovett among the younger. They were radicals but not revolutionaries; they looked forward to great changes which they believed that enlightened working men would be able in time to achieve; they were optimists and rationalists prepared to think in long-term strategies. They stood a long way from the half-starved weavers and operatives who hung on the words of Oastler and Feargus O'Connor.

In 1831 Place was sixty years old. His last major political campaign was the organization of the popular movement for reform in 1830-32, though he remained quite active during the rest of the decade. He supported the campaign against the newspaper stamp duties which were partially removed in 1836. He had connections with Lovett's London Working Men's Association, and he shared in the drafting of the People's Charter, though he, like Lovett, did not understand or sympathize with the attitude of the 'physical force' men. He believed, as we have already seen, that there had been great moral and social improvements since his boyhood in the 1770's.[39] He seems to have thought that one result of this had been the progressive differentiation of a small group more provident and more intelligent than the majority of the workers. The point comes out in an interesting way in his evidence to the select committee on education of 1835, most of which deals with his opinions about standards of health and education. In the course of his examination he was asked about the increase of drunkenness and prostitution among the 'lower class'. The interchange with the questioner goes on as follows

> I should not use the word lower class there, there is a great distinction to be made; drunkenness has certainly decreased among the more respectable part of the working class, but I do not think it has decreased among those who are absolutely dissolute, they have been always much the same, but there is a great distinction now. The working people are no longer indiscriminately mixed with the dissolute, as they were in former times.

> Therefore, taking the mass of respectable mechanics and the dissolute together, the aggregate of drunkenness is on the whole less?—Yes; and the number that get drunk much less in proportion to the population. London has increased in an unparalleled ratio.[40]

The implication of his answers is clear. The working class should not be confused with the dissolute, because there are those among them who set themselves a much higher standard. Place, of course, had a strong interest in education. Nor should it be forgotten that he was one of the pioneers in disseminating practical knowledge of contraceptive methods.[41] Though this activity gained him great odium in his own time, there was no policy more valuable for those who wished to improve their condition than the ability to control their reproductive powers.

Place and Lovett were on friendly terms, though their ideas were in many ways very different. William Lovett was not, like Place, a Londoner born. He was a Cornishman from Newlyn who came to London as a young man and learned the trade of cabinet making. His career and interests, as he set them out in the autobiography which he wrote as an old man,[42] offer an epitome of the working-class activities of his time. He began to be interested in cooperative movements and working-class politics about 1830. In 1831 he joined 'The National Union of the working classes and others', the objectives of which included the reform of Parliament and 'the free disposal of the produce of labour', and which was 'organized somewhat on the plan of the Methodist Connexion' with a class leader to each thirty or forty members.[43] He was connected with the campaign for an unstamped press led by Hetherington and Cleave, and he was one of the founders of the London Working Men's Association whose deliberations gave birth to the People's Charter. In the Chartist movement Lovett stood on the moderate wing. He was secretary of the convention of 1839, and, after its removal to Birmingham, signed the resolutions protesting against the actions of the police brought down from London and against the restriction of the right of the people to meet in the Bull Ring. This led to his arrest and to his imprisonment for twelve months in the county gaol at Warwick.

After his release he moved away from political activity and concentrated on education and on international questions. He proposed the foundation of a 'National Association of the United Kingdom, for promoting the political and social improvement of the people' which should establish circulating libraries, print tracts and pamphlets, erect public halls and schools, and found normal schools for teachers and agricultural and industrial schools for orphans.[44] Such schemes were far too ambitious to be realized in full, but Lovett managed to open his National Hall, capable of holding 2,000 people in 1842, and some years later to start a day school there, which for some time he managed himself with the help of an assistant.[45]

Lovett was an idealist who saw better popular education as a step towards 'the coming age of freedom, peace and brotherhood'.[46] Many of the politicians, the clergy, the inspectors who wanted more and better schools would have shared the same hopes, but there was a clear difference of emphasis between them and people like Lovett and Place. Those who possessed political and economic power saw education as a means of preserving the existing social structure. It would be difficult to find in Lovett's writings a coherent educational doctrine to set against such ideas, but he and those who thought like him clearly wanted much more from education than that. Something of their aspirations towards a more open society comes out in the prospectus of Lovett's school at the National Hall:

> the object in forming this school is to provide for the children of the middle and working classes a sound, secular, useful, and moral education—such as is best calculated to prepare them for the practical businesses of life—to cause them to understand and perform their duties as members of society—and to enable them to diffuse the greatest amount of happiness among their fellow-men.[47]

v) Religion and philanthropy

It all depended in the end on how men interpreted 'their duties as members of society'. The radicals believed that too much emphasis was placed upon obedience, and many, though not all, of them deeply distrusted the introduction into the debate of religious teachings depending on supernatural commands rather than logical arguments. The position, as it appeared from the opposite ends of the debate, is very well summed up in two comments from Lancashire. The Oldham working-class leader John Knight said in a speech in 1830:

> He was not so ardent an admirer of the system upon which the Sunday Schools were at present conducted . . . in a word, instead of teaching the poor, or endeavouring to excite a free and independent spirit among them, the conductors of these schools might be considered as preparing the children for slavery and degradation.[48]

Ten years later John Clay, chaplain of Preston gaol, wrote in his annual report that he had been observing a group of Chartists and Socialists, who belonged to the lower ranks of society and who were self-educated:

> ... and are fully possessed with the notion that they are playing and have yet to play, an important part in public life;—while they are at the same time absurdly insensible to their ignorance in the most elementary subjects. The mysteries of spelling and grammar are impenetrable by them, but they will undertake to unloose the knottiest point of policy.[49]

The position of religion in the whole debate is a complex and difficult one. As one of the most powerful social disciplines of the day it was a powerful factor in many of the movements for self-help and self-improvement, yet some of those who were deeply interested in these aims distrusted its influence very much. Among them was Francis Place. Brian Harrison has worked out one aspect of the question by examining Place's attitude to the findings of the select committee of 1834 on drunkenness—and temperance was a virtue strongly advocated by powerful religious interests. Harrison argues that Place's attitude was determined by his dislike of Evangelicalism and of any policies which attempted to influence the working classes by notions of terror and fear rather than by an appeal to reason. Individuals, Place thought, must be educated to recognize their own interests, not schooled to rely on divine aid and the wise leadership of their superiors.[50]

The line of thinking represented by Place and Lovett—meliorist, secularist, anti-religious, confident in the power of human rationality—is an important strand in Victorian radical thinking, but it set its sights very high and was too demanding, too arid perhaps, for many people who needed more help on the way than this school of thought was inclined to give them. The power of religion flowed through every aspect of English life and wove a most complex network of relationships. Significantly, Samuel Smiles called mutual improvement societies 'the Educational Methodism of our day', and it was in one such group in Leeds that his famous book on *Self-Help* found its origins.[51] One of the greatest of the self-improvement bodies was the Young Men's Christian Association, founded in 1844, and the strongly Evangelical nature of its foundation, springing from a network of prayer meetings and chapel services, Sunday schools and ragged schools, is very clear.[52] Teetotalism provides another interesting example. The movement, which began in England at Preston in Lancashire in the early 1830's, had strongly Radical Nonconformist origins,[53] and is of special mark among such reforming movements because it began far from the capital and was fostered by humble people of modest station. It spread in a social sense upwards and outwards, though it always remained strong in the artisan and middle-class circles in which it had begun and it retained its strong links with Nonconformity.

Some prominent self-made men like Thomas Cook the travel agent, John Horniman the tea merchant, and publishers like Cassell and Collins were attracted to it,[54] and its members developed links with many other reforming and humanitarian movements. Indeed it is generally safe to argue that people who were strongly interested in one of these groups tended to have affiliations with many others. On the national scene Shaftesbury is the obvious example, and his religious and philanthropic interests were paralleled by many unknown men and women throughout the country. The religious interest, composed of the many interlacing networks of the pious and the charitable, could on occasion wield a formidable influence.

Religious beliefs—and the denominational rivalries which accompanied them—also spread over into politics. Political Nonconformity became a powerful force in education, in the opposition to church rates, in the movement to disestablish the Anglican church. There was a revivalist flavour to the programme of the Anti-Corn Law League which enjoyed active support among Nonconformist manufacturers and business men. Nonconformity had its links with working-class politics, and it has often been pointed out that these borrowed the organization of the Methodist chapels. What is more, the workers harnessed to political leadership the talents developed by the class leader and the local preacher; for example, chapel communities provided many of the early trade union leaders. Working-class activism was, however, not always welcome to the ministers and leading men of the chapels. It was, after all, not so long since Jabez Bunting had warned them that Methodism hated democracy as it hated sin. There was a dilemma here which it was not easy to resolve.

Radical Nonconformity, though it stood for political and religious freedom, stood also for closer social controls. Its supporters enforced the severe discipline of factory management which Engels called a slavery 'more abject than that of the negroes of America because . . . more strictly supervised'.[55] It demanded a closer control of public amusements and entertainments, an attitude which replaced an earlier type of Radicalism which, to take an example used by the Webbs, had attacked the authority of the justices to licence alehouses as an undesirable exercise of monopoly power.[56] Later Radicals were more inclined to think that in such cases restriction was more in the public interest than free trade.

Strong principles of regulation were built into all forms of working-class political and religious activity. The union demanded subscriptions, and its orders to strike or to return to work had to be obeyed. The chapel made demands for attendance at worship, for the renunciation of certain kinds of conduct and the acceptance of others, for almsgiving and for personal service. The associated organizations like cooperative societies and building societies[57] certainly brought benefits, but they demanded thrift and planning, the preference for long-term advantage against immediate pleasure. The working man who wished, and was able, as many were not, to participate in these many kinds of voluntary organization, imposed severe disciplines upon himself and his family by so doing. The pleasurable thing about them was that, unlike the disciplines of the factory, they were self-imposed.

Some relief was given to those who could not help themselves through the philanthropy which was a distinctive expression of the religious consciousness of the age.[58] Philanthropy may be defined as the desire to do good to others, the obligation of personal charity and service enjoined on all Christians—and accepted by many who were not Christians. It clearly links with social reforms in the broader sense; a man of philanthropic tendencies might well believe that he could do most to help his fellow human beings by promoting better sanitation or better housing. The word is used here not so much to suggest this kind of commitment to wider causes which might not involve any particular commitment to help individuals, but rather the provision of gifts and services to the needy on a personal basis where this was possible, and, where this was not directly possible, gifts to voluntary bodies or to individuals who themselves provided such personal services. Philanthropy thus implies the direct contact between donor and recipient, and the idea of warm kindness and self-giving love implicit in the idea clearly appealed to many people who were not especially moved by the claims of a reform programme which might take a long time to bring about results. In theory at least—though this was often difficult to achieve in practice—one major appeal of philanthropy was its immediacy. The beneficiaries came directly into contact with the donor.

Great pride was expressed at the time at the large number of charitable agencies, though there were many critics who asked whether the money was always well spent. Charitable giving of this kind satisfied the consciences of many pious people, but it conflicted with the creed of self-help because it was very difficult to be sure whether the recipients were 'deserving'. It was disliked by economists who wanted to remove, not to palliate, the causes of misery and distress, and by working class reformers who disliked the atmosphere of subservience connected with it. In a society of such wide social and financial differences the gulf between giver and receiver was a chasm indeed. Perhaps philanthropic giving actually strengthened class divisions. It was very easy to believe that generous personal giving made it unnecessary to tackle evils, the removal of which would have freed the poor to do more to help themselves. Philanthropy could in fact lead to a kind of social quietism which did nothing to take away the causes of social injustice, though it might be generous in remedying their actual manifestations. Moreover it worked in a very arbitrary way; those who benefited were those who suffered from afflictions which happened to arouse the sympathies of the charitable or who were in situations where their poverty could be easily noticed.

Yet for all its limitations as a remedy for social ills philanthropy was an essential strand in movements for reform, especially through its appeal to the religious public. Like foreign missions, it called out the crusading spirit of the time which has already been mentioned.[59] It was of the greatest real use when the element of personal self-sacrifice was linked with an interest in improving the whole system of human relationships. One such link was the concern of some of the clergy of the Established Church for social improvement. Clergymen like G.S. Bull of Bierley were active supporters for better conditions for Yorkshire factory workers. Others were good friends to the cause of sanitary reform like the Staffordshire incumbent Charles Girdlestone, who worked through two cholera epidemics and was an early supporter of the movement for better housing for the workers.[60]

Of all the religious bodies the Quakers were the most famed for this combination of personal service and an interest in wider public causes.[61] They were a small group and so they worked with other like-minded people; there was no movement completely dominated by them. Nor of course did all Quakers agree, for instance, on a subject like teetotalism; they always acted as individuals. However there are some causes in which their contribution was of particular importance. The first of these was the Peace Movement. The Peace Society had been founded in 1816, and the movement had a major revival between 1846 and 1854, when the Crimean War marked a major setback to the campaign for international arbitration and more harmonious relationships between states. There were links too between the peace and the anti-corn law movements. The latter had strong internationalist undertones and appeared to many people to combine philanthropy with self-interest. It is worth noting that Quakers generally opposed the limitation of factory hours. An old concern was anti-slavery, and a newer objective was the temperance movement, both in the moderate form of the renunciation of spirits and in the more extreme form of complete teetotalism. The Friends who became teetotallers were the first recruits from the higher ranks of society. They gave the movement a financial backing and an authority which it had not possessed before. Finally, it was the Quakers who first began the systematic instruction of illiterate adults, though the numbers influenced by their First Day Schools were always comparatively small. The first important step here was the foundation of a school at Birmingham by Joseph Sturge in 1845. The Friends First Day School Association followed in 1847. When the Quaker record is looked at as a whole, it makes an impressive tally of good works for so small a body.

VI. Poor Law, education and police

i) Edwin Chadwick and his policies

If there is one person whose ideas are central to the movement for social reform between 1830 and 1854, that person is Edwin Chadwick. For intellectual power, for the grasp of broad ideas and for knowledge of detail, there was no one in his generation to touch him, and he did more than anyone else to shift the government of England towards the concept of a tutelary state with strong central agencies, communicating with well-organized local bodies through an inspectorate and official memoranda. It is not too much to say that he opened up an entirely new vision of what public policy could achieve, and, although some of his ideas seemed to run into the ground in the 'fifties and 'sixties, he charted a direction which was never completely lost and which has determined many of the objectives of social policy in this country during the last century and a quarter.

To consider Chadwick as the initiator and organizer of change is to return to the major question of the influence of Jeremy Bentham on the reforming movement which has already been discussed in an earlier chapter.[1] Chadwick as a young man had been Bentham's secretary, and, with Southwood Smith, had helped him to complete the Constitutional Code. Chadwick was one of the main creators of the New Poor Law, and two distinctive features of that law—the controlling power of the central government department and the idea that paupers should always be treated less favourably than the poorest independent labourer—were Benthamite.[2] Because Bentham worked out an idea, this does not mean that it had not been developed by someone else as well, and the famous principle of 'less eligibility' provides an excellent example of this fact. A similar type of argument can be applied to Chadwick's ideas. His legal studies, his knowledge of poverty in London no doubt taught him a great deal, but the architecture of his mind, the broad design of his approach to policy was Benthamite, and it is difficult to believe that they would have been the same had he not known Bentham and worked on the Constitutional Code. Writers tend to throw the words 'Benthamite' and 'Utilitarian' about rather loosely when they are searching for the origins of reforming ideas in this period. In most cases it seems that Benthamism was 'in the air'. Politicians and publicists absorbed it, mixed at very different levels of concentration with ideas of many different kinds. Yet there are a few people on whom the Benthamite mark may be traced rather more clearly than through this kind of diffused influence, and Chadwick was the most important of them. Like the master he embraced the whole range of social and preventive policies in a concept of governmental activity which could be applied in many different fields. Apart from Utilitarianism, there was no other concept at that level of generality available for him to use in the intellectual climate of his time.

The first and most obvious contrast between the two men is that Bentham was a theorist and Chadwick a practical man of affairs. He did not have the purely intellectual qualities to outline a whole theory of public policy, as Bentham had done over half a century or more ago. On the other hand he had a remarkable grasp of detail, and an ability to conceive schemes and to put them into practice, which made him an outstanding administrator. Yet in one sense he shared the generalizing qualities of Bentham's mind in a way which limited his practical success. He could both conceive a general scheme and plan the details, and, because he had an inflexible conviction that he was right, he could be impossible to shift once he had made up his mind. This quality was a source of strength, but it could also be a source of weakness, since it meant that he found it difficult to compromise, or to accept change in a situation as a result of new evidence.

Much of this general cast of mind arose no doubt from his own natural temperament, and would have been so had he never met Bentham. It is possible, however, that this kind of temperament was strengthened by the influence upon him of Utilitarian doctrines. Bentham had presented to him as a young man a complete scheme of social policy which seemed to cover all possible eventualities. The very detailed way in which Bentham worked out the statements of his own Constitutional Code suggests that, had he been forced to make practical decisions, he might have found it as hard to compromise as Chadwick did. It is at least possible that the whole style, so as to speak, of Chadwick's administrative policies may have been influenced by his acceptance of a very comprehensive yet equally inflexible scheme of thinking. It was a concept of uniformity and regularity in government which fitted with difficulty into the practical pre-occupations of English politics.

Chadwick took an active part in most of the social reforms of the period. He was one of the commissioners who produced the Poor Law Report of 1834. He and Nassau Senior were the most active members of the commission, and they wrote the report between them.[3] Disappointed in his hope of becoming one of the executive commissioners appointed under the New Poor Law of 1834, Chadwick was persuaded to become their secretary, a position which he found extremely frustrating because the commissioners systematically excluded him from exercising any real influence over policy. While the poor law enquiry was still in hand, Chadwick and his fellow Benthamites Thomas Tooke and Southwood Smith were appointed commissioners to conduct the enquiry of 1833 into the employment of children in factories. Six years later he drafted the report of the royal commission on the establishment of a constabulary force in the counties, a report in which he made use of ideas he had already worked out in a review article of 1829 on preventive police.

By the end of the 'thirties Chadwick was disillusioned with poor law administration. He felt more and more that his superiors had no real policy to deal with pauperism, but were confined to a series of short-term expedients. His own interests gradually shifted into the field of public health, since it was already clear that there was a close connection between poverty and disease. An important step was taken when three medical men, Arnott, Kay(-Shuttleworth) and Southwood Smith, made enquiries for the poor law commissioners into conditions in East London, which for the first time revealed to the general public something of the horrors of disease and misery in the poorer districts of the capital. In 1842 Chadwick published his own report on the sanitary condition of the labouring population, a massive work of investigation and synthesis which made a deep impression on the public and which opened up an entirely new vein of social enquiry with which Chadwick's name will always be associated.[4] For the following decade public health attracted more attention than any other social problem, and Chadwick, whether for praise or more often for obloquy, was the central figure in the debate. The problem of public health proved to be a central issue in social enquiry because, even more than the problem of pauperism, it extended into every geographical area, every class, every sphere of interest.

If these practical problems were to be solved, some method of cooperation had to be found between the new ideas of directive government and the traditional autonomies of the English representative system. Here Chadwick faced his greatest problem; however excellent his ideas in themselves, he had to convince both parliament and the welter of local bodies, vestries, town corporations, improvement commissioners, water companies who shared the existing responsibility. David Roberts considers that Chadwick did not favour centralization on the French model, but preferred a balance of power between central and local authorities, the former to determine general policy, and the latter to deal with day to day problems.[5] The Poor Law Report of 1834 is not very specific on the matter—in so far as its recommendations can be taken as expressing Chadwick's views. They say a great deal about the powers of the central department, but not very much about local administration except for statements that parishes should be combined together for various purposes including the organization of workhouses. The local authorities set up under the Act of 1834, the Guardians of the Poor, were elected bodies which in practice exercised a good deal of power.

Ten years later, when Chadwick had become absorbed in public health problems, he had come to believe that all such local representative bodies were ineffective. What was needed, he believed, was a combination of strong central control and local management in the hands of persons appointed, not elected, and preferably officials rather than local notabilities. His experience of representative and coopted bodies of all kinds and of the water companies had been uniformly unfavourable, and his recommendations for change all tended in the direction of a greater concentration of power in official hands. In a memorandum of 1844 he suggested the appointment of medical officers of health with extensive powers to control sickness and to enforce the law against nuisances.[6] He suggested in the same year the establishment of a central authority, acting on the advice of a responsible legal officer who would direct local enquiries and would nominate for appointment the members of the local public health commissions.[7] Particular difficulties had arisen in London where the tangle of existing local bodies was the most complex, the most difficult to manage and the most corrupt. In a plan of 1850 for the control of London's water supplies Chadwick dismissed the idea of municipal management, and suggested that the task should be put in the hands of a 'small board of paid and skilled officials'. Such a small group would have the skill and authority to push business through at many times the speed of the thirteen existing boards of commissioners of sewers.[8] Nor did Chadwick have much more respect for Parliament than he possessed for local municipalities and water companies. After his retirement he wrote:

> In the present condition and practice of legislation . . . no measure based on administrative principles, partaking of science or system, goes into the House of Commons that as a general rule, does not come out worse than it went in.[9]

During the last century most of what Chadwick campaigned for has come to pass, and, from the point of view of the modern age, he had right on his side in many of his campaigns. No man could have undertaken what he tried to do without bringing torrents of opposition upon himself. Yet it must also be said that a man prepared sometimes to bow to the wind might have achieved rather more. He tried too resolutely to brush aside the prejudices of conservative, traditionalist, aristocratic England; he made no real attempt to win over his opponents by the gentler arts of persuasion and management. He made up his mind and, once he had done so, he was impossible to shift. His inflexibility was ultimately a source of weakness rather than of strength.

Some of this must have been just a matter of personal temperament. Some of it may have arisen from the fact that, in political terms, he was an outsider dealing with aristocratic politicians who had little sympathy with what he stood for. Something of this absolutist cast of mind must also have come from his Utilitarianism. The point has often been made that Benthamism was not really a creed of liberty. Once prejudice and tradition had been broken down by the reformer, the state was left unhindered to exercise, in the name of the greatest good of the greatest number, an unhindered domain over its citizens. Though the principle of utility certainly operated to remove some restrictions, it could be invoked to favour the introduction of others in their place. In the reformed age human lives were likely to be more dominated by public authority than they had been under the ancient régime. Perhaps there was more 'laissex faire' in the England of Blackstone than in that of Chadwick. Chadwick had his successes and his failures, but many of the failures sprang ultimately from the fact that the English are not sympathetic to government based on a theory which claims to embrace the whole of human experience. They understand the need for theories and for logical argument, but they do not welcome them in an undiluted form. Bentham himself might have had to learn that lesson had he been a man of affairs. Chadwick certainly had to learn it. For better or for worse, the country preferred more pragmatic remedies than he was prepared to advise.

ii) The New Poor Law of 1834

A recent writer on Chadwick has said that he has been unfortunate because 'of all his work, it is the Poor Law which is best remembered and which his name first calls to mind'.[10] The pre-occupation of the generation before 1830 with the problem of poverty and the steadily rising level of the poor rates has already been studied in an earlier chapter.[11] The Poor Law Commission of 1832-34 under the chairmanship of the Bishop of London, C.J. Blomfield, produced a programme to tackle the problem of pauperism. There was much in their report which had been said by the select committees of the 'twenties. Essentially what they did was both to make a convincing case against the abuses of the old system and to suggest practical measures for the implementation of the policies which they proposed. Though their study of the subject of poverty was in some ways incomplete and superficial, the report was strong both in the negative and in the positive senses. It was not enough to diagnose what was wrong, for that was well known. What was essential was to suggest a positive policy which promised to have a good chance of success. This the commissioners were able to do, and their proposals were accepted by Parliament with very little discussion. Their report was a successful piece of salesmanship as much as a penetrating analysis of the problem of pauperism. It convinced the majority of the ruling classes that here was the key to the problems which had beset English society since the beginning of the French wars.

The great source of abuse, the report argued, was the system of outdoor relief paid to the able-bodied on their own behalf or on that of their families.[12] This relief was given in four principal ways: through the payment of house-rent for cottages occupied by the poor; through gifts of money, especially the making up of wages according to scales related to the price of bread; through the subsidizing of wages by the 'roundsman' system of employment; and through the agreement of ratepayers to employ labourers according to some tariff fixed according to the circumstances of the parish. Very little relief was given through the parish itself providing work. The granting of outdoor relief to the impotent poor—the aged, the sick and young children—led to fewer abuses because, the commissioners argued, less profit could be made out of maladministration,[13] and in fact their recommendations concentrated on the problem of the able-bodied. There was little change after 1834 in the system of relief for the aged and sick.

Outdoor relief for the able-bodied had, it was claimed, made the poor discontented and unwilling to work. Not only did it lead to evergrowing expense, but it made the law difficult to administer because of the pressures which the poor could exercise to obtain generous treatment for themselves. The more generous the allowances, it was said, the more discontented and disorderly the poor became. Nor would it be advantageous to turn over to indoor relief within the workhouse unless the workhouses themselves were reformed. In their existing state they were quite unsuccessful in disciplining their inmates because their management was very unsystematic.

> ... in by far the greater number of cases, it [the workhouse] is a large almshouse, in which the young are trained in idleness, ignorance and vice; the able-bodied maintained in sluggish sensual indolence; the aged and more respectable exposed to all the misery that is incident to dwelling in such a society, without government or classification, and the whole body of inmates subsisted on food far exceeding both in kind and in amount, not merely the diet of the independent labourer, but that of the majority of persons who contribute to their support.[14]

The more relief was given, and the greater the pressure on the poor rates, the more rural labourers became hostile to those who had to administer the law and the more they deteriorated as workmen. Clearly the commissioners thought that nothing effective could be done without a better system of practical management because, under the supervision of the parish overseers, it was very difficult for checks against overexpenditure to operate. The overseers had neither the time nor the incentive to do their work properly. They were often subject to threats or even to actual violence. The parish vestries, whether they were closed or open, felt no real responsibility to maintain control, and were often tempted into corruption or various kinds of dishonesty. It was, for instance, difficult for small tradesmen to stand out against the clamour of the poor when the poor were the tradesmen's best customers. At a higher level the magistrates had allowed a bad system to take root; it was, after all, quarter sessions which had introduced the Speenhamland system. Somewhat removed as they were from the immediate pressures of parish life, they sometimes did harm by interfering with the decisions of the overseer when they were unlikely to have detailed knowledge of relief matters. The commissioners argued that the jurisdiction of the magistrates should be used only sparingly, and should not form part of the routine of administration. In the light of all these criticisms it is not surprising that the report put great emphasis on the unified national system of poor relief with a strong central body administering general rules to which local bodies had to adhere.

Such was the commission's analysis of the basic problem. What did they think should be done about it? First of all they disposed of the remedies which they thought inappropriate. They did not favour adopting a national basis of chargeability for the poor laws, because they thought that this would remove barriers to expenditure and would increase the total burdens on the public. The standard of relief would in fact become the standard of the most extravagant. One set of problems which they did not tackle because they did not wish to alter the parochial basis of rating were the ancient abuses connected with the law of settlement. The commissioners did not believe that it would be possible to help the labourers by giving them plots of land to occupy; either the plots would be too small to make any real difference, or, if they were larger, the labourer would be exposed to new dangers as a petty farmer without adequate resources. No scheme of forcing the ratepayers to employ and pay the labourers could be put into action without being unfair to someone. By its very nature a labour-rate system would break down the essential distinction between pauperism and independence. Since it would create all kinds of vested interests, which would expand as it operated, it would have the further disadvantage of making future reforms even more difficult to achieve.

Thus the commissioners rejected a national rating system, the creation of allotments and a labour-rate. They might have argued, as many people like Malthus and Thomas Chalmers had done, that a compulsory system of poor relief should be abandoned altogether, and that the relief of the poor should be turned over to private charity. In fact they did not take this course, an important point to which we shall return later. They began their positive suggestions for remedial measures with the statement that a compulsory provision for the relief of the indigent could and should be preserved. This provision was to be controlled, however, by the principle of less eligibility; this principle, so crucial for the social policy of the following generation, is important enough to be stated in their own words.

The first and most essential of all conditions, a principle which we find universally admitted, even by those whose practice is at variance with it, is, that his [the individual relieved] situation on the whole shall not be made really or apparently so eligible as the situation of the independent labourer of the lowest class. Throughout the evidence it is shown, that in proportion as the condition of any pauper class is elevated above the condition of independent labourers, the condition of the independent class is depressed; their industry is impaired, their employment becomes unsteady, and its remuneration in wages is diminished. Such persons, therefore, are under the strongest inducements to quit the less eligible class of labourers and enter the more eligible class of paupers. The converse is the effect when the pauper class is placed in its proper position, below the condition of the independent labourer. Every penny bestowed, that tends to render the condition of the pauper more eligible than that of the independent labourer, is a bounty on indolence and vice. We have found that as the poor's rates are at present administered, they operate as bounties of this description, to the amount of several millions annually.[15]

Nor, the commissioners claimed, was this a matter of theory, because where measures of this kind had been taken, they had been successful, both Southwell and Bingham were quoted as examples of this fact.[16] The absorption of paupers into productive work had been followed by a rise in wages because more diligent work increases the general wages fund. Increase in population had been checked because the number of improvident marriages had been reduced, and crime had diminished. Where men had been refused poor relief, they found it in their own interest to be sober and prudent.

What the commissioners wished to do was to extend the attempts at reform which had already been made and to create a central agency to direct the whole system. All relief to the able-bodied should be given in well regulated workhouses, and this should apply in the towns as well as in the country. The greatest obstacle to efficient administration under the present system was the incapacity and ignorance of the parish officers and their exposure to intimidation by the paupers. This necessitated much more central control; it could be put right only by the creation of 'an especial agency ... to superintend and control' the execution of the law.[17] Local officials should be given no discretion in the distribution of relief. If they had to work under general regulations, these would be obeyed because it would be clear that there was no way of evading them.

The key to reform, therefore, would be the establishment of a central board to control the administration of the law with a body of assistant commissioners as its local agents. Three commissioners and eight to ten assistant commissioners were suggested. The central board should be given power to frame uniform regulations for the management of workhouse and the nature and amount of relief. The board should be enabled to incorporate parishes in order to provide new workhouses better organized and staffed than the existing houses, and in order to ensure that the incorporated parishes appointed and paid permanent officials. The board was not itself to appoint such officials, but it should have powers to remove unsuitable people from their posts. Most of the detailed recommendations of the report need not concern us here, but the general statement about the duties of the central board is important because it provides a model for the new kind of tutelary government of which the Poor Law Report is the first herald. The executive commissioners were to act on the widest possible information and without any tendency to be swayed by bias or intimidation. They would operate with clear objectives, powerful means of obtaining those objectives, and clear rules of practice. They must be given a wide discretion, and while they kept the confidence of Parliament and government they should enjoy wide powers to bring the new system into force.[18] Their enthusiasm and their integrity would be the key to success in the struggle against pauperism.

The act of 1834 kept very close to the proposals of the commission. A body of poor law commissioners was set up, the first central administrative agency with a specific duty to enforce a national programme of social policy, and assistant commissioners were appointed. Local management was based on unions of parishes, each of which was to have an elected board of guardians of the poor with power to select their own officials. The new system got going rapidly in the southern counties, but much difficulty was experienced in the north, particularly in Yorkshire. Part of the difficulty arose from the fact that the new law was not introduced into the northern counties until the late 'thirties when the country had run into a major depression. There were also serious limitations to the new poor law policy in its application to industrial areas. Though there are references to the towns, it is very noticeable that the report is written largely in terms of the situation of the rural labourer, and gives little attention to urban problems. In 1830, it is true, agriculture was still England's greatest industry, and agricultural problems 'loomed largest in men's minds. The Webbs, for example, pointed out that the labourers' revolt of 1830 had increased the desire for reform because it was argued that rioting was worst in those areas where the allowance system was most generally in operation, that is, in southern England.[19] Certainly the authors of the report were very conscious of the dangers arising from agrarian unrest. Yet the problems in the agricultural counties were in general those of pauperization. The problem in the industrial areas was that of seasonal unemployment to which the sacred principles of less eligibility and the workhouse test offered much less satisfactory solutions because they provided no means of dealing with distress brought about by changes in the trade cycle and the movement of international markets for textiles. In fact, as we shall see, the new principles were in many areas enforced only to a very limited extent.

The Poor Law Commission had claimed that, if the measures which they advocated were put into effect, 'the expenditure for the relief of the poor will in a very short period be reduced by more than one-third'.[20] The statistician G.R. Porter calculated that in the year 1831-2 the sum expended for the relief of the poor was equal to an average payment for the whole population of 9s. 11½d. per head. For the year 1848-9 the similar average payment per head was 6s. 6½d., or a saving of 30% on the payments in 1832, which represented a real saving of 40% if the increase in population was taken into account.[21] It would, of course, be an over-simplification to argue that this change represents a simple relationship of cause and effect, yet the change, whatever the reasons for it, is a striking one.

The New Poor Law was always extremely unpopular. It was criticized as harsh and bureaucratic. The workhouses were satirized as bastilles in which married couples were separated from one another and the inmates tyrannized over by insensitive officials like Dickens' Mr. Bumble the beadle. *The Times* attacked the system over a long period, and there was a major scandal in the 'forties when it was established that the paupers in the Andover Union workhouse were so starved that they fought among themselves for the rotting bones which they had to crush for manure.[22]

The Andover scandal arose from the mismanagement of an inhumane workhouse master. In practice the changes between the old and the new systems were not as great as the report of 1834 had proposed. The new policy had concentrated on the problem of the outdoor relief of the able-bodied. There had been no real consideration of the problem of poverty in general and no statistical enquiry. The system of relief for the impotent poor was not much changed. The commissioners under the new law did not exercise the omnipotent bureaucratic authority of which their critics complained. They lacked the power to make the guardians initiate new policies.[23] They did not introduce the reformed workhouse system with separate classification for the different types of pauper which had been recommended in the Poor Law Report. There were continued problems about recruiting for the unions officials who were efficient and honest and the guardians made some very bad appointments.

Nor were the poor law commissioners themselves men with the vision and the foresight to carry out far-reaching policies. Between their hesitations and the obstructiveness of the guardians, Chadwick, their secretary, who did have a picture of broad social policy, soon found that there was little he could do. The administration of the system tended to become more and more formalized and dominated by routine. The extent of innovation can easily be exaggerated. A recent writer has described what he calls 'the savage changes which did occur in 1834 as no more than an extension of an established method, devised and revised from time to time in order to care for and discipline the various classes of poor people'.[24] The continuity between old and new is brought out in several local studies. In Lancashire, though the total amount spent on poor relief was low, outdoor relief continued to be given in aid of wages and the workhouse test was not enforced. The workhouses continued to be chaotic and insanitary and were not reformed until the 'fifties and 'sixties. Few paid staff were employed by the guardians, who were opposed to central interference.[25] A similar point is made by a recent study of Co. Durham which shows that local considerations rather than central policy were predominant in the granting of relief. It was in fact the commissioners who pressed upon local people a reasonably enlightened policy.[26]

One major result of the Report of 1834 was to reaffirm the principle that the system of state-financed poor relief should continue. Nassau Senior, who had a major influence on the report, had earlier expressed the view that the poor laws should not be reformed, but abolished altogether, though he abandoned this opinion in the early stages of the enquiry.[27] Such an enormous change in national habit would probably have been impossible after two centuries under the old law, but even had it been possible, it might well not have been good economics. The Edinburgh medical professor, W.P. Alison, to whom Kay-Shuttleworth had served as an assistant, wrote an interesting pamphlet in 1840 on the management of the poor in Scotland.[28] Alison argued that, because of the existence of a legal provision for poor relief in England, the condition of the English poor was better than that of the Scots. They had greater motives to practice prudence and restraint. They were more contented and more inclined to work hard. Below a certain level of misery, Alison argued, people do not practise restraint at all; they simply behave like animals. Nor in a complex society could the problem of poverty be left to individual charity; it was unavoidable that the problem of destitution should be dealt with by the public purse if degradation and misery were to be avoided, and disease was not to spread. These were the kinds of arguments which appealed to Chadwick, and which strengthened the case for maintaining the compulsory system. The decision to do so was of the greatest importance for the future development of social policy in England. Imperfect the New Poor Law may have been, but it did reaffirm the principle that the state had an obligation to ensure some basic standard of livelihood for its citizens. From that concern developed most of our modern programme of public welfare.

iii) The Beginnings of national education

The Poor Law Report spoke of the need, after the law had been reformed 'to take measures to promote the religious and moral education of the labouring classes'[29] and several of the assistant commissioners recommended a national system of education as a means of dealing with pauperism.[30] Something was done after 1834 for the education of children in workhouses though very much less than people like Kay-Shuttleworth, who wanted to collect them away from the houses into district schools, desired to achieve.

There was widespread interest in education during the 1830's, as is evidenced by the fact that three House of Commons Select Committees investigated the subject—in 1834, 1835 and 1837-8. The general claim that better education reduces crime came up again and again and there is no need to say any more about it here. Certain other themes recur regularly. Very little confidence was placed in the influence of the parents who, it was argued, were likely to obstruct rather than to promote the education of their children.[31] There was some difference of opinion about the respective emphases which should be placed on moral and on secular instruction. The Scottish educationalist James Pillans, professor of humanity at Edinburgh, criticized the schools of the National Society for their concentration on religious teaching and the extremely limited nature of the general information given to the children.[32] On the other side another witness to the 1834 committee, Benjamin Braidley, who had been connected with church Sunday schools in Manchester, claimed that, although a good literary education increased the comforts of life, no education really promoted the welfare of the nation unless it was based on sound moral and religious instruction.[33]

Braidley's view was the more popular at the time. Better education, it was believed, produced moral fruit in more industrious and more tractable workmen. Bishop Blomfield, chairman of the poor law commission, who was anxious that church schools should give effective secular instruction, pointed out that the evidence which the commission had collected proved the superiority of educated over uneducated labourers. In the agricultural riots 'the most desperate of the offenders were always the most illiterate'. Further the bishop, perhaps looking back on his first see of Chester, compared the two manufacturing towns of Stockport and Oldham. In one, where a large proportion of the population was under instruction, the workers were industrious and tractable. In the other, where the proportion of workers under instruction was much lower, the reverse was the case.[34] The evidence of Kay-Shuttleworth on this subject is of particular importance since it was he, as first secretary of the Committee of Council for Education after 1839, who really organized the educational planning of government. Superior artisans, he thought, valued education but the great majority of working men did not. Like many of his contemporaries he was very frightened of the power of trade unions and of political agitators. The authority of these men derived largely from the ignorance of the workers about their real interests, a situation which education alone could remedy.

> ... the best objects of the education of the poorer classes cannot be attained, unless whatever secular instruction is given to the poor be combined with careful moral and religious training.[35]

In his evidence to the 1837-8 select committee Kay-Shuttleworth argued that it would be best if the whole cost of education could be provided by the parents, but that a school-rate was necessary to guard the schoolmasters against loss.[36] By that time government had already entered the field. The first grants to the National and British Societies had been made in 1833. In 1839 the Committee of Council for Education was set up to administer the grants, and soon afterwards the first H.M.I.s were appointed. The Minutes of 1846 organized the pupil-teacher system and involved the government deeply in financing the training of teachers. The public commitment to popular education was to grow enormously in the twenty years after 1840.

It is not always remembered that another form of educational control came about through the Factory Acts. The crucial act of 1833 not only limited the hours of children under the age of 13 in the factories to which it applied, but it also provided that they were to attend school. Since no measures were taken to supply such schools, the law was extremely difficult to enforce. In 1839 the reports of the inspectors pointed out the bad condition of many of the schools.[37] When in the next year factory inspectors gave evidence to Ashley's select committee of 1840, they considered that the educational provision of the law was frequently a mockery.[38] In 1843 Graham's proposed factory bill made definite provisions for part-time schooling, but the bill had to be dropped because of the Nonconformists' opposition to the school management clauses which, they considered, gave undue influence to the Church of England. However the act passed in a revised form in 1844. Children's working hours were arranged on a half-time basis, and it was provided that they must attend school during the remainder of the day. The inspectors reported that education for factory children was more effective after the act of 1844 partly because, with half a day free, they could attend the ordinary National and British schools.[39]

Half-time schooling was a very imperfect system and it applied only to a minority of the children at work, but it was something, and it would not have come about without the compulsion of the state. The proper limits of state authority in educational matters were keenly debated. There were many Nonconformists who took up a completely voluntarist view, arguing that education, like religion, was something which should be left entirely to the conscience of the individual. Henry Brougham told the select committee of 1834 that he was against education by public provision because this would lead to the withdrawal of private benevolence, and because a national system of education might lead to the control of opinion by government.[40] Yet in an age which publicized with such vigour the advantages of laissez-faire and self-help there was a surprisingly strong current of opinion which urged that government had a duty to ensure that the people were properly instructed. It was expressed by G.R. Porter in his economic survey, *The Progress of the Nation,* a book of strongly free trade sympathies, when he wrote:

It would appear to be the duty of every government to see that its subjects are taught their duties as men and as citizens, and thus to provide for the security of all.[41]

The report of the hand-loom weavers' commission, of which Nassau Senior was chairman, pointed out in similar fashion that the commitment to provide education which was contained in the Factory Act should be extended to cover children in other kinds of work. Parents, guardians or masters should be required to show that children under their care attended school or possessed the average information of educated children of the appropriate age. The state should provide inspectors and teacher-training establishments out of the national revenue, while other expenses should be met out of local rates and by fees paid by parents. It was also suggested that a royal commission should be set up to look into the question of a system of national education.[42] The same kind of argument was put forward by politically conscious working men. The London Working Men's Association declared in an address published in 1837 that it was the duty of government to provide the best possible system of education for all classes; 'the erection of schools and colleges should be at the expense of the nation'.[43]

Since opinions of this kind were being put forward in the 'thirties and 'forties, it remains to answer the question why it took so long for government to assume general responsibility for national education. A good deal was done in a rather piecemeal way, but no national legislation was passed until 1870, and even then the elected school boards shared the task with the voluntary societies. To avoid repetition, it will be most convenient to discuss the whole issue in a later chapter which deals with the passage of the Forster Act.[44]

iv) Police and the Constabulary Report of 1839

For another forty years after 1830 local initiatives remained of great importance in education because early and mid-Victorian England was still a highly localized society. It was the activity and conscientiousness of the parish clergyman, the landowner, the board of managers which determined whether there was to be a school at all and how well it was to be supported. The educational setting mirrored the general scene. It has been pointed out, for example, that even after the increase in general legislation in the 'thirties, local acts of parliament remained the normal method of carrying through administrative change.[45] Two general acts affecting local government were particularly important during the 'thirties. The first of these, the New Poor Law, has already been discussed. The second was the Municipal Corporations Act of 1835. The reform of the old town councils formed a natural complement to the reform of the old parliamentary system with which the boroughs had been so closely connected. It is important to note that there was a major difference between the two laws. The Poor Law set up a central authority with an inspectorate and supervisory powers over the guardians. The borough law created no central supervisory authority and provided no measures to ensure that the corporations reached a minimum standard of efficiency. In fact the reformed town councils enjoyed only limited powers. It was to be a long time, for example, before they gained control over the various improvement commissioners and an even longer period before they took an active part in creating a healthier environment. One of their difficulties was that their financial powers were limited.[46] Yet the Act of 1835 did preserve the idea of a general authority for the borough with power to levy a rate, and, as the century went on, the town corporations gradually acquired more and more of the powers which had been given to 'ad hoc' bodies.[47]

One task entrusted to the town councils by the Municipal Corporations Act was the power to raise a police force. There was at the time a widespread belief that crime was increasing. One recent writer argues that it is almost impossible to decide whether this was so or not, though he thinks it possible that population growth provided greater opportunities for the criminal.[48] According to G.R. Porter there was a striking increase in the number of persons committed for trial—4,605 in 1805, 27,816 in 1848—and an increase in the number of convictions from 58.8% of committals at the beginning of the period to 74.03% of committals at the end.[49] Of course an increase in the number of convictions could have arisen simply from more effective police methods and from an increase in the population.

Measures against crime could take two forms: a more efficient preventive police and an improved prison system which attempted to reform the criminal. A new prisons act (1835) provided for closer supervision by the Home Office and for the appointment of prison inspectors.[50] The method of organization which the inspectors favoured was the 'separate' system. New prisons were built at Pentonville (1840-2) and at Reading (1844), and a corridor of separate cells was opened at Preston in 1843.[51] It was in these three prisons that the chief attempt was made to combine reformation with punishment. Separation and solitude were the key to reform because they broke up associations with other prisoners and thus made it possible for religious influences to operate on the mind and will. Religion, education and practical training would all cooperate together in the work of reform.[52] Much thought was also given to the problems of young offenders. If the inspiration for the separate system had been American, in the case of the reformatories it was German and French.[53] An important step here was the opening of the Philanthropic Society's farm school at Redhill in 1848. In 1854 the Youthful Offenders Act authorized the establishment of reformatories by private groups, and in 1857 another act set up industrial schools to which magistrates could send young vagrants who were in danger of becoming criminals.[54]

Effective police forces were not established throughout the country until the Act of 1856. The Metropolitan Police, despite many early difficulties, had already established its worth. A select committee of 1833-34 praised it as one of the most valuable of modern institutions because of its influence in repressing crime and in giving security to person and property.[55] Its officers were often detailed to help in the formation of provincial forces.[56] Its powers were clarified and its numbers and its area enlarged by the Metropolitan Police Act of 1839, which abolished the Bow Street Runners and the constables of the stipendiary courts, and transferred to the new force the Thames police and the duties of court police.[57] Borough forces were set up in a number of towns, but it seems that there was a less sharp break with the past than there had been in London, and in many places the level of efficiency was still low in the 'fifties. There was no system of central inspection, it was very difficult to get good officers and the pay was poor. There were dangers that the police forces would be exposed to political interference, and the fear still survived that an efficient force was a danger to liberty.[58]

Though something had been done in London and the towns the country districts remained largely unpoliced. The whole subject of crime and disorder was investigated by a royal commission, which reported in 1839 and the report of which is one of Chadwick's major state papers.[59] It began by analyzing the various types of crime, which were to be divided broadly into two classes: attacks on property, and robbery and violence. Many of these offences, it was argued, were committed by vagrants and mendicants who wandered about the countryside, using trampers' lodging-houses as their bases. They tended to concentrate in rural districts because better policing had made it more difficult for them to stay in the larger towns. Since the traditional system of local constables had proved quite ineffective in dealing with these problems, there had been a considerable growth of voluntary associations to deal with crime, among them the police forces of the various railway companies. This kind of voluntary policing was undesirable, the report argued, because it led to overlapping of functions and excessive expense. Moreover it handed over to private persons, who might use the powers for their own advantage, what should have been a major public responsibility.

Crime, it was argued, arose, not from want or destitution but rather 'from the temptation of obtaining property with a less degree of labour than by regular industry'.[60] Particular stress was laid on violence and intimidation arising from industrial disputes, in which trades unions and militant agitators used coercive methods to maintain their interests against their employers. Again this industrial violence did not spring from poverty; it was caused by the few and the well-paid, not by the many. Sometimes the harm done by intimidation was economic, sometimes it threatened actual breach of the peace. There was a serious danger that the pressure of workmen's combinations would drive capital abroad. In the manufacturing districts—and Oldham was particularly mentioned— agitators had stirred up feeling against employers, disorders had taken place, manufacturers were arming for their own protection, and the law could not be enforced because witnesses were too terrified to give evidence.

The only remedy for the insecurity of property and the danger of intimidation was a well-trained and well-organized constabulary. The next question the commissioners had to consider was how such a force might be organized. One model which had been used in a number of instances was a force covering quite a small district, and a detailed examination was made of a scheme set up in Cheshire under an act of 1829, based on the petty sessional divisions and controlled by the magistrates. In the judgment of the report this arrangement had not been successful. The number of men employed was too small and they had not been properly trained. The administrative areas were too small, and there was no proper relationship between them so that it was impossible to provide the steady flow of information which was essential to good police work. The minimum area for successful policing was the county and it was essential, if criminals were not to slip through the net, that there should be proper co-ordination between town and country districts. Nor was it desirable, as in the Cheshire example, to confuse the judicial responsibilities of the magistrates with the control and management of the police, and the distinction between the two had been rightly made in London when the Metropolitan Police had been set up.

It was the London system, the report concluded, which offered the model for the new kind of trained constabulary. The expenses would be moderate and money would actually be saved because of the reduction in crime of all kinds which would ensue. The new police would be able to perform many tasks other than the purely coercive. They might deal with accidents and calamities of all kinds, including problems of vagrancy and destitution; they might act as firemen, serve writs, and help to enforce the customs and excise laws. In fact, they would perform a general 'social service' function in addition to their duties in preventing crime.[61]

Great emphasis was laid by the report on comprehensive planning. Separate county forces would not meet the situation. There should be a single force throughout the country, based on a unified system controlled by commissioners of police. Within this general structure the county units should act as far as possible like the Metropolitan Police divisions. The finance should be provided one quarter from the Consolidated Fund and three quarters from the county rates. The policemen should be appointed by the senior officers of the force not by the magistrates, they should be properly trained, and they should be moved periodically from district to district so that they formed no undesirable local attachments. In such a national force the dangers arising from local jealousies and local acts of arbitrariness would be much reduced. It was clear, however, that such sweeping changes could be made only gradually, not least because the number of trained police in the country was so small. The report suggested therefore that the system should be introduced permissively when a county quarter sessions asked for this to be done. However one important reservation was made, very much in line with the fears expressed of industrial violence and coercion:

a power should be given to Her Majesty's Government to provide for the preservation of the peace by an efficient constabulary force in those of the manufacturing or other districts where any free deliberation on the subject is prevented by the influence of the interests adverse to good order or legal restraints.[62]

Not surprisingly these very radical proposals were implemented only to a very limited extent. The County Constabulary Acts of 1839 and 1840 enabled county quarter sessions to decide whether or not to set up a police force. Though the Home Secretary was allowed to frame general rules, there were no provisions for coordination between the various forces, no powers of inspection or power to enforce minimum standards. By 1851 little more than half the counties had been covered and the forces were very unequal in value.[63]

So Chadwick's scheme for a unified national system remained an unfulfilled ideal. Nevertheless the Constabulary Report fills an important place in the story of tutelary government with which this chapter has been largely concerned. The scheme, like the New Poor Law and the plans of the 'forties for sanitation and water supply, bears the hall-mark of Chadwick's breadth of view, his ability to conceptualize a whole area of policy and to produce a coherent scheme. The Constabulary Report itself pointed out that the plan of 'a central control in combination with local management' had already been successfully tested in the administration of poor relief.[64] The two reports, from their different standpoints, share the same views about the links between idleness, vagrancy and crime. In the view of the report of 1839 the mendicants who frequented the trampers' lodging houses 'obtain more money with less labour than is obtainable by means of honest industry by a large body of labourers'.[65] A more efficient police force, by making it more difficult for these people to live by robbing and cheating, would be reinforcing the principle of less eligibility which was enforced by the guardians and their officers. Crime and idleness must cease to pay; if that could be achieved, there was more chance that hard work would replace them.

Both reports expressed fear at the dangers arising from working-class disorder. In 1834 this fear related principally to the agricultural troubles of 1830, in 1839 to the industrial districts and to workers' combinations. The question was very much in people's minds whether a more efficient police force, even if it were successful in putting down disorder, might endanger liberty since it would greatly increase the power of the state. The Constabulary Report concluded by examing this question. It pointed out that the evils which had been studied were in themselves a worse danger to the liberty of the subject than any measures likely to be taken by government. The real danger lay, not in public authority being over-aggressive but in its being impotent to act for the public good.

The safe course for maintaining the freedom of the subject appears to us to be, not to render the authorities impotent, but to make them strictly responsible for the use of the power with which they may be invested for the public service. The securities respecting which the greatest anxiety should be manifested, are the securities that the power which the Legislature may confer for the general advantage shall be fully used.[66]

Here the true Benthamite note is sounding. Individual claims, when these operate against the common good, are not to be preferred to public power. Provided that the public realm is duly responsible for what it does, its authority should be enlarged so that it may be used to promote the common good.

VII. The Living conditions of the people

i) Working-class traditions and Chartism

The Constabulary Report was published in the same year as John Frost's rising at Newport, and it has been argued that the government took action about the rural police in 1839 because of the fear caused by the Chartist disturbances and the impossibility of relying on the military to keep order.[1] While the Report of 1839 saw the police as instruments of public control, the radicals saw them as instruments of public repression. The Chartist Convention at Birmingham interpreted the actions of a force of London police in putting down meetings in the town as

> a wanton, flagrant, and unjust outrage ... upon the people of Birmingham by a bloodthirsty and unconstitutional force from London acting under the authority of men who, when out of office, sanctioned and took part in the meetings of the people.[2]

A public meeting at Oldham, a town picked out for special notice in the Constabulary Report,[3] complained of the County Police Act of 1839:

> The evils arising from the said act is the placing of such police under the immediate control of justices ... the whole power of appointing police was taken away from leypayers and they were left to the tender mercies of a set of men from whom they knew what to expect when they had power ... it was their duty to foil the magistrates in putting this Act into force.[4]

The last chapter was devoted to examining the process of social reform as planned by those who controlled the organs of government. In this chapter emphasis will be laid rather on the living conditions of working people, studied particularly through the movement for factory reform and the campaign for better public health. It is only possible on occasion to disentangle the point of view of the workers themselves from that of the middle-class investigators who studied them, because in most cases we know about the lives of the workers only through what external observers have told us. Even when working men and women themselves provided information, they did so in reply to questions devised by people with a different set of values and a different background. The structure of the question determines the answer given.

It was very difficult for poor people in relation to sanitary problems to do more than make simple statements about the existence of dirt and disease because the problems were so complex that the workers could do very little to solve them. The factory question is different because here the workers had a point of view and could take action. They could do nothing about a tainted water supply, but they could, and did, withdraw their labour as a protest against cuts in wages. The factory campaign had close links with other movements like Chartism and the resistance to the New Poor Law. It has already been shown that working-class protest developed against a background of disorder and violence which sometimes erupted into riot and even rebellion. Chartism throughout its history had revolutionary undertones. It represented a revolt against intolerable conditions as well as a policy which aimed at improving them.

In some ways the record of Chartism appears to have been one of complete failure. The movement was never united. The division between 'moral force' and 'physical force' men persisted throughout, and Feargus O'Connor, who came increasingly to dominate, proved to be an unwise and increasingly unsuitable leader. The influence of local issues was very strong, and Chartism appealed to different social groups in different places.[5] Yet the failure of Chartism can be exaggerated. It was the first political movement in which working men played a large part. Success, when the workers were poor, uneducated and disunited, could hardly have been expected, but the effort and the publicity had their ultimate importance. Even after 1850, when the Chartist rump was advocating socialist policies which gained very little support, Chartist groups were active in local government in towns like Leeds and Sheffield.[6]

Perhaps it would be truer to define Chartism rather as a series of movements than as a unified movement in itself with a common purpose. Indeed much of its historical importance derives from its symbiotic character, to the way in which ideologically it both took in and gave out, and increased working-class self-reliance by doing so. It had drawn much of its initial support from the movements in the industrial areas for factory reform and against the New Poor Law. It had links with the cooperative movements. The moderate wing of Lovett and his friends made, as we have seen, major contributions both to popular education and to movements for peace and international understanding.[7] Chartism as an independent movement may not have had much importance after 1850 but its inspiration spread out into many other liberal/reforming causes. According to Brian Harrison,

> many Chartists entered into organized temperance, and other mid-Victorian liberal crusades—the Garibaldi procession, the demonstrations for the North in the American Civil War, the Reform League, the Liberation Society, the Financial Reform Association, the National Education League, Josephine Butler's

campaign, the Bulgarian atrocities agitation, the attack on newspaper taxes, Home Rule.[8]

Chartism indeed was rather like a river in limestone country which
disappears into the ground only to reappear a few miles further on.

All the working-class movements of the 'thirties and 'forties had certain
common characteristics which it is important to understand. The most
important fact of all is that the workers were conservative, indeed
reactionary. Indeed it was the business men who were the economic
radicals because they had everything to gain from new methods, while the
workers feared that they had everything to lose. Bewildered as the
industrial workers were in a period of very rapid change, they did what
people in such situations usually do—they looked back to an idealized past
in which economic and social conditions had been fairer to poor men. It is
not until the 'fifties and 'sixties that the labour aristocracy began, so as to
speak, to acclimatize themselves to the new conditions. One particularly
good example of a traditional institution which came under heavy attack
during this period was the industrial family unit. Working people had
inherited from the days of the domestic system the idea of the co-working
family, and they struggled desperately but unsuccessfully to preserve it.
Before the factory age the weaver did not work alone. He was aided by
his wife and his children who were all partners in a common enterprise,
which might indeed be agricultural as well as industrial, for, in the West
Riding, the family in many cases worked some land as well. The
relationships between parents and children in this older age should not be
idealized for parents, as well as mill owners, could be bullies and tyrants,
and much of the ill-treatment of children in the early factories seems to
have been at the hands of adult workers rather than employers.

Yet the family unit, whatever its faults, represented some notion of
independence and self-respect, some concept of shared activity under
parental guidance which the workers were extremely reluctant to give up.
The comments of the Hand-loom Weavers Commission on the working
group which had suffered most bitterly from the process of change
brought this out very clearly. Men liked the weaving trade, the
commission thought, because they had considerable control over their
conditions of labour and because the family could all work together. The
trade was over-stocked not only because it was easy to learn but also
because it appeared to offer maintenance to the whole family unit. In
another sense families were imprisoned within the trade, whether they
liked it or not, because the power of workers' combinations made it
difficult for them to enter other kinds of industry.[9]

Nor was the idea of the working-family unit limited to the traditional
manual trades; in many cases it was also carried over into the early
factories. In the 1820's, the family unit was preserved in the Lancashire
cotton mills because many of the women and children who assisted the
male spinners were their near relations, though this broke down as larger

mules were introduced, demanding larger working groups, as the country became rapidly urbanized and as firms which combined both spinning and weaving increased in number. Strikes against the introduction of more complex machinery were linked with the desire to protect the position of the head of the family.[10] The operatives' aims, it has been said, were

> to halt the flood of children and to protect the traditional economic relationships between parent and child by linking their hours and consequently maintaining the existing conditions of work.[11]

The workers could achieve their ends only by limiting the working hours of both parents and children because the family relationship could be preserved only if parents and children worked together in this way. The Factory Act of 1833, which will be discussed later,[12] aimed at different objectives and was opposed by the workers as a result. Its purpose was to differentiate between the hours of adults and children. The former were not to be touched; the latter were to be shortened so that children might work with adults in relays. This naturally made the family relationship much more difficult to preserve. Moreover, even in their free time the children were to be taken out of the control of their families because it was provided that they should attend school. The school provisions, though they were ineffective, were another blow at the self-sufficiency of the family economy. It was natural that after 1833 the workers continued to press for the ten-hour day for all labour.[13]

The traditionalism of the working-class attack on factory conditions and the New Poor Law was very clearly expressed by Richard Oastler, 'the Factory King', who launched the Yorkshire movement for shorter hours in 1830 and who dominated it during the rest of the decade. Oastler was a Tory traditionalist. To him the New Poor Law and the harsh working conditions of the factories were to be fought because they took away from working people the security and decency of life which should be guaranteed to them, as much as to their richer neighbours, by the institutions of society. A Tory, he wrote,

> is tenacious of the rights of all, but most of the poor and needy, because they require the shelter of the constitution and the laws more than the other classes.[14]

His practical policies, as set out in newspaper articles of 1834-5, expressed the same ideas. He wanted to repeal the new poor law, to establish regional tribunals to fix hours and wages, to promote small holdings and the resettlement of men on the land. He advocated the abolition of indirect taxes, the introduction of a system of direct taxation, and a graduated tax on capital. Better education should be provided for adult men and women.[15]

Oastler was an orator accustomed to sway the great meetings which whipped up the poor law and factory agitations. His speeches and writings have a clear note of apocalyptism and violence. During the ten-hours campaign of 1833 he told an audience in Manchester that things could not go on much longer in their present state because there were limits to human endurance:

> If the mill owners will drive me to use the word, let them—at their own bidding and not at mine let them dread *the dagger and the torch* .... I have ceased to reason.[16]

and in his pamphlet, *The Law and the Needle,* against breaches of the Factory Act, he warned that, if the law were still to be violated,

> I will in that event put a little card about *Needles* and *Sand* and *Rusty Nails*, with proper and with very explicit directions, which will make these law-breakers look about them and repent that they were ever so mad as to laugh at the Law and the King. These cards of mine shall then be the catechism of the factory children.[17]

This pamphlet led Ashley to break off relations and permanently shattered Oastler's friendship with John Wood, the Bradford manufacturer who had been one of the staunchest supporters of factory reform. Though extreme it was not untypical, and the same tone could be paralleled in the speeches of other leaders like Feargus O'Connor and J.R. Stephens. It was the kind of language which made a direct appeal to the audiences to which it was addressed, partly because it was reminiscent of the language of evangelical religion. It is striking how close this kind of political oratory comes to the sermons of religious revival There is the same denunciation of the sinner, the same catalogue of the sufferings of God's people, the same aspiration towards a state of future bliss. It was an age when the power of religion made many of the great movements into semi-religious crusades, not least among them the Anti-Corn Law League. Prosaic as its objectives seemed to be, bitterly opposed as it was by many of the Chartists, the free trade campaign held all the passion and drama of an evangelical cause and made the same appeal for loyalty and total commitment.

The Anti-Corn Law League succeeded at much the same time as Chartism, as an organized movement, failed. The free traders had their eyes fixed on the future; the Chartists and ten hours campaigners looked in many ways to the past. The last major project which grew out of Chartism was Feargus O'Connor's land movement, which aimed to set up agricultural colonies in which working men could till their own farms.[18] The project evoked great enthusiasm but its financing was insecure, there were legal difficulties about title and the scheme finally collapsed. Its interest lies in its aspiration to escape from a capitalist machine-dominated society into a purer world where men would till the ground in independence and self-respect. The idea lingered on long after the failure of the Chartist colonies; it was reborn later in the century in Jesse Collings' 'three acres and a cow'. The Chartist land scheme showed the atavism of those working men and of some at least of their leaders, who hoped to escape from the employer and the landlord into free communities where men would be their own masters. It is doubtful whether such communities had ever existed. They were certainly alien to the capitalist temper of early Victorian England.

ii) Working people in factories and mines

The textile factories represented to contemporaries one of the major triumphs of the capitalist ethos, though, as we have seen, there had long been concern about the conditions of the children employed in them.[19] Before considering the arguments for and against freedom and restraint, it is probably convenient to sketch very briefly the course of legislation between 1830 and the early 'fifties.[20] In December 1831 M.T. Sadler introduced a bill which proposed that children under nine years of age should not be allowed to work at all, that those under eighteen should be limited to a ten hour day and that those under twenty-one should not work at night. In August 1832 a select committee of the House of Commons under Sadler's chairmanship produced a mass of evidence highly unfavourable to the manufacturers. However Sadler lost his seat in the general election of that year, and a new approach was taken by the Royal Commission of 1833 which maintained the idea of a minimum working age but advised, not a universal ten-hour day for young people, but a shorter day for children under the age of thirteen together with a limitation of hours for young people between the ages of thirteen and eighteen. This approach was adopted by the Factory Act of 1833; the provisions of that act about the appointment of inspectors and the provision of schooling have already been discussed.

The next substantial changes came with the report of the Royal Commission on Children's Employment which looked into the situation both in the mines and in manufactures other than textiles. In 1842 the Mines Act prohibited the employment of women and of children under the age of ten below ground. Meanwhile pressure had continued to achieve the ten hour day. By the act of 1844 the minimum age of employment in textile factories was fixed at nine, and hours were restricted to six and a half up to thirteen years and to twelve up to eighteen, while women even above that age were not allowed to work for more than twelve hours. The act's provisions about half-time schooling have already been discussed. In 1847 John Fielden's bill for a ten-hour day for women and young persons was finally passed into law, but it was evaded because the manufacturers found that they were able to work longer periods by using relays.

In 1850 Ashley carried an act which secured the ten and a half hour day with cessation of work at 2.00 p.m. on Saturdays, though this compromise solution to the relay problem was very unpopular with the operatives themselves because it gave up the principle of ten hours. In 1853 another act limited children's labour so that it must take place within the hours worked by women and young persons, and so the fixed normal day was at length established. Although formally the rules did not apply to men, they did so in practice because it was impossible for them to work without the assistance of women and young persons. Even after 1853 protection applied in few areas outside the textile factories and, to some extent, the mines. The extension of restrictive legislation to cover factory processes of all kinds and workshops did not take place until the 'sixties.

There are some interesting points of contrast between the evidence collected by Sadler's committee and the report and evidence of the royal commission of 1833. The Committee's evidence leant heavily towards expressing the workers' viewpoint. Its predominant tone is a very humanitarian awareness of human suffering, reminiscent of much of the evidence collected by the earlier committee of 1816. The workers, disappointed at the abandonment of Sadler's bill, refused to cooperate with the royal commission which certainly took a very different view of factory management from that put forward by many of the Sadler committee witnesses. The difference between the two documents is a good deal more profound, however, than the question whether one is more or less sympathetic with masters or with men. I have already used the term 'humanitarian' to describe the Sadler report. For the royal commission report I should choose the word 'clinical', a very appropriate word for the production of three Utilitarians like Chadwick, Tooke and Southwood Smith.

The royal commissioners tried to make a balanced judgment. They did not gloss over the fact that abuses existed and they made practical suggestions to deal with the problem of child labour. But the tone is analytical, the mood coercive. The report is yet another essay in the extension to a new field of the programme of tutelary government. The provisions about inspection and schooling all suggest a closer system of checks and controls. It is not enough, the commissioners seem to be saying, to bewail the sufferings of the factory children; the problem is not primarily one of showing sympathy but of providing practical relief while ensuring that the country's essential economic interests are protected. To harmonize these two rival demands is a problem of practical statesmanship.

Some of the points which stand out most clearly from the Sadler Committee evidence are the prevalence of cruelty to children, the extent of immorality in the mills, the number of cases of physical deformity as the result of excessive labour, and the claim that masters are not concerned whether children are fatigued. The evidence concluded with an absolute battery of medical testimony about the physical and surgical consequences of over-working children. Oastler told the committee that he had never heard a single argument produced 'which was not exactly the argument of the owners of slaves'.[21] G.S. Bull of Bierley made much of the difficulty of securing any decent education for factory children. He bewailed both the weakening of parental authority and of filial affection and said that he would favour the re-introduction of the domestic system because the parent could then regulate the work of the child.[22] The tone of the questioning was far from impartial, and the witnesses were often flagrantly 'led' by the questioner.[23]

The Report of the Royal Commission was moderate and judicious in tone, but its criticisms of the abuses of child labour were none the less telling for that, and it made clear recommendations for tightening the law. The Report gave many examples of the long hours worked by the children, though it pointed out that they were often encouraged by their parents to work those hours. It cited examples of both good and bad factory conditions, though it considered that modern mills were much better to work in than the older mills, which were dirty and unventilated. The commissioners considered it to be clearly established that the children were very fatigued by their long hours of work, which led to physical pain, to stunted growth and to physical malformations. The supporting medical evidence was a good deal less unanimous in tone than that collected by Sadler's committee, since some of the witnesses spoke favourably of the health of the factory workers. Charles Loudon, the medical commissioner for the North-East, stood unequivocally on the other side:

> ... I think it has been clearly proved that children have been worked a most unreasonable and cruel length of time daily, and that even adults have been expected to do a certain quantity of labour which scarcely any human being is able to endure.[24]

A case had, therefore, in the commissioners' view, been made out 'for the interference of the legislature on behalf of the children employed in the factories',[25] while it was clear that the existing law was not observed. They were not, however, in favour of the general limitation to ten hours per day because that had been intended to involve a limitation of the working day for adults as well as for children. The discussion about the limitation of the hours of adults showed the same deep suspicion of the trades unions as was displayed six years later in the Constabulary Report. The operatives were, it was claimed, using the sufferings of the children as a cloak for measures designed to shorten the labour of adults. It was in the interest of the agitators to keep up the struggle so as to provide occupation for themselves.

Broadly speaking, then, it was desirable to limit the hours of children and young persons, undesirable to limit the hours of adults, and some means had to be found of treating the two groups separately. There ought to be an age below which children should not be employed at all. Above that age children should be worked in double sets, a solution which was not free from difficulty but which had the advantage of clearly differentiating their work from that of adults. The Report recommended therefore that children under the age of nine should not be employed at all in mills and factories. Between the ages of nine and the beginning of the fourteenth year they should not be employed for more than eight hours daily and they should not do night work. After the fourteenth year the body has become much stronger, the sense of independence has grown, and young people may be treated as adults.[26] If the law was to be duly enforced it would be necessary for the government to appoint inspectors, and arrangements should be made that children should spend some of their free time by going to school since one of the major evils of the present system was that factory children had no opportunity to receive instruction. The changes which they proposed would still, the commissioners argued, leave the factory working family in a better condition than the families of many other urban workers and of the labourers in the country.[27]

There was keen debate at the time about the merits and demerits of the factory system, and the contrasting viewpoints are very clearly set out in the writings of Peter Gaskell, a surgeon who practised at Bredbury near Stockport, and of Dr. Andrew Ure, the Scottish chemist and scientific writer.[28] Gaskell, though he did not exaggerate the evils of factory conditions, was a severe critic of them. The factory system, he thought, had harmful moral effects on the workers, which might be much reduced by better education. Factory labour broke up family ties. It made the household a less comfortable and congenial place because women factory workers did not know how to manage their homes. It tended to increase crime, it led to heavy drinking and to the physical deterioration of the stock. The development of machinery tended to throw adults out of work and the children who replaced them had to work hours which were far too long. As steam power developed, it became increasingly difficult for labour to find a market. Like many of the critics who have already been discussed, Gaskell was particularly concerned by the workers' loss of independence, taking as examples of this the truck system of paying wages and the practice linked with it of masters building cottages for their workers. Both tied cottages and truck were profitable for the master. For the worker, on the other hand,

. . . the moral evils of the truck and cottage systems are analogous. By reducing the labour to a mere machine—by destroying his personal independence—by cutting off his claim to self-respect—they degrade him to a condition of mere slavery, compared with which the West Indian slave may indeed congratulate himself on his good fortune, for his is a state to be a thousand-fold desired in preference.[29]

Ure would have regarded arguments about West Indian slaves as quite beside the point, for his book is a paean of praise for the 'perfection of automatic industry',[30] and 'the benignant power of steam'.[31] It was a positive advantage of more sophisticated machinery, Ure claimed, that it enabled the labour of men to be replaced by that of women and children, though this kind of change worked to the advantage not to the detriment of the workers. Factory work was better paid than hand work, and did not involve such hard labour. The more complicated and expensive the machinery, the less the danger from foreign competition and the greater the inducement to the mill owner to keep up the wages of his workpeople. The health and appearance of factory operatives were good and the mill owners had set their face against the over-working of children. In the light of the report of the Factory Commission credulity is somewhat strained by Ure's description of child workers in the mills:

> The work of these lively elves seemed to resemble a sport, in which habit gave a pleasing dexterity. Conscious of their skill, they were delighted to show it off to any stranger. As to exhaustion by the day's work, they evinced no trace of it on emerging from the mill in the evening; for they immediately began to skip about any neighbouring play-ground, and to commence their little amusements with the same alacrity as boys issuing from a school.[32]

Like Gaskell, though his conclusions were very different, Ure's final standard of judgment related to the moral effects of the system on the workers. The wise manufacturer knew that factory discipline would be most effective if the operatives were moral and contented people who could be trusted to work with zeal and care. It was therefore in the mill owner's interest 'to organize his moral machinery on equally sound principles with his mechanical'.[33]

It would have been difficult to apply the 'lively elves' image to the conditions unveiled by the Children's Employment Commission. It produced two reports, the first of these dealing with mines, particularly coal mines, and the second with trades and manufactures generally. The most important of these trades, as listed by the commissioners, were metal manufactures; earth-ware, porcelain and glass; lace and hosiery; calico printing, bleaching and dyeing; paper; draw-boy weaving, winding and warping; tobacco; and miscellaneous trades including dress-making and needlework. In all these occupations the hours were very long. In the coal mines most children and young people seem to have worked about twelve hours per day, though, if the time taken getting to and from home and to and from the work-place be added, the total effective day was often thirteen to fourteen hours.[34] In the manufacturing industries, twelve hours was general, though considerably longer periods of work were quite common.[35]

In the coal mines eight to nine was the ordinary age of starting work though much younger children were often employed. A collier from the North-East testified:

Some of six years old go down now. Lads six years old can keep doors well enough, and soon learn as well as old persons the ways of a pit.[36]

There was some evidence that the age at which children started work was tending to fall, as a result of parental pressures to get them to work as soon as possible. The mines enquiry also investigated the work of women as well as of children and young persons. The numbers of all these people employed was considerable, though it varied a good deal in proportion from area to area. In Yorkshire, Lancashire, and Northumberland the proportion of people under eighteen to adults was one-third; in Leicestershire, Derbyshire and South Durham it was two-sevenths. In Scotland it varied from one-quarter to almost one-half. Where women and girls were employed underground, the proportion of women to men again varied greatly. Very much the highest proportion was in East Lothian in Scotland where among adults it was one to three and among thirteen to eighteen year olds one to three and a half.[37]

The employment of women underground was confined to Lancashire and Yorkshire, to South Wales and to Eastern Scotland, an area which seems to have endured the worst conditions of all. It was a particular evil in that area that girls were employed in carrying heavy loads of coal in baskets strapped to their backs up long series of ladders from the work-face to the base of the mine-shaft. One single journey undertaken by one of these children was calculated, in height and distance, to 'exceed the height of St. Paul's Cathedral; and it not unfrequently happens that the tugs break, and the load falls upon those females who are following'. The whole picture, in the sub-commissioners' view, was one of 'daily physical oppression and systematic slavery which I conscientiously believe no one unacquainted with such facts would credit the existence in the British dominions'.[38] These conditions become easier to understand when it is remembered that until 1799 most of the Scottish colliers had been serfs tied to their employment.[39] Particular horror was expressed in the report at the demoralizing practice, followed in all the areas where women and girls worked underground, of men and women working together in teams, the women scantily clothed and the men often stark naked.

Children, when they went to work in the pit, were usually made responsible for opening and shutting the trap-doors which regulated the ventilation of the mine. This was not arduous physical work but it meant very long hours of darkness and loneliness. As they grew older and stronger, they were employed in drawing the coal tubs by belt and chain worn round the waist, and in 'putting' or 'hurrying', that is pushing the tubs along the wagon ways. There was plenty of evidence that children were exhausted by the heavy labour and the long hours, made worse in some areas by the common practice of night work. In the West Riding, for example.

> the great majority say that they are always tired, and the language which many of them use to express their sensations shows that they feel their labour to be extremely oppressive.[40]

The seams were often narrow and damp, the drainage and the ventilation poor. Children were often ill-treated by adult workers and by the 'butties' who sub-contracted for parts of the work. Accidents were very common, one particular source of danger in some areas being the practice of placing children in charge of the winding machinery.[41] The physical condition of the colliers was generally good because wages were high, but by the age of forty to fifty they were physically worn out and had to stop work. It was rare, it was said, to see an old collier.[42]

Much of what was said in the commissioners' second report on trades and manufactures repeats what had been said in the Mines Report. Work began at about the same age. There were the same details about long hours, bad conditions of work, and brutal treatment by adult workmen who usually paid the children and controlled their labour. The main difference between the two groups seem to have been that, whereas the physical condition of the colliers was generally good, the children in manufacturing trades were often poorly fed and stunted in growth.[43] The conditions in some trades were picked out as especially bad. In the lace industry hours were irregular and often very long, and wages were poor.[44] In the metal trades of the Wolverhampton district children were often very badly treated by their masters.[45] In London milliners and dress-makers during the season sometimes worked all night and quite commonly had time for only four hours sleep.[46] The second report concluded by considering, in characteristic fashion, the moral condition of the children and young persons whom they had been studying. Most of what they said followed the themes which have already been stressed. They were highly critical of working-class family life. There was a lack both of parental control and of filial affections. Parents rarely expressed any desire for the working hours of their children to be limited. Rather they were anxious that the children should go to work and that they should receive the profits of the children's labour. Coarseness of manners and gross immorality were prevalent, leading in many cases into crime and prostitution, while the workers were the easy victims of agitators. One root of the poverty and crime so common among the working classes was their neglected homes. Girls who had gone straight to work as small children had never learned the domestic skills and were unable to make comfortable homes for their husbands and children. The workman was often driven, with disastrous results, to find consolation in the beer-house.

Once again, as we have seen so many times before, social problems were associated with the grave deficiencies in education and in moral and religious training. In South Durham, for example, there had been an enormous extension of the collieries and many new towns and villages had grown up but 'for the secular, moral and religious instruction of these masses, thus suddenly brought together, no provision has been made'.[47] The profound ignorance resulting from this neglect is suggested in this thumb-nail sketch of a collier lad, James Taylor, eleven years of age:

> Has heard of hell in the pit when the men swear; has never heard of Jesus Christ; has never heard of God, but has heard the men in the pit say 'God damn thee'. Does not know what county he is in; has never been anywhere, but here, i' th' pit, and at Rochdale; never heard of London; has heard of the Queen, but dunnot know who he is.[48]

Children who went to work so young had no chance of gaining any schooling before they were employed and, after they had started work, they were too tired in the evening to learn. It would be important, the commissioners reported, that, if children's hours of work were limited, means should be found to enable them to attend school in their free time.

Some of this neglect of education could be attributed to the parents. At Birmingham, for example, where mechanics were earning from two to five or six pounds per week, they made no provision for the future . . . 'these large wages were but too often wasted in vice and extravagance'.[49] But the commissioners did not find the mill owners and manufacturers guiltless. With few exceptions they recognized no obligation to promote the welfare of their work-people. The connection between master and man was no more than an economic bond, even though the minority among the masters who had shown a more profound concern had found that better educated workmen were more industrious and more tractable. The final conclusion of the commissioners was a gloomy one. They could see no means adequate to improve the physical and moral conditions of the children and young persons employed in mines and manufactures.[50]

This conclusion, at the end of a massive investigation which had uncovered social material of an entirely new kind, shows how intractable contemporaries considered these problems to be, and it was indeed to be another generation at least before real progress was made in improving the general situation of children and young people. This could be accomplished only by expanding the tutelary functions of the state, and, in a halting and piecemeal fashion, something was done in the late 'forties to extend the range of state activity in areas where private individuals could not look after themselves. In 1847 the Poor Law Board was set up; this did not represent any development of a more aggressive policy, but it did put the work of poor law administration under the charge of a responsible minister. In 1847 Parliament passed the Ten Hours Act and in 1848 the Public Health Act to ensure better sanitation and water supply. In 1846 another act had created the Railway Commission, a central board which took over powers previously exercised by the Board of Trade, though it is true that its powers were extremely limited.[51] None of these acts went very far, but they do collectively represent a steady expansion of public control over the lives of the citizens.

Yet in the end the results of all this were less than the expectations. The Ten Hours Act was persistently evaded, the General Board of Health had insufficient powers, far too little was done for the education of the people. By about 1850 the reformed parliamentary system of 1832 had reached an end-point in its development. The particular grouping of interests which had resulted from the Great Reform Act had accomplished as much as it could achieve. The necessary momentum for new measures would not be found until the parliamentary system was further reformed. This tendency towards political stalemate was strengthened by the course of party politics. The great split in the Conservative party over the repeal of the Corn Laws ushered in twenty years of weak governments. Cabinets on the whole were weak, private members were powerful and, in such a situation, there was a built-in likelihood that radical changes would be difficult to achieve.[52]

iii) The Public health movement

At the end of the 'forties there was, on the one hand, a tendency to extend public control in matters of social policy. There was another tendency to call a halt to further change. The last of the great social campaigns of the period, the public health movement, had to operate against the pressures produced by these opposing forces, pressures which in the end brought Chadwick down and ended a stage in the history of social policy. The public health movement was the fourth major area of policy, alongside the poor law, factory reform and constabulary reform, with which Chadwick's name will always be connected. The campaign bore the characteristic stamp of Chadwick's mind. It was constructively based on a broad conception of the issues involved. He propounded sanitary policies which tackled all parts of the problem and left no loose ends. He thought out an administrative structure at both central and local levels which should be intelligently related to basic environmental and geographical factors. As usual his virtues of comprehensiveness and broad planning won him a number of enemies. Any part of such comprehensive plans would antagonize some powerful interest. The whole policy was bound to offend a whole legion. Nor were the plans free from Chadwick's characteristic dogmatism. They showed his usual inability to compromise, or to modify his views.

Chadwick's interest in public health had developed as a result of his exclusion from policy making in poor law administration. The first stages in awakening public interest had been the enquiries of Arnott, Southwood Smith and Kay-Shuttleworth into sanitary conditions in East London in 1839.[53] Chadwick's own Sanitary Report of 1842 was the result of two years of exhaustive work, and it put the whole discussion of public sanitary policy onto an entirely new footing. Before the Report itself is discussed, something more must be said about Chadwick's basic ideas because they dominated the whole of his subsequent policy up to 1854. Like the fashionable medical opinion of the day, he believed that disease was carried by impurities in the atmosphere. He wrote in the Report:

> The first extracts present the subjects of the inquiry in their general condition under the operation of several causes, yet almost all will be found to point to one particular, namely, atmospheric impurity, occasioned by means within the control of legislation, as the main cause of the ravages of epidemic, endemic and contagious diseases among the community, and as aggravating most other diseases.[54]

The great problem, therefore, was to get rid of impurities before they could decompose and this led Chadwick to formulate a cyclical theory of water supply and sewage removal in which all the parts closely cohered.[55] The key to the solution of the whole problem, as he saw it, was the provision of a sufficient supply of pure water driven through the pipes at high pressure. This water would provide abundant water to drink and make it much easier to cleanse both houses and streets. Houses should be supplied with water-closets and house drains, linked to the main sewage system by infall pipes which were well constructed and which would not block up. In this way houses and privies would be kept pure and fresh, while the water under pressure would flush out sewers effectively. Finally, as it left the town, the manure could be collected and used as fertilizer on the fields of the neighbourhood. The circuit was complete. Pure water at high pressure would provide for drinking, for cleansing and for sanitation, and the end product would be of considerable economic value.

It was, in its very completeness, a very Chadwickian concept, and one which, in practical terms, presented many problems. First of all, though many water companies were in existence, they normally provided water only on certain days a week and at certain times. They did not provide it either in the quantity or at the pressure which Chadwick desired. Many houses in poorer districts had no water supply at all and no proper means of sewage disposal. They all too often had overflowing cesspools or shared, with many other houses, privies which it was impossible to keep clean. Little was known about the planning of drainage schemes. Where sewers did exist the levels were often very badly regulated. Traditionally, sewers had been large brick-arched constructions which Chadwick wished to replace by the smaller egg-shaped type developed by John Roe, engineer to one of the London commissions of sewers.[56] Roe's sewer was very much cheaper than the traditional model and the smaller egg-shaped type became a major feature in the Chadwickian canon of orthodox sanitary doctrine.

The first two basic ideas, then, were the atmospheric theory of infection and the cyclical theory of water supply and drainage. The third, of which less need be said because it ran on very parallel lines to his ideas on poor law and police, was the importance of proper central direction of sanitary planning, combined with efficient local organization. In this instance there was another important factor which did not arise in the other cases. The administrative area must coincide with the natural boundaries set by contour and natural drainage. Sanitary administration must be based on sound geography if it were to be effective.

The Sanitary Report was complemented by another report of 1843 on interments in towns, which exposed the terrible conditions of the over-crowded graveyards of London.[57] It was a subject on which Chadwick felt especially strongly, and to which he was to return, though he failed to achieve his objective of creating a municipalized service on the lines which existed in France and Germany. The Sanitary Report itself is most easily dealt with section by section, using the local observations made by medical witnesses to illustrate Chadwick's own comments. Evidence was presented about the filthy housing of the poor and the related deficiencies in drainage and water supply. It was clear from the local reports that many of the worst examples of poor housing were in rural areas,[58] but the main problem, as it presented itself to Chadwick, was an urban one. The refuse from towns might, he claimed, be sold as liquid manure, and Edinburgh was named as an example of a city where this had been attempted.[59] The water undertaking at Bath and the gas undertaking at Manchester were cited as examples of the benefits accruing from municipal management of public utilities. In the hands of skilled officers they would be much more expertly conducted than private companies which depended on the part-time services of local solicitors or business men. Moreover municipal control would save the expense of dividends and enable profits to be applied to public improvements.[60]

The next topic to be discussed was the effect of overcrowding on the general living conditions of the people and on mortality rates in different areas. Disease on the scale at which it was prevalent was extremely expensive to the community. Since adults were cut off in their prime, a high proportion of the population of a town like Manchester was youthful, and such a population was not likely to be steady in its habits and well instructed in its morals but 'credulous, irritable, passionate, and dangerous, having a perpetual tendency to moral as well as physical deterioration'.[61] This conclusion recalls earlier warnings about working-class violence and the pressure exerted by workmen's combinations.

The local reports provide valuable information about particular places. Among the larger towns, Birmingham, although it had its share of filthy courts and poor drainage, seems to have enjoyed better conditions than most, as it had a low incidence of fever and few cellar dwellings, while the workers had good wages and most families occupied a separate house.[62] In Manchester there were many damp and unwholesome cellars where conditions were always the worst. Moreover the poor of the town lacked any public parks or places of recreation.[63] The worst conditions of all seem to have existed at Liverpool where Chadwick had pointed out the very high death rates. According to Dr. W.H. Duncan, who later became the town's first medical officer of health, 1/25th of the working population were annually affected by fever,[64] which he called 'an inseparable accompaniment of extreme poverty affecting large masses of the community'.[65] Like Manchester Liverpool had many cellar dwellings. The courts, hidden away behind the street frontages, were deep in filth of every kind which was rarely removed. Many houses indeed had neither yard nor privy nor ash-pit of their own. Where the poor were most closely packed together, fever was most prevalent, the worst conditions existing among the Irish who sometimes kept pigs and donkeys in the cellars and garrets into which their families were crowded.

The later sections of Chadwick's Report dealt with the beneficial effects of preventive measures and the practical steps by which they were to be achieved. Good water supplies and efficient sewage would be comparatively cheap to install and would actually save money because they would greatly reduce the cost of medical attendance. The provision of schools and of better housing would provide employers with a more stable work force. The interests of employers would be furthered by the very measures which improved the health and morals of the workers since men who were healthier and happier would work harder and produce more.

What was proposed was within the power of parliament to achieve if it took the proper measures. Existing bodies like the commissioners of sewers must be swept away. A unified authority must be set up for each area to consolidate all public works under skilled professional management. Chadwick expressed himself rather dubiously about the establishment of Boards of Health to do this work. He preferred the policy of extending the powers of the poor law medical officers and of appointing a new class of superior medical officers to be in charge of a considerable area. This new group of officers might inspect schools, factories and workshops, keep a careful record of the registered causes of death and enquire into particular unhealthy districts and trades.[66] As we have already noted, he preferred to entrust the task of reform to skilled officials.

The Sanitary Report made a deep impression on public opinion. It was followed by a royal commission on the state of the towns, by a good deal of propagandist activity, for instance through the Health of Towns Association founded in December 1844, and, after a series of delays, by the passage of the Public Health Act of 1848. The Health of Towns Commission made enquiries into conditions in London and in the fifty towns with the highest mortality rates. It produced two reports; the first was brief and was accompanied by very full evidence, the second contained the recommendations. Though Chadwick was not a member, both the enquiry and the reports closely followed the lines of his thinking.

From the mass of evidence presented in the first report several major points stand out. First of all the members and officials of the existing commissions of sewers were generally examined in an unsympathetic, even hostile way.[67] Secondly there were two authoritative statements of the views of the reformers, one by Southwood Smith from the scientific and medical viewpoint, the other by Thomas Hawksley from the engineering viewpoint. Thirdly, complementing Hawksley's evidence, there was evidence from other professional men about the importance of properly made plans and surveys as the pre-requisite for sound development.

Southwood Smith had been for ten or fifteen years the most prominent of medical propagandists. Like Chadwick, he had worked for the elderly Bentham, he had written for the *Westminster Review*, he had been a member of several commissions, and he had a wide knowledge of the poorer districts of East London. His evidence to the Health of Towns Commission sets out with particular clarity the need for a controlling body to manage public health. If, he argued, the legislature could make regulations about building houses in order to prevent fires, there was no reason why it should not make regulations that houses should be well drained and clean. The knowledge on the subject of public health which scientists possessed could not be left to spread on its own:

> It has been justly stated that it is only when the public health is made a matter of public care by a responsible public agency, that what is understood can be expected to be generally and effectually applied to the public protection.[68]

Such an agency should be responsible for the exercise of the authority delegated to it and it should be served by skilled agents. It should operate by general regulations covering the whole country.[69] However great the evils which existed, it was perfectly possible, by wise public policy, to remove them.

Southwood Smith's comments about conditions in the town slums ran on very similar lines to those of the Sanitary Report. Fever was most prevalent where the commissioners of sewers had not penetrated, and he stated once again the atmospheric theory of its origins.[70] Every year in England preventible typhus carried off twice as many people as the casualties of the allied armies in the battle of Waterloo.[71] Fever was particularly likely to strike at people between the ages of 20 and 40, when family responsibilities were at their height, a judgment which recalls

Chadwick's observations about the youthfulness of the people of Manchester. The effects of dirt and disease enfeebled and debilitated the poor, and children in particular. They predisposed the poor towards crime; those areas which were the haunts of disease were the haunts of the criminal classes too.[72] By treating men and women like beasts, they were reduced to the level of beasts, without intelligence, humanity, domestic affections, or moral and religious feelings.[73] Nor did Southwood Smith neglect practical remedies. The costs of improvement should be spread over a number of years so that existing owners and occupiers did not have to bear it all. No house should be let 'in which water is not laid on, and to which there is no privy sufficiently screened from view'.[74]

The provision of privies and the costs of improvement involved the practical skills of the engineer, and here the evidence of Thomas Hawksley was of great importance. Hawksley was a Nottingham man, who at the age of 23 had become engineer to the Trent Bridge Waterworks company in that town, a company which had been a pioneer in supplying a constant provision of water under pressure. Hawksley told the commission that his company had found this system more economical both in the use of water and of staff, while it facilitated the use of smaller pipes. To introduce water into the homes of the poor, he argued, served not only to remove offensive matter and to reduce the danger of disease. It improved the whole quality of their lives because nothing was so debilitating for them as the squalor in which they were forced to live. The financial problems of introducing water supply into the homes of the poor were not difficult. A constant supply could be introduced, on terms remunerative to the company, at a cost of one penny per week. The work should not be undertaken on terms less favourable to the investor than the normal rates because, if this were done, the benefit would accrue to the landlords who would be able to charge higher rents for improved accommodation.

Hawksley claimed that, if proper measures of this kind were taken, it would be possible to reduce mortality rates by 20%.[75] Like Chadwick he put great emphasis on the importance of skilled management and on the control of local bodies by a national authority. All too often drainage work was in the hands of mere tradesmen and, even when competent persons were employed, they were usually controlled by people with no knowledge of the subject. One major problem arose from the competition between rival gas and water companies in the same town. This difficulty made Hawksley support the establishment of a national body acting to promote the interests of the community as a whole. All acts of parliament which dealt with local improvements should, he thought, be prepared by a central commission after a local enquiry had been held.

One final aspect of the evidence is the stress laid by professional witnesses on good surveying and map-making. If water supplies and drainage were to be materially improved, the first practical step was to make comprehensive surveys. Hawksley had argued this. So did Captain

Dawson, R.E. who had supervised the surveys made for the commutation of tithe, and Captain Vetch, R.E. who had been instructed in 1842 to plan a new system of drainage for Leeds.[76]

The second report recommended the enactment of new legislation. The Crown should have power to inspect and to supervise the execution of the necessary sanitary measures which should be undertaken by local authorities armed with additional powers and controlling areas co-terminous with the natural drainage areas. Drainage, the paving and cleansing of the streets and the provision of an ample water supply should all be placed under one administrative body.[77] The local body should appoint its own officials who should be properly qualified for their duties. If the municipal authority of the place or a proportion of the inhabitants so petitioned, the Crown should have power to order an inspection and to ensure that the law was carried out. The local sanitary body should have the power to levy rates to carry out necessary improvements and should be empowered to spread the cost of such improvements over a specified term of years. They should also be able, with the approval of the Crown, to raise loans on the security of the rates. They should have power to take action against nuisances and to deal with smoke and chemical fumes emitted from factories. Owing to the special importance of good water supply, the local body responsible for drainage and cleansing should have the duty to ensure a constant provision of water at high pressure, either by contracting with water companies or by other means. The water companies should be required to comply with the demands of the sanitary body, which should be allowed to purchase private water undertakings when the owners wished to sell them. The recommendations covered a number of other suggested powers, such as the power to widen streets, to control cellar dwellings, and to cleanse premises which had become infected. One important proposal was that the local body should have power to appoint a medical officer to inspect the sanitary condition of the town and to ascertain the causes of disease.

The Public Health Act of 1848 had been watered down as it passed through Parliament, but it did retain some of the powers suggested in the Commission's report. The Act established, for a period of five years, a General Board of Health consisting of three members with the First Commissioner of Woods and Forests as president.[78] The first president was Lord Morpeth; the other two commissioners were Chadwick and Lord Ashley, and Southwood Smith was later added as medical member. The General Board could act to set up a local board only on the petition of one-tenth of the rate-payers so that the new system of health administration was only permissive in nature. Indeed Chadwick had argued that the one-tenth provision would make the act almost inopera-tive.[79] However, the General Board did have special power to act when the death rate from all causes had reached the figure of 23 per thousand, so that they had some sanction for taking the initiative in the worst areas. A preliminary enquiry would be made by an inspector who would submit a report to the General Board. The Act would then be applied by Order in Council, or, in districts where a local act was in force or where boundaries were to be altered, by a Provisional Order which had to be approved by Parliament. In municipal boroughs the Town Council was to be the Public Health Authority, but in other areas a new local board of health was to be set up, elected by plural voting on a system which gave more votes to the larger property owners. The local board was to appoint its own officials, though the surveyor could be dismissed only with the approval of the General Board. The local board could, if it wished, appoint a medical officer of health, though to do so was not made compulsory, and in fact few were appointed. The local board could raise loans but, by a provision which gave the General Board one of its main powers of control, the approval of the central body was required for this to be done.

The scale of the General Board's operations was modest. In July 1853 a return showed that they had received petitions from 255 places, 164 of which had been brought under the act.[80] One of these places was Birmingham, but many of the larger towns stood aside. Manchester and Liverpool had taken separate powers under local acts of 1844 and 1846 respectively,[81] as Leeds had done in 1842.[82] In the great county of Lancashire, which contained many industrial towns with serious health problems, only 26 townships took advantage of the act, and by 1858 only 400,000 of the county's 2½ million people came under Boards of Health.[83] The inspectors' reports to the General Board give a very interesting picture of conditions in towns and even villages all over the country. The report on the middle-sized Yorkshire industrial town of Rotherham is cited here as an example of the whole class.[84]

The superintending inspector, William Lee, reported that the townships of Rotherham and Kimberworth (within the much larger parish of Rotherham) displayed the usual combination of filthy courts and cottages, of fever and disease, and of defective water supply. In one especially bad district there had been a number of cases of cholera, and throughout the town such drainage as existed was so defective that it did more harm than good. The water supply was good in quality but very defective in quantity and did not reach large parts of the town at all. Lee calculated that, where water had to be fetched and carried, about 12 to 15 gallons per house were used by the same class of persons who used 40 gallons per house where water was piped 'with the disadvantages of an outside tap, and intermittent daily supply'.[85] Many of the houses in the town were very old and dilapidated, and—a very common complaint—there were some 30 to 40 nauseous and overcrowded common lodging houses, which were often refuges for criminals. Like the burial grounds which so appalled Chadwick in London, the parish churchyard was in such a disgusting state that it should be closed at once.[86]

To deal with these conditions, Lee suggested that the Public Health Act should be applied to the townships of Rotherham and Kimberworth and a local board of 12 members created. A new water supply and drainage system should be constructed, the courts and byways should be re-paved, the streets washed and cleansed, and all the burial grounds, except the General Cemetery, closed: a familiar situation and a familiar set of remedies, the interest of which lies in its very ordinariness. Lee's report had mentioned the cholera, and a cholera outbreak was the first major problem which the General Board had to face. It had no powers to compel the Guardians of the Poor to take action against the epidemic, and very soon, as it tried to enforce its various policies, it became unpopular with the many interests which resented it as an instrument of meddlesome bureaucracy. It was constantly criticized by *The Times* and many of the powerful group of civil engineers attacked the practicability of its schemes. There was controversy over the size of pipes and the best materials for making them. Bad publicity was created by events at Croydon which had been one of the first places to put the Board's schemes into effect, but which was then smitten by a serious outbreak of fever. An enquiry reached the conclusion that the outbreak was due to the new plan for sewerage and to the use of pipe drains and pipe sewers.[87]

The most crucial events for the success or failure of the new policies took place in London, where a new Metropolitan Commission of Sewers had been set up in December 1847 of which Chadwick was a leading member. There were bitter rivalries in the commission between him and the representatives of the old sewer commissions and the parish vestries. In 1850 Chadwick produced a new scheme for the water supply and drainage of the metropolis, and he returned to his old plan for a system of publicly controlled cemeteries and the prohibition of burials in churchyards. Both schemes roused a host of opponents, and both schemes had to be given up. The Treasury refused to advance money for the purchase of private cemeteries. The water scheme was never implemented, and the Metropolitan Water Supply Act of 1852 left the whole provision in the hands of the water companies.

By 1852 hopes for any comprehensive reform in London had been dashed. There was growing opposition to the General Board in the country at large, and after 1850 even the head of the General Board itself was hostile. Chadwick's supporter, Lord Morpeth, was succeeded by Lord Seymour who rarely attended but was an opponent in so far as he took any interest at all. The Board was in any case due to expire in 1854, and feelings against it, and particularly against Chadwick, grew steadily fiercer. It was in fact Seymour, who had left office in 1852, who demanded the removal of the present Board members and successfully carried an amendment against the government's bill to reorganize the Board. This was the end, and on 12 August 1854 Chadwick ceased to be a commissioner. Though he lived until 1890 this was the end of his active career. His conception of a new structure for public health had been remarkably farsighted, but success in practical terms proved very difficult to achieve. The cause of sanitary improvement was to make slow progress in the next thirty years.

PART III

ACHIEVEMENTS AND FAILURES 1830-1880

VIII. The Mid-Victorian social structure

i) A New sense of optimism

By the time that Edwin Chadwick had been displaced the political and social tensions of the 'forties had greatly diminished, and England was launched on an easier age, very often described by W.L. Burn's phrase 'the age of equipoise'.[1] The contrast between the 'thirties and 'forties on the one side and the 'fifties and the 'sixties on the other can easily be exaggerated. Although for many of the workers circumstances were a little easier, many of them remained desperately poor. Problems like public health and popular education remained unsolved, and others like urban housing were if anything growing worse. Working-class self-help achieved great successes through the organization of cooperative and friendly societies, but the development of trades unions, which was part of the same story, produced new economic and political problems for a society which lacked any concepts to harmonize individual and group activity.

Yet, serious as these and many other problems were, men did feel in the early 'fifties that they had moved from the shadows into the sunlight. Force and violence had drawn back to be replaced by reasoned debate and ordered progress. If one event epitomized the general change in atmosphere, it was the Great Exhibition of 1851, which consecrated the power and success of industrial Britain. Burn makes the point that the Exhibition was both the symbol of commercialism and utility and the culmination of the romantic age.[2] It was a fairy palace of the arts and sciences, which promised to unite both Britain and foreigners in a new era of peace and progress.[3]

The sense of excitement, compounded of a mixture of commercial success, hopes for economic advance, and aspirations for moral betterment which the Exhibition produced was characteristic of the mid-Victorian age. Hard work and material achievement were endowed with moral values. Financial success, the enrichment of human personality, and the realization of moral goals were all seen as different facets of the same activity in a way which a more critical age finds difficult to understand. It is too superficial to stress the materialism; what the mid-Victorians valued was not so much the rewards as the struggle itself. The Great Exhibition seemed to mark a sunny plateau on which, for a time, man could luxuriate in enjoying what had been achieved by earlier struggles and in nerving himself for further efforts. The flavour of that summer of 1851 is very well conveyed by the comments of two visitors from widely differing social backgrounds. A young Manchester engineer wrote to his wife:

We reached the Crystal Palace at 12 o'clock and found our largest conception of its wondrous extent and magnificence more than realized. There was not the same variety about this great show which sometimes one feels on the occurrence of a great pageant. I felt that it was a place to worship in, not intellect not industry, but the God who has made men so much better than the brutes. Endless as are the productions of human ingenuity and skill which abound on every side, it is not a place for self-glorification. Of its varied wonders I can attempt no description—Eastern romance is in fact here. Every country under heaven is present. The mind and the affections are expanded and a brotherly feeling to other nations rises in one's heart.[4]

So much for a young professional man, one of the new aristocracy of industrialism. The reaction of a Coventry artisan, who was allowed a week's holiday to visit the Crystal Palace, was not very different.

This was then the longest journey I had ever undertaken, and the delight and pleasure of seeing this varied collection of products from every part of the world was unbounded. However much the wonderful structure of glass and iron in which the exhibition was contained might have been admired—it seemed almost a realization of one of the gorgeous pictures of the Arabian Nights—the treasures it contained interested me most. They surpassed anything previously conceived or read about, and they kept my mind in a continual state of excitement for some time.[5]

One cause which the Great Exhibition seemed likely to promote was that of international peace and arbitration, a subject in which much interest was shown in the late 'forties and early 'fifties. Richard Cobden had brought forward resolutions in Parliament in 1849 and 1850. Several international peace conferences had been held, and many Quakers like Joseph Sturge and John Bright were active in the cause. The hopes for a more peaceful world were to be short-lived; within a few years the Crimean War (1854-6) put an end to the peace movement.[6] The Crimean War marks the beginning of a period when foreign and imperial affairs loom much larger in English politics than they had done during the previous forty years. Though the military and diplomatic consequences of the war were not great, it had two major consequences for English social history. By making Florence Nightingale and her nurses into national heroines, it helped to give a new position to women in the national life. By revealing the weaknesses of the civil and military establishments, it stimulated the movement for administrative reform.

During the twenty years after the Peace of Paris (1856) national attention was actively taken up with overseas problems. The Indian Mutiny of 1857 roused deep-seated feelings of national pride at the courage of the beleaguered troops and civilians and less admirable passions of revenge against the rebels. In 1859 came the decisive struggle in the campaign for Italian unity. Two years later the American Civil War began. Educated men and London society in many cases favoured the South, and the workers of Lancashire, who favoured the North, had to overcome the hard years of the cotton famine. In the 'sixties came the rise of Prussia and the victories over Austria and France which transformed the European balance of power. In 1874 Disraeli became Prime Minister for the second time. The purchase of the Suez Canal shares and the Queen's assumption of the title of Empress of India marked a stage in the development of later Victorian imperialism. The latter years of the ministry were dominated by the Eastern Question, by Gladstone's campaign against the Bulgarian Atrocities, by the Congress of Berlin, and by the Prime Minister's return with 'Peace with Honour'.

The quarter-century between 1854 and 1880 marked a major shift in the national concerns. The 'thirties and 'forties had been obsessed with political reform, with the struggles of rival groups for power, with the tensions imposed by the growth of a new industrial society. The repeal of the Corn Laws in 1846 marked a stage in the long-continued debate over national economic policy, which by the early 'fifties had hardened firmly into the mould of free trade. Before 1850 the country's mood had been introspective, absorbed in the contemplation of its internal problems. Burn suggests that in the early 'fifties there was a slackening of interest in domestic politics and an increased concern for foreign countries 'as markets, as fields for investment and travel and as sources of knowledge and influence'.[7]

The replacement of an inward-looking by an outward-looking mood perhaps reduced the demand for social change because it took the national attention into paths different from those of the two previous decades. The political and social atmosphere became easier, tension declined, and the fear of disorder and violence markedly lessened. In an easier age there was more elbow-room for men to think, to debate, to argue without the pressing fear that argument might lead to riot, and to eventual overturn of the social fabric itself. Although social reform was considerably slowed down in the 'fifties, changes also began in areas untouched before, while new social groups were able to enter into the debate.

ii) Social groupings and individual initiatives

The period from 1850 to 1865 was one in which individuals and groups were remarkably active in promoting reforms. Yet this private activity was hardly matched by public initiative, for the age of Palmerston's political dominance was on the whole a period of weak government. That this was so is something to do with Palmerston's own standpoint. A more deep-rooted reason for the situation was the weakening of party allegiances after the repeal of the Corn Laws, and the late development of clearly defined Conservative and Liberal parties. The slow-down in the pace of change was very noticeable in a number of areas which have been discussed. The Poor Law Board, established in 1847, took few creative initiatives. Despite the pioneering work of Chadwick, progress in improving public health standards was delayed. Popular education, which had taken great strides as a public service under Kay-Shuttleworth, slowed down under Lingen and operated once again on restrictive and formalized lines under the Revised Code of 1862.

One reason for this situation lay in the fact that the society of the 1850's had moved faster than its political institutions had been able to adapt to change.[8] Many reform bills were produced but, until the events of 1866-7, they came to nothing, for it proved very difficult either for the politicians to agree that reform was necessary or on what was to be done once the necessity had been accepted. The same fate befell the many bills brought forward to promote the education of the people. It was widely urged that the government should take action, but it proved impossible to obtain agreement about what government was to do. An effective education act was not to be passed until the problem of parliamentary reform had been settled for that generation in 1867.

From the point of view of the social reformer the 'fifties and 'sixties were a frustrating period. Unitl the later 'sixties at any rate the record looks a rather barren one as compared with the record of the Age of Reform (1830-50). Yet in many ways the Age of Equipoise achieved more than it initially appears to have done. Social reform was actively going on, but it was more diffuse in its nature, more sophisticated through its response to the demands of a more complex society. Two examples will serve to make the point. The first is the much greater part played by women in social movements. The second is the extension of reform into secondary and higher education, which was closely linked with the reform of the governmental structure. The mid-Victorian decades were the period when women for the first time play a major part in social movements. This was a change of immense importance. It provided new opportunities for the middle- and upper-class woman whose horizons had been narrowing for at least a century as society more and more came to regard women as purely ornamental appendages. It immensely enriched the pool of talent on which society could draw. It provided new skills and insights in nursing, in education, in housing problems. The women's movement affected the activities of government but it sprang entirely from voluntary effort—it was indeed one form of the self-help of which the age was so proud.

One major field which was transformed by the activities of women was nursing. After Miss Nightingale's triumphs at Scutari she published *Notes on Nursing* in 1859, and the foundation of the Nightingale Nursing Home at St. Thomas' Hospital followed a year later. It was a nurse trained at St. Thomas', Agnes Jones (1833-68), who went to work at the Brownlow Hill poor law institution in Liverpool, and who pioneered higher standards of nursing in poor law hospitals. The medical profession itself was entered by women like Elizabeth Garrett (Anderson), who qualified after years of struggle in 1865.[9]

Apart from nursing, women made their greatest impact in education. F.D. Maurice and the Christian Socialist group had been among those who first made it possible for women to gain an academic training comparable with that of men. Both Frances Mary Buss of the North London Collegiate School and Dorothea Beale of Cheltenham Ladies' College had studied at Queen's College, Harley Street, where Maurice lectured. Emily Davies, who first set to work to scale the barriers of the ancient universities, was a friend of Elizabeth Garrett. Education spilled over into social work with Mary Carpenter, who was a pioneer in establishing reformatory schools. With Octavia Hill women's activities spread out into the housing of the poor, the fight to preserve common land, and the foundation of the National Trust.

For very understandable reasons women played an important part in the agitation against the Contagious Diseases Acts. Josephine Butler, the most striking personality involved in that campaign, urged, in her essay *The Constitution Violated*, that women were deprived by the acts of their basic rights, and that this could not have been done had they possessed the vote.[10] In 1869 Mrs. Butler helped to found the Ladies' National Association for the Repeal of the Contagious Diseases Acts, which was also supported by Mary Carpenter, by Harriet Martineau, and by Florence Nightingale.[11] Such women's associations were a new development. Some, like the one just mentioned were national. Some, like the North of England Council for Promoting the Higher Education of Women, founded at Leeds in 1867, were regional.[12] Others, like the Manchester and Salford Ladies' Sanitary Reform Association, established in 1862, met a purely local need.[13] All represent a much higher level of public activity by women which would never have been thought of in the earlier part of the century.

Some successes had already been gained by 1850, in the long campaign to provide a national system of elementary education, but, by that date, very little had been done to remedy the equally grave defects in secondary and higher education. Between 1850 and 1870 a good deal was achieved in this field, though progress was slow. There was no question at the time of the state providing such education, yet it took a greater and greater share in determining policy, if not by providing institutions and paying the fees, at least by strictly regulating and controlling schools and universities which remained independent institutions. The process began with the royal commissions of enquiry into Oxford and Cambridge, established in 1850, and it continued in the following decade with the Clarendon Commission on the public schools and the Taunton Commission of the endowed grammar schools, and with the legislation which followed their reports.

There were many reasons for this new reforming activity. One obvious motive was the desire to clean up and improve old institutions which had fallen behind the demands of the age. The enquiries did not reveal any great corruption but they exposed inefficiency and waste which was adhorrent to the temper of the time. Closed fellowships, the abuses of the schoolmaster's freehold, the profits enjoyed by corporate bodies from the renewal of leases for lives were all evils which, to the mind of an age very conscious of efficiency and the benefits of competition, needed to be cleared up. To some critics, notably to Matthew Arnold, the weaknesses of England's secondary schools and universities compared very unfavourably with the higher standards of other European countries, notably of Germany, the educational Mecca of the day.

Too much can perhaps be made of the effect on English opinion of these foreign comparisons, and Arnold's views were not typical of the opinion of this time. A more serious factor was the growing feeling in mid-nineteenth-century England that a richer, more highly developed society with a greatly expanded upper and upper middle class needed more effective educational institutions than the ancient universities and grammar schools or the private schools which had tried very hard to fill the gaps left by their chartered competitors. Changes were in some ways rather slow; for example, school and university curricula stayed·close to the traditional models and the newer subjects like the natural sciences took a long time to find favour. Yet Oxford and Cambridge were much more efficient institutions in 1880 than they had been in 1850, and by 1880 the new provincial colleges were beginning to appear. The ancient public schools had been reformed and many new ones had been founded. Many of the grammar schools took on a new lease of life after the Endowed Schools Act of 1869.

The change from the situation in the 'thirties was very striking and, had it not taken place, England would have found it even more difficult than she did to maintain her place in the more competitive international world of the late nineteenth century. There was a close connection too between better education and more efficient government. The movement for administrative reform got under way in the 'fifties, and was strongly supported by the university reformers who saw a reformed public service as providing suitable careers for the graduates of expanding universities.[14] Public appointments by competitive examination represented the same kind of intellectual free trade as college fellowships opened to free competition. Mr. Gladstone, who had supported the Oxford University Act of 1854, introduced open competition into the civil service in 1871. Academic and administrative reforms worked together to achieve higher standards among the upper class group which managed so much of the nation's affairs.

During the twenty years between 1850 and 1870 the dominance of that upper class group was at its most unquestioned, both because the group itself was more broadly based and because class tensions had lessened. This was the period in which Bagehot claimed that deference was a major characteristic of English society. The divisions between landed and industrial wealth were growing less marked. Though their assimilation was the fruit rather of the later than of the mid-Victorian years, the process was beginning. J.G. Fitch, when he reported to the Taunton Commission on the West Riding grammar schools, noted that manufacturers habitually sent their sons away to distant schools like Rugby and Westminster. 'It is the object of the father, as a rule, to withdraw his son from local associations, and to take him as far as possible from the sons of his own neighbours and dependants'.[15] The public schools were an important influence in drawing together the sons of the well-to-do from all social groups.

The pattern of deference was as influential among the new rich as among the old. In the early years of industrialism the manufacturer had ruled over the factory village with a sway as despotic as that of any landowner. Robert Owen may have been a benevolent despot at New Lanark; the nature of the case made him a despot none the less. Something of the same tradition lingered in the towns of the later industrial society. A recent article has pointed out the way in which, in industrial Lancashire, the mill-workers tended to identify themselves with the political views of their employers, who engendered, not only a particular political loyalty but a whole social and cultural atmosphere.[16]

This means that the dividing lines in society tended to run vertically, separating off interest groups and connexions, rather than horizontally, dividing classes. The men of the time argued that there was considerable mobility between social groups and that the divisions within them were often as significant as the barriers between them. The attitude of the time is well summed up by Palmerston in his speech in the Don Pacifico debate; though the words are familiar, they bear quoting:

> We have shown the example of a nation, in which every class in society accepts with cheerfulness the lot which Providence has assigned to it; while at the same time every individual of each class is constantly striving to raise himself in the social scale—not by injustice and wrong, not by violence and illegality, but by preserving good conduct, and by the steady and energetic execution of the moral and intellectual faculties with which his Creator endowed him.[17]

In these words Palmerston accepts the ideas both of stability and of tension—each class is resigned to its lot, while each individual is striving to improve his own position. From about 1850 until his death in 1865 the equilibrium held. The ruling minority was firmly in command. The fact that its own position was so unchallenged made it feel generous to those who were struggling to win their own place in the sun. In the later 'sixties the equilibrium began to break down. Intellectuals like J.S. Mill and Walter Bagehot began to fear the tyranny of mass opinion once political democracy was achieved. In the early 'sixties it had seemed that such an event was very far away. The passing of the Second Reform Act of 1867 represented a crucial change in the pattern.

We are not here concerned with the political changes themselves but with their effects on the movement for social reform.[18] In a book published in 1967 Paul Smith looked at the relationships between the Conservative party and social reform at this time.[19] He argues that Conservative conversion to reform in 1866-7 was partly caused by the working-class agitation of 1866 and by the pressure of trades unionists who believed that the franchise was necessary to enable them to protect their own interests. The act itself created no political or social upheaval ,but it altered the conditions of politics because

> both parties now had to compete for working class votes, and working class interests, aspirations, and needs took on a novel importance, becoming increasingly part of the staple of the political contest, instead of one of its peripheral inconveniences.[20]

One of the major changes after 1867 was the restoration of strong governments, able, if they wished, to take decisive measures, in place of the weak governments which had characterized the period after 1846. The Gladstone government enacted the Education Act of 1870. Disraeli, in his Crystal Palace speech of 1872, defined the three objects of the Conservative party as 'the maintenance of the country's institutions, the upholding of the empire ... the elevation of the condition of the people'.[21] Paul Smith denies that Disraeli's government of 1874 came into power with any distinct social policy of its own, but in R.A. Cross it possessed one of the greatest home secretaries of the century, and it had major achievements to its credit in trades union legislation, in public health, in factory regulation, and in housing.

The legislation of the Disraeli government closed the era of social legislation which had begun in the 1830's. By 1880 the state had become more and more actively involved in establishing the basic conditions of tolerable living for the people. It is noticeable, for instance, that discussions about factory legislation in the 'sixties and 'seventies generally assume that such control serves the common interest and is of value to manufacturers as well as to operatives. By that time English society had accepted a broader responsibility for the concerns of its weaker members than would have seemed possible fifty years earlier. In more and more areas it had become clear that the state must actively intervene since the task was too complex to be left to individuals and groups.

In 1869 Stafford Northcote told the Social Science Congress in his presidential address that 'social questions are assuming such large dimensions that they cannot be adequately dealt with except by the employment of the central administrative machinery'.[22] The mid-Victorians were not reluctant, if they thought it necessary, to make use of state power, but in most cases their belief in self-help and personal initiative made them lay stress on individual activity. They believed in a balance between the individual and the collective operating within an expanding economy. The social legislation of the 'seventies was based on the maintenance of that balance, though it was clearly becoming increasingly fragile. The best example of this was the keen debate over the rights of trades unions. The right to strike was not disputed, but what of the possible intimidation to which strikes led and of the interference with the employer's control over his business? After 1800 England moved into a more uneasy age when international competition was keener and domestic issues like the rise of Socialism and the problems of the great cities more contentious.[23] The mid-Victorian balance of classes and interests was breaking down, and, so far as social issues were concerned, a new period began.

iii) Ruling Elites and Working Classes

The great mass of mid-Victorians earned their living by manual labour, and their general economic position had improved. 'Average real wages (allowing for unemployment)', writes E.J. Hobshawm, 'remained pretty unchanged from 1850 until the early 1860's, but rose by about forty per cent between 1862 and 1875. They sagged for a year or two in the late 1870's, but were back to the old level by the mid-eighties and after that climbed rapidly.'[24] Such general averages cover enormous differences within the working class. Only about fifteen per cent belonged to the aristocracy of labour, the skilled men who were prominent in cooperative societies and trades unions. At the other end of the scale was the mass of real poverty surveyed at the end of the century by observers like Charles Booth and Seebohm Rowntree—the casually employed, the workers in sweated industries, the sick and the old. Though the agricultural labourers escaped from some of the evils suffered by town dwellers, they suffered from hardships enough of their own and their standards of living remained very low. The wage-earning classes as a whole were not increasing their share of the national income, and the middle classes were gaining a more than proportionate share of increasing wealth.[25] They and the upper classes alike were adopting higher and more ostentatious standards of living, and there was considerable pressure upon them to earn and to spend in a lavish way.

At the top of the social pyramid, weakened by the agricultural depression at the end of our period but hanging on to much of their authority up to the First World War, was the ancient landed aristocracy. If the mid-Victorian age was a deferential one, the supreme type of deference-situation was that which centred round the landed estate. If the aristocracy exhibited many examples of conspicuous, and indeed useless consumption, they were on the whole a hard-working and conscientious group of people. Their distinguishing mark, says F.M.L. Thompson, was 'acceptance and discharge of the authority and responsibility which absence of any apparatus of centralized administration left to them'.[26] By the 'sixties and 'seventies they held political power by the will of a large popular electorate, but their influence persisted, partly because they were constantly reinforced by new wealth from commerce and industry which merged, as it had done for centuries, with the traditional wealth of the land.

By the middle of the century the landed interest was far less prominent than it had been in forming public opinion, and much of its role in that area had been taken over by the rapidly expanding group of intellectuals and professional men who wrote for newspapers and reviews, became administrators, doctors and factory inspectors, and broke into the charmed circle of political power. The fruit of university reform and open competition in the civil service was to put the running of the country more and more into the hands of the highly educated rather than of the nobly born. However, as with so many Victorian dichotomies, the contrast can be exaggerated. Administration certainly became more expert, but the difference was an intellectual rather than a social one. The same kind of people carried on but they had been equipped with a more thorough intellectual training for the job. It is noteworthy that, in the early years of the civil service examinations, the civil service commissioners laid great stress on their success in recruiting young men who had enjoyed the education of gentlemen.[27]

The landed aristocracy probably held their place in the institutions of the new age better than is often argued, but they were not very prominent among the promoters of social reform. There were exceptions of course. The most prominent of them is the great Lord Shaftesbury; others at a lower level of importance were Sir John Pakington, who campaigned for many years for an education act, and Sir Charles Adderley, chairman of the Royal Sanitary Commission of 1869. As a group the merchants and manufacturers were more heavily committed to social reform than the aristocracy, for it is a great mistake to regard the men of industrial wealth as devoted to nothing but money-making. Many of them had very wide public interests. Among the Anti-Corn Law leaders, Richard Cobden, with his interests in international peace and arbitration, in education and in land-reform stands pre-eminent. Many others, like Joseph Chamberlain of Birmingham or A.J. Mundella of Nottingham and Sheffield, moved through making a fortune to activity in their own areas and then into national politics. Some like Titus Salt, the Bradford manufacturer who built the model town of Saltaire, remained essentially local figures.

The men of landed wealth and the manufacturers shared one important characteristic in common. Their wealth and interests were based in a provincial centre not in London, and , though they might also enjoy power at the capital, they maintained the ancient English tradition of locally-based influence. The professional men and intellectuals were, on the other hand, much more likely to be based in London, and their growing influence increased the marked central pull of London in mid-Victorian life. Even those, like the factory inspectors, who worked in the provinces, had strong links with the capital, or, like the medical officers of health,represented a professional opinion which was metro-politan in inspiration. The essential social difference between these professional men and either the industrialists or the landowners was that their power was based on holding office not on owning property. They were not, in general, men of wealth; they enjoyed surrogate power on behalf of organizations. In many cases they represented either the state or the local authority, and the power which they wielded tended more and more to reduce the traditional freedoms of the property owner. In the country districts, for example, the professional police forces and the medical officers and relieving officers of the Guardians had steadily lessened the independence of the gentry.[28]

The professional men filled a wide range of posts. In London they staffed the civil service and formed opinion through the press. They were the factory inspectors and the inspectors of schools, the chief constables of counties and the medical officers of health. They were the headmasters of public schools and grammar schools, and even the humble schoolmaster, trained under the regulations of the Education Depart-ment, had his foot on a very low rung of the same ladder. All of them were, in one sense or another, experts, and Victorian society was becoming more and more influenced by skilled opinion. The expert view was heard through John Simon's reports as medical officer to the Privy Council.[29] It produced its own pressure group in the Social Science Association (1857-86), which concerned itself with law reform, edu-cation, penal organization, public health, and social and economic conditions.[30]

Pressure groups were not always successful. The civil service was reformed, though not as a result of the propaganda of the Administrative Reform Association (1855-57) which had a brief moment of success as a result of the calamities suffered in the Crimea.[31] The later Victorian civil service, after the introduction of competitive examination, became more efficient, but efficiency did not thereby increase its range of action or its activity in promoting social policies. Indeed the great administrators of the pre-reformed age, like Chadwick or Kay-Shuttleworth or John Simon, took a far more active share in promoting change than their successors were to do. As social administration became more regularized, it seems to have become more mechanical. The Local Government Board, founded in 1871 by the fusion of the Poor Law Board and the Medical Department of the Privy Council, was dominated by poor law officials and took a narrowly administrative line. So far as the medical side of its work was concerned, the attitude of the new department was to contract powers of central control and to reduce national supervision over disease. John Simon, who had built up a national reputation at the Medical Department for his enquiries into public health problems, found the situation so frustrating that he retired in 1876.[32]

Simon was a doctor and a medical scientist who had built up a national position as a scientific expert. He had carried forward the public health campaign after the fall of Chadwick, and had laid great emphasis on the medical and scientific pre-requisites for a national policy. The team he assembled to carry out medical enquiries—Buchanan, Edward Smith, Whitley, Burden-Sanderson, Greenhow, Ord, Bristow, Hunter, Holmes—showed how much the trained scientist could contribute to solving national problems. At a more local level it has been shown that the London medical officers of health were among the first to recognize the importance of overcrowding in creating the problem of the slums.[33] The medical men provide the best example of the growth of the trained expert, but not the only one. The natural sciences, using the term in the broadest sense, had developed to the point where they both engrossed an increasing share of the national attention and could be applied to solving specific problems.

A good example of the latter situation is provided by the Alkali Acts of 1863-81, passed to deal with the emission of acid fumes from chemical works. The first inspector, R.A. Smith, was himself a distinguished chemist who had studied in Liebig's laboratory at Giessen and was a co-worker with A.W. Hoffman and Lyon Playfair. Smith and his assistants quickly built up a position as advisers to the chemical manufacturers who collaborated in extending public control. The story provides an example of the extension of public supervision over industry in a way which aroused no controversy. It also shows that scientific knowledge had practical applications and that the expert adviser was in a position to render service to industry.[34] During the 'seventies the claim of science to increased public recognition was being strongly pressed. There was a great deal of propaganda in favour of government aid for science through the endowment of research. In 1875 the Devonshire Commission on scientific instruction and the advancement of science recommended the creation of a ministry of science and education and the establishment of a national technical laboratory and physical observatory. In 1876 the Royal Society was given an increased research fund, though the movement died away after 1880, since the politicians were not deeply committed to supporting science and many of the scientists themselves were suspicious of governmental control.[35]

The place of the expert in the middle and late Victorian world was an uneasy one. In one sense, as the example of the Alkali Acts administration shows, a more sophisticated society needed more skilled agency. Fitzjames Stephen wrote to Lord Lytton in 1879: 'This is not the age for public life. It is emphatically the age for engineers, men of science, lawyers and the like'.[36] On the other hand the reformed system of secondary and higher education took little account of the need to learn specific scientific or technological skills. It was still believed that the traditional subjects like classics and mathematics trained the mind better than any others, and that a man whose mind had been effectively trained could quickly apply himself to any appropriate skill which he needed to learn. The point comes out very clearly in the criteria used for recruitment to the civil service. As we have seen, at the higher levels the aim was to attract young men of breeding with good university careers behind them. The civil servant recruited by competition was not an expert, but the traditional gentleman brought up to date.

Perhaps Fitzjames Stephen's contrast between political skills and professional expertise really reflects a cleavage between the two activities which had come about as a result of the movement towards a more democratic political system. Before 1867 the role of the politician and the administrator had been imperfectly differentiated. Government was not regarded as a highly professionalized business and administration was a craft which men very often entered after they had worked in one of the liberal professions. Both politicians and administrators were members of a small élite, very conscious of the fact that it controlled the national destinies. After 1870 this harmonious and homogeneous world steadily broke down. The politicians had to appeal more and more to a mass electorate and to respond to the demands of mass parties. The administrators ceased to be men of independent professional experience and became bureaucrats, dedicated throughout their working lives to maintaining the official machine.

The breakdown of the political administrative synthesis which had dominated the 'fifties and 'sixties engendered a strand of criticism by many of the intellectual liberals who were becoming increasingly fearful about the future after the 'leap in the dark' of 1867. Fitzjames Stephen's *Liberty, Equality, Fraternity* (1873) is a powerful criticism of Liberal ideals, more particularly of J.S. Mill's *On Liberty* of 1859.[37] Mill himself had expressed his fear of majority tyranny and wished to introduce proportional representation to lessen the danger. The most interesting exponent of this general attitude was the banker and economist, Walter Bagehot. He had in his *English Constitution* of 1867 contrasted the dignified and the efficient elements in the British system and had argued that Cabinet government worked because the real rulers could operate behind the deference paid to the ornamental parts of the structure. Bagehot was hostile to an egalitarian society; he believed in what he called 'removable inequalities', in a system in which many people might be worse off than others, but in which all might hope to make some advance in their station.[38] In his very interesting book, *Physics and Politics*, he discussed the laws of development in human societies and concluded that the highest form was represented by 'government by discussion, which has fostered a general intellectual tone, a diffused disposition to weigh evidence, a conviction that much may be said on every side of everything which the elder. and more fanatic ages of the world wanted'.[39] He probably believed that the rule of the educated minority before 1867 had guaranteed those advantages; he feared that they were endangered through the extremes fostered by democracy.

The reign of democracy meant the increased power of the working class. The skilled workers and their families formed but a small group. These were the people who joined trades unions, cooperative and friendly societies, who were accessible to the argument that through self-help they might be able to improve their position in life. They had risen above the worst poverty, though through misfortune or old age they could easily fall back into it. The great majority of the workers had never emerged from poverty at all, and, although they were constantly being urged to help themselves, they found it remarkably difficult to do so because they had not reached the point of elementary well-being from which providence became possible. Since they were so often in need, they were the objects of the philanthropy which was such a characteristic feature of the age.[40] The concepts of self-help and of philanthropy epitomize much of Victorian attitudes towards the working classes. There is an important difference between the two ideas. The former implies that the individual has the ultimate control over his own destiny; it is a positive idea. The second implies that the individual's condition is so mean that someone has to take the essential decisions on his behalf; in that sense it is largely negative. Reforming bodies like the Charity Organization Society, fearful of the debilitating effects of indiscriminate almsgiving,[41] were always trying to change the negative idea into the positive, but circumstances made their efforts unsuccessful in many cases. So many of the poor did not have the reserves of skill and good health and decent housing which might have enabled them to stand on their own feet.

The concepts of self-help and of philanthropy will be analyzed more fully later. Here we need to consider how far the individualism implied in the first idea related to the dominant philosophies of the time. In one sense, as we have already seen, the idea of self-help reconciled men to the capitalist order and gave them a stake within it. The workers, like their social superiors, found that the ends which they desired to achieve were to be obtained only by joint action. The kind of shared activity which promoted the anti-slavery movement, the Health of Towns Association or the Anti-Corn Law League was paralleled by the activity which produced cooperative and friendly societies. The difference between working-class and middle-class activism arose from the fact that it was rare for the latter to limit the individual freedom of the manufacturer or the business man. Society treated his economic interests with hallowed respect.

In the case of the working class it was different. No man, it is true, had to shop at a cooperative store or save with a friendly society, but there might be considerable pressure on him to join a trades union or not to break a strike. The trades union leaders urged in the late 'sixties that the violence and intimidation in the Sheffield trades, which necessitated an enquiry by the Royal Commission on trades unions, were not characteristic of the national unions as a whole.[42] What they said was in the great majority of cases no doubt true, but the middle-class opinion of the time was very conscious of the danger. To the Sheffield workman it seemed that he was simply protecting himself by the only means which lay to his hand; to his critics there was the threat that collective action meant collective tyranny.

The issue was a much broader one than the problems of the Sheffield saw grinders. To the workers only collective action, which might sometimes mean coercive action, could safeguard their livelihood by limiting the number of apprentices, banning piece work and settling minimum rates of wages. To the majority of the members of the royal commission on trades unions of 1867 such activities not only harmed the employer who paid the men's wages, but they prevented the really industrious workman from getting ahead. The point is very clearly made in an exchange during the royal commission's hearing between J.A. Roebuck, who is asking, and the union leader, Robert Applegarth, who is answering the questions:[43]

So that you do really interfere with a man's judgment of his own interests; you say, we the trade interfere and tell you that you shall not be governed by your own judgment?—In matters like that we believe it to be on the whole very injurious for the men to act in that way.

How should you like me to interfere with you as you interfere with those men?—If you were a member of my society, and you, in conjunction with a majority, decided that I must conform to certain regulations I should be bound to do so; but if we are to be left to do as we like the sooner we dissolve our society the better.

It is clear that the commissioners accepted the right of a man to withhold his labour, since the individual might make that decision for himself, but they were very unhappy about the collective results of individual action. They thought of a trades union as representing merely a number of individuals banded together for certain purposes. They never faced up to the idea that an organized group is not simply a number of individuals but a unit which has a drive and momentum of its own apart from the men who compose it, and to which they, in some circumstances, need to be subordinated. The mid-Victorians should not be criticised too harshly for not having solved problems with which the later twentieth century is still grappling. With their individualist pre-suppositions it was very difficult for them to understand the point of view of an organization which was arguing in collectivist terms. The great debate over the place of the trades unions in society which was taking place at the end of the 'sixties provides a very good example of the way in which the consensus of laissez-faire was breaking down.

iv) The Development of public power: local government, police, railways

The change is clearly represented in the ideas of the Oxford philosopher and Liberal reformer T.H. Green. In his lectures on the principles of political obligation, first delivered in 1879, he propounded the idea of freedom as a positive activity, as the right to act and to enjoy in the company of others. Freedom, he argued, can only mean the freedom of individual persons, but it can be realized only through influences which the state supplies. It would have been a mockery to speak of the state as a realization of freedom to an Athenian slave; 'and perhaps it would not be much less to speak of it as such to an untaught and under-fed denizen of a London yard with gin-shops on the right hand and on the left'.[44] The division, Green argued, between the individual and the state was an unreal one.

> To ask why I am to submit to the power of the state, is to ask why I am to allow my life to be regulated by that complex of institutions without which I literally should not have a life to call my own, nor should be able to ask for a justification of what I am called on to do.[45]

The positive idea of freedom—that it is something done or enjoyed in the company of others—involves the idea of control. The state helps to make a town free from epidemic disease by sanitary regulations which may bear hardly on individuals. The trades union hopes to free its members from poverty by prohibiting them from working with non-unionists in order to keep up the rate of wages. Even the advocates of so personal a cause as that of total abstinence find that, in order to save individuals from the tyranny of drink, they promote schemes for control of the liquor trade or for total prohibition. The idea that freedom is a positive good contains a paradox which Green and the philosophers of the Idealist school were never able to resolve.

Central state planning lost a good deal of its momentum in the 'fifties, but the pace quickened again in the 'sixties. Individual and group action, organized into the good causes in which mid-Victorian England was so rich, developed steadily throughout. A more detailed examination of state policy in areas like factory reform and public health will follow in later chapters. Here three briefer examples, taken from railway policy, police and local government, may help to explain the nature of public controls as the mid-Victorian understood them.

State activity meant the attempt to regulate the standards of society in accordance with an accepted national policy. The Medical Act of 1858, passed after years of controversy, set up a General Medical Council and controlled the qualifications for practising medicine and surgery.[46] The Prisons Act of 1877 took prisons out of the hands of local authorities and vested them in the hands of the Secretary of State, working through a body of prison commissioners. 'In no other branch of public administration', wrote the Webbs, 'has such a change been made in England.'[47] Sometimes, as in the case of the Taunton Commission on the endowed schools, the original proposals for state control were a good deal more extensive than the changes which were actually made. The Commissioners proposed the establishment of a national authority for secondary education with subordinate authorities and a Council of Examinations. All that was actually achieved by the Endowed Schools Act of 1869 was legislation for the reform of individual endowments.[48]

Public activity involved the work of both central and local government, and the relationship between them was difficult and complex. In earlier decades local bodies had been left considerable freedom to decide whether or not to adopt reforming measures. As time went on they were more and more required to adopt standards nationally set so as to ensure that people in some parts of the country were not under-privileged in relation to those in more favoured areas. The great problem of mid-Victorian local government was that its efficiency was so limited and its reputation so low. The civil servant Tom Taylor, addressing the Social Science Association in 1857, argued that the danger in England was not centralization, but the kind of localism which tried 'to establish the rule of unmitigated selfishness and petty wisdom under the specious name of local liberty'. Central action was required, Taylor argued, to confer powers for local improvement cheaply and effectively, to promote such improvement by disseminating general information, and to act as a court of appeal against local oppression or default.[49]

Many of the speeches on the Education Bill of 1870 addressed themselves to local government questions because of the proposal to set up school boards. The speakers stressed two criticisms: that the ratepayers were very parsimonious, and that they were open to jobbery.[50] Even in the major cities municipal administration tended to be mean and vacillating. E.P. Hennock, in a recent study, has argued that in Leeds there was a burst of activity after 1850, but that this was not maintained. The council's policy was indecisive, largely because the pressures towards economy were very strong. They refused, for example, to increase the police force between 1879 and 1893, they sold the task of emptying ash-pits in 1876 to a contractor on terms which made it almost certain that the work would be scamped, and they did nothing to control the building of back-to-back houses.[51] The situation in Leeds seems to have improved in the 'nineties. If Beatrice Webb is to be believed, conditions at Manchester were no better at the end of the decade. The scale of the council's work had outgrown its organization and the machine was disorganized. The council had no real head and the officials lacked influence. The committee chairmen were sometimes able, but in other cases 'grotesquely unfit'. Even the abler administrators, Mrs. Webb thought, 'were merely hard-headed shopkeepers divided in their mind between their desire to keep the rates down and their ambition to magnify the importance of Manchester as against other cities'.[52]

The evidence does not at the moment exist to make a full assessment of the record of later nineteenth-century local government, but it is clear that parsimony and parochialism affected the level of performance in many places. The great example on the other side, pointing forward to what local government might achieve under imaginative management, was that of Birmingham. Municipal government in Birmingham in the 'fifties ran on similar lines to that of Leeds in the 'seventies and 'eighties. The change towards a new approach came about in the 'sixties, partly through the influence of Nonconformist ministers like George Dawson of the Church of the Saviour and R.W. Dale of Carr's Lane, and partly through the increasing interest in local affairs of business men like Joseph Chamberlain. Dawson and Dale preached the duty of public service to the town as a major responsibility of the Christian community. Chamberlain brought to the work the skill and enterprise which had made him a large fortune.[53]

The first public cause which the Birmingham group took up was that of education. The National Education League, founded in 1869, campaigned for national, unsectarian and compulsory education with state aid and inspection and local management. The League played an active part in the campaign which produced the 1870 Act, though the act itself did not meet many of its demands.[54] The education programme was one of the roots of the new Radicalism which Chamberlain took into the House of Commons in the mid-seventies. Before his interests became centred at Westminster, a good deal had been achieved at home. New measures were adopted to deal with sanitary problems. In 1874-5 Chamberlain steered through the purchase of the gas companies and of the water company, and the bold plan to build the new Corporation Street was an attempt to improve the amenities of the central area. The work of these years went a long way to justify the claim made by J.T. Bunce, editor of the *Birmingham Daily Post* and collaborator of the reformers, that 'the work of the town, according to its means, should be done with such completeness as to leave no source of danger or evil unchecked, no material defect uncured, no intellectual want uncared for'.[55] Chamberlain struck a new note when he argued, in proposing the introduction of a bill to take over the water undertaking, that 'all regulated monopolies, sustained by the state . . . should be controlled by the representatives of the people and not left in the hands of private speculators'.[56]

One of the major services where the power of central and local government overlapped was the police. Here central control tended to expand, though the process was slow and, even after the Police Act of 1856, the Home Office lacked any directing policy for the local police forces. The County Constabulary Acts of 1839 and 1840 have already been discussed.[57] The Municipal Corporations Act of 1835 had required the boroughs to establish police forces, but progress in the counties was comparatively slow. By 1841 only 24 counties had adopted the act and only four more followed between 1841 and 1856.[58] A uniform system was not set up without a struggle. A select committee on police in counties and boroughs (1853) reported that the permissive act of 1839 had failed to provide a system adequate for the prevention of crime and the security of property. The committee favoured the consolidation of the smaller borough forces into the counties and the sharing of management and control between the counties and the larger boroughs. They suggested that the government should make a contribution towards the cost of an extended police system and they recommended urgent legislation.[59]

Palmerston's Police Bill of 1854 proposed the establishment of police forces in all counties and the appointment of government inspectors. Boroughs with fewer than 20,000 inhabitants were to lose their separate forces and the powers of the Home Secretary over the remaining borough forces were to be increased. However no provision was made for a government grant-in-aid.[60] The bill, described as 'subversive of the independence and rights of local self-government', was strongly attacked by the boroughs, led by Manchester,[61] and was withdrawn. Another bill of 1856, introduced by George Grey who had become Home Secretary, was also opposed by the boroughs and was fought hard in Parliament, but it passed into law and was to form the basis of the modern police system. County Quarter Sessions were required to provide a police force. The Treasury was to meet one quarter of the cost of police pay and clothing, provided that a certificate of efficiency was given by the inspectors of constabulary whose office the Act created, and who were to make reports to the Home Secretary. The only major provision of the original bill which did not pass into law was that the Home Secretary might make regulations for the borough forces.[62]

Of the 59 country forces which were established under the act of 1856 all but seven had qualified for grant in 1857 and six of these qualified the following year.[63] In the boroughs the effect of the act was slower. Most of the larger boroughs qualified for grant within two years, and by 1870 many of the smaller forces had been consolidated into the counties.[64] But inefficiency remained a problem in the smaller towns, and some very small forces survived. Certainly the act of 1856 achieved higher general standards and the device of the grant-in-aid was to be of crucial importance for local government finance in a later period, but the amount of centralization in police management after 1856 can be exaggerated. The Home Office had no active policy, and the inspectors, who lived in their districts and worked from their homes, were not always consulted on matters of general interest.[65] Little was done to achieve cooperation between the different forces. In the boroughs the powers of the watch committee remained very great, and were sometimes, for instance in relation to licensed premises, corruptly exercised. In some cases boroughs refused the grant, which amounted only to one-quarter of the cost of pay and clothing.[66] In 1874 the grant was increased to one-half of these costs, and in 1888 the Local Government Act abolished separate forces in towns with a population of under 10,000. The same act established in counties the Standing Joint Committees, representing the justices and the new county councils, to control the police.[67]

Central government, in dealing with the counties and boroughs, was dealing with institutions enjoying powers and traditions coeval with its own. The industrial age had brought into existence new institutions, enjoying great wealth and power in their own right, which had to be fitted into the general administrative structure. Of these institutions by far the most important, with national affiliations as far-reaching as those of government itself, were the railways. Parliament took great interest in them, but it did not control them very closely. The railways department of the Board of Trade had been established in 1840. This was replaced in 1844 by the Railway Board which aimed to guide Parliament through all the railway bills of the session and to recommend whether each scheme should or should not be adopted. Had the plan succeeded, the influence of government would have been brought directly to bear on railway development, but the scheme quickly came to nothing. The Railway Board's reports on railway bills were given up because Peel would not support a policy which led to government supervision of a whole class of private bills.[68]

Railway bills were indeed private bills in the technical sense, but they had very wide public implications. The consequences of a negative government policy were noted by the statistician G.R. Porter. In his judgment private enterprise, in the case of the railways, had led to great public inconvenience. He did not suggest that government itself should have built railways but that it had a responsibility to reconcile conflicting interests and to ensure that the revolutionary changes in communication were carried through smoothly. These needs might have been met by 'a preliminary inquiry made by competent and uninterested professional men, with a view to ascertain the comparative advantages and facilities offered by different lines for the accomplishment of the object in view'. Great sums of money might have been saved if Parliament had refused to consider any railway bill until it had been examined and reported on favourably after such an investigation.[69] Such extensive government control over private enterprise was perhaps impossible to achieve in the 1840's. Certainly after 1844 there was no major development of the Board of Trade's legal power over the railways, but its influence over the companies steadily increased through the administrative actions of its officers. It enquired into accidents, it studied systems of communication on moving trains, it promoted safety measures like the use of the telegraph for traffic control. In railway policy, as in so many areas of mid-Victorian administration, it was the steady pressure of executive action, far more than legislative enactment, which increased central power.[70]

The railways in turn exercised considerable influence on public policies.

As chartered interests with monopoly powers, for instance the power to acquire land by compulsory purchase, they strongly affected the general interest, particularly through their acquisition of land in the cities. The effect of railway development in towns and cities was often drastic. In building their lines and goods yards and stations they destroyed urban property on a large scale, made many people homeless and increased the problem of urban over-crowding.[71] They frequently drove their lines through populous working-class districts because it was comparatively easy and cheap to do so. H.J. Dyos has shown that in London, the most thickly populated and the most seriously affected area, 51 railway schemes, affecting over 56,000 persons, were implemented in the period before 1885 with no provision for re-housing the displaced. Within these totals no less than 37,000 displacements took place between 1859 and 1867.[72] The problems of urban housing will be discussed later,[73] but it is clear that urban 'improvements' in general, and railway construction in particular, made the housing situation in inner urban areas worse than it would otherwise have been. Nor did the railways provide better housing opportunities by moving workers out of the city centres. Until the latter part of the century the workers were too poor and too much bound to the providers of casual employment in the central districts to be able to travel, and the railway companies were not interested in providing workmen's trains. The first major attempt to force a railway company to meet this social need was the bill for the Great Eastern's Liverpool Street extension which was authorized in 1864 only on condition that the company ran cheap workmen's trains daily. This requirement was to have a far-reaching effect on the growth of later nineteenth-century working-class suburbs in East and North-East London.[74] In general the railways did a great deal of harm to the city environment. It is true, of course, that they existed to provide a transport service and to earn dividends for their shareholders and not to preserve working-class houses. Yet their effect on urban patterns of living brings out one of the many clashes between public and private interests of which men were becoming increasingly conscious in the 'seventies. The railways destroyed much more living accommodation than was provided under the Cross and Torrens Acts, which made the first official attempt to deal with the problem of urban housing.

i)Pressure groups and moral crusades

The last chapter was concerned with analyzing the process of change in English society between 1850 and 1880 and with considering some basic assumptions about the public domain and the extent of its activities. The link between private aspirations and public policies was provided by the pressure group, or the crusading individual, desiring either to change some particular law or to represent the claims of a wider interest. Many examples have already been cited in the last chapter: the Social Science Association, the Administrative Reform Association, the National Education League, the group which pressed in the 'seventies for greater recognition for science. Such groups played a very important part in bringing about social change at a time when these matters did not form part of the programmes of the political parties, as they were increasingly to do after 1870. Many more examples might be given of campaigns, successful and unsuccessful, waged by the advocates of reforming causes. Samuel Plimsoll fought to amend the Merchant Shipping Act in the interest of greater safety at sea. The United Kingdom Alliance, founded in 1853, stood for the total prohibition of the liquor traffic.[1] The Lancashire Public School Association (1847) and the Manchester and Salford Committee on Education (1851) produced different solutions to the problem of providing education for the people which, though they were not implemented at the time, helped to make the subject into a national issue.[2]

Though pressure groups were active in all aspects of the national life, they were especially busy in promoting the many philanthropic causes which were so characteristic of the age. The idea of philanthropy has been defined as the desire to do good to others, particularly when this involved personal service, the direct contact between donor and recipient and the idea of warm kindness and self-giving love implicit in that relationship.[3] The greatest and most characteristic of the philanthropists—not least because of his own deep personal involvement in the causes to which he gave his name—was Lord Shaftesbury. His activities during a long life—the humane treatment of lunatics, factory reforms, public health, ragged schools, the problems of poverty in London, the improvement of common lodging houses—form a roll-call of the causes which stirred the Christian conscience of his day.[4]

The general atmosphere of philanthropy was deeply religious. Men recognized no distinction between moral and social reform, since it was believed that social reforms could succeed only if they were based on renewed personalities.[5] The philanthropists tended to pursue a policy of moral absolutism, seeing the world in clear blacks and whites and anathematizing all those who did not support their cause. In many cases this led to a narrow and exclusive attitude from which Shaftesbury himself was not free and he was a man who moved in the great world and was concerned with a wide range of national affairs. Many more humble philanthropists—business and professional men, the clergy, middle-aged ladies—had no such safeguards. As J.F. Stephen claimed in a *Saturday Review* essay, they were content for evils to exist if they could find means for removing their bad consequences. They tended to look on their fellow creatures, 'not as men and women' but as persons to be 'in some form or other restrained or re-modelled'.[6] For them the moral imperative to do good extinguished the right to freedom of choice and limited the possibilities of compromise.

This absolutist approach was linked with a deep individualism because the philanthropist, as has already been suggested, was aiming to revolutionize personal lives. He aimed to dig a very sharp divide between the old man and the new, and such an appeal, as religion has always known, could succeed only if it struck down to the deepest roots of human personality. Yet the philanthropist's attitude to state intervention was a somewhat uneasy one since he often tended to advocate it to promote the causes in which he was interested. In the temperance movement, for example, there were serious tensions between those who believed in legislative prohibition of the drink trade and those who stressed the moral persuasion of individuals to abandon drink.[7] The concept of positive freedom, which has already been discussed,[8] fitted in very well with the ideas of the prohibitionists. T.H. Green himself was a supporter of local option to control the drink trade because he saw such controls as creating a wider freedom. Limiting a man's right to drink too much protected the interests of his children and their chance of enjoying a better standard of life.[9]

From the premise that the state could never be indifferent to such issues might follow very extensive measures of interference with personal habits. Brian Harrison has argued, however, that there were severe limitations in practice to the kind of interventionism which the United Kingdom Alliance desired.[10] They looked on legislative measures rather as breaking a habit than as imposing a regular system of control. The whole development of the Victorian administrative state was based on the establishment of such controls to ensure that the law was carried out. Once Parliament had legislated the real work began through public enquiries, through the visits of inspectors, through detailed regulation. The moral reformers stood aside from such things because they were not interested in them. They were concerned to strike at what they saw as particular evils. After the great blow had been struck, they expected the evil to disappear and the individual to adopt reformed habits. If they were advocates of state intervention, it was a very different kind of intervention from that advocated by those who wanted closer control over public health or over working hours in factories.

Two of the most distinctive of the moral reform crusades were those waged by the United Kingdom Alliance for the reform of the drink trade and by Josephine Butler and her associates for the repeal of the Contagious Diseases Acts. From the point of view of state activity, their objectives appear to have been directly contrary. The prohibitionists wanted more state activity in order to control the evils of drink. Mrs. Butler and her friends wanted to abolish one existing form of state power—the control over women in garrison towns—as offensive to the personal freedom of women and to the moral interests of men. Yet the two attitudes, apparently so different, share important common characteristics. Both exhibited a revulsion from what they saw as grave evils, combined with a reluctance to get involved in the practical measures of administrative reform. They did not wish to ameliorate the evil condition, but to sweep it away.

Brian Harrison argues that the teetotallers failed to investigate the drink problem systematically, and that they tried 'to avoid contamination from evil by shunning all contact with it'.[11] Their unwillingness to become involved in practical measures for regulating the trade came out in their attitudes towards the Licensing Bills of 1871 and 1872, promoted by H.A. Bruce, Home Secretary in Gladstone's government, which aimed at tightening up government control of the trade, reducing opening hours, and creating a more effective system of supervision of public houses. The act, as finally passed in 1872, reduced the permitted hours, though many of the other provisions for control were abandoned. The proposal to create a special system of police inspectors to control public houses was struck out by the House of Lords. The teetotallers had given the bill little help, because they were not interested in detailed methods of improvement like the proposals for inspection. From the absolute point of view that the drink trade was evil, it was a matter of little concern that it should be better administered.[12]

The movement against the Contagious Diseases Acts shows even more clearly the division between the practical man—doctors, army officers, administrators—concentrating on choosing the best among unacceptable alternatives, and the moral reformers who were not interested in amelioration, but simply wanted to sweep away the evil altogether. The first of the acts for the regulation of prostitution in port and garrison towns and for the medical inspection of women who were suspected to be suffering from venereal disease were passed in 1864 and 1866, and another act of 1869 increased the number of towns to which the act applied. The system of public control of prostitution existed in many other countries. It was defended as providing the lesser of two evils, not only by doctors but by public figures like John Morley and the theologian F. D. Maurice, though both of these changed their minds during the course of the agitation. The two people whose names are particularly connected with the campaign against the acts were the Halifax solicitor James Stansfeld, who had been President of the Poor Law Board in Gladstone's government of 1868, and Mrs. Josephine Butler, who had already been active in promoting the higher education of women and—a very different good cause—in helping prostitutes and poor women on Merseyside. Mrs. Butler joined the movement against the acts in 1869. Stansfeld declared himself in favour of the repeal of the laws in the summer of 1874. He carried the motion in the House of Commons in April 1883 that 'this House disapproves of the compulsory examination of women under the Contagious Diseases Acts', and he moved the successful private member's bill which repealed the acts three years later.[13]

Mrs. Butler's agitation is a very good example of the increased public activity of women which has already been mentioned.[14] Much of her case was based on the feminist position that the law discriminated against women. The state, she argued, should not interfere with the work of reclamation since only personal effort could cure moral corruption. Because she believed that the acts were an offence against God's laws, she was interested in no practical measures other than repeal, and she underestimated the need to produce supporting evidence to win over the unconvinced. She made her position clear in her statement to the royal commission on the acts set up in November 1870:

> We know that to protect vice in men is not according to the Word of God. We hold that the practical working of an Act, which is vicious in principle is not fit subject for an enquiry, and therefore we do not require your verdict any more than if it were to tell us whether there is a God or not. You may be sure that our action in this matter will continue to be exactly the same, even if the Commission pronounce the Acts highly moral. We shall never rest until this system is banished from our shores.[15]

Mrs. Butler argued that individuals and private societies were bound to do all they could to attack the vices of common life and to prevent immorality. The interference of the state in such matters would only slacken their efforts and reduce the sense of personal responsibility for moral evil.[16] The deeply religious sentiment of the campaigners is very obvious. When Stansfeld's motion of 1883 against the acts was being considered by the Commons a continuous vigil of prayer was maintained. 'As men and women prayed', Mrs Butler wrote, 'they suddenly burst forth into praise, thanking God for the answer, as if it had already been granted.'[17] Those who are so deeply convinced that God is on their side can display harsh feelings in the fight against evil. The Hammonds made the point that James Stansfeld contributed a great deal to the movement through his refusal to accept extreme positions; for instance, he rejected the view of some of the repealers that venereal disease was God's punishment for vice and that it was wrong to try to check it. He favoured the provision of hospital treatment against those members of the group who argued that to provide such treatment would encourage vice by giving to the victims of this disease a special position of privilege.[18]

The movement against the C.D. Acts and the teetotal movement were both inspired by people who wanted to protest against the system and not to pursue moderate policies of change within it. These characteristics marked the teetotallers even more strongly than the opponents of the C.D. Acts. Brian Harrison has emphasized the tendency of the temperance movement to become an enclosed withdrawn body. It was strongest among manufacturers and artisans its leaders tended to be Nonconformists.[19] It represented those social groups which had a long tradition of being 'agin the government'.

ii) Philanthropy and its critics

Victorian philanthropy placed a heavy emphasis on personal service, and the idea of individual endeavour to relieve distress was closely related to the basic social and religious assumptions of mid-Victorian society. Many philanthropists, however, came to feel a nagging fear about such undirected and private efforts. What of the dangers of helping the undeserving, of accentuating rather than relieving the problems of pauperization? Men and women who wished to do good to their fellows more and more came to believe that what was needed was not indiscriminate alms-giving but careful case-work to assess the need and to provide means to meet it, which, so far as possible, forced people to rely on themselves. Charity, they believed, needed to be organized. The organizers themselves were deeply committed individualists, but through their activities they helped to develop the framework upon which a welfare state was later to be built.[20]

Much of the organizers' effort was concentrated in London because there the social problems were the most extreme and the giving most generous. The Metropolitan Visiting and Relief Association, which aimed to relieve the poor through district-visiting societies 'after due inquiry into the circumstances of each particular case' had been founded as early as 1843.[21] The idea of closer control and of systematic visiting of the poor really took hold during the 'sixties. One of the pioneers was William Rathbone of Liverpool, who had already created the first district nursing system (1859). In 1863 he founded the Liverpool Central Relief Society, and in 1867 he published *Social Duties, considered in reference to the organisation of effort in works of benevolence and public utility*, in which he called for the organization of voluntary activity.[22] In London, the Society for the Relief of Distress, founded in 1860, was one of the precursors of the most important of these bodies, the Charity Organization Society, founded in 1869.

The C.O.S. played a very large part in the charitable policy-making of the next half-century and its long serving secretary, C.S. Loch (1875-1913), was a leading figure in the world of philanthropy. Many saw the society in its early days as a promising agent for solving an intractable problem. Others, like Canon Barnett and Beatrice Potter (Mrs. Sidney Webb), reacted against the extreme individualism which it represented, and by the end of the century the society had become increasingly out of sympathy with the main currents of social change.[23] The society's policy rested on systematic case-work and investigation and the employment of a professional staff. It acted on the principle that the poor must be expected to meet all the ordinary contingencies of life themselves, relying on charity only for cases of exceptional misfortune.[24]

The society operated through district committees which kept detailed records of cases considered. An application for assistance was taken down in set form: full details about the applicant's address, employment, health and other personal details; replies of employers, clergy, schoolmasters, and similar referees to enquiries made either by post or by interview; and the applicant's home was visited either by the paid agent or by a voluntary worker. Finally the district committee or a sub-committee would make a decision in the case: to refer it to another charity or to the poor law, or to grant some form of relief which was always followed up by regular visits to the family. The method aimed to combine a systematic and pro-fessional approach with the personal concern which would—hopefully—help the family to help itself. Unless that goal of self-reliance was achieved, the whole effort would, in the eyes of society, have been a failure.

The central office of the society had its own distinct tasks. It prosecuted the promoters of bogus charities. It maintained a reference library and did a good deal of printing and publishing. It maintained pressure on ministers and on the press, and carried out special enquiries, inves-tigating, for example, night refuges, soup kitchens, housing, the training and care of the handicapped, care of idiots and imbeciles, and the working of medical charities.[25] Its policy was epitomized in the ideas of C.S. Loch. In his view the man who became dependent had lost something of his manhood, and charity if it was to fulfil its true purpose, must ensure that manhood was preserved. The society might, he hoped, produce a new alignment among all those who were concerned with poverty. Its work would open up new opportunities for the exercise of personal influence—upon the poor themselves and upon the agencies, like the churches and the poor law guardians, who were trying to help them. The society might become a great synthesizer of charitable effort, its goal to create 'a church of charity, undeclared it might be and invisible, but in a very real sense actual—a peace-making, unifying body'.[26]

Another exponent of the idea of scientific charity who had close connections with the C.O.S. was Octavia Hill, who worked in the peculiarly intractable area of the housing of the poor.[27] She was a grand-daughter of Chadwick's associate, Dr. Southwood Smith, who had considerable influence on her childhood, and she was much affected as a young woman by the ideas of F.D. Maurice and of John Ruskin. Miss Hill became interested in housing through the working women who came to the kitchen of the school which she and her sisters ran in London, and in 1865 Ruskin bought three houses in a court for her to manage. This was the small beginning of what became an extensive undertaking. Both she and Ruskin began with the assumption that the houses should be made to pay. She would allow no arrears and no sub-letting, and she turned out those who fell into debt. By coming herself to collect the rents she established a personal contact with the tenants. She did her best to clean up the houses and she provided a room for a club-room and a playground for the children. As the scale of her enterprises grew, she gave increasing attention to training other workers, dividing up the responsibility for her properties among them.

In later life Miss Hill's interest in amenity and good environment led her to work for the preservation of open spaces and to become one of the founders of the National Trust, but that falls outside the limits set to this book. Her combination of efficient management and personal care was very characteristic of all those who wished to ensure that good works should lead to greater independence and not to loss of self-respect. The practical problem, which was never solved, was this: how far down the social and economic structure could the maxims of self-help apply? In Octavia Hill's own field could the really poor pay regular rents at all? She herself was anxious that housing standards should not be raised too high in order to help the really poor tenant who could pay very little. But the core of the problem in London was the mass of the casually employed for whom regular payments were impossible because they earned no regular wages. By the end of the century it was becoming clearer that no private individuals could create Loch's 'church of charity'. That could be done only by the state and through a concept of public power which was quite unacceptable to Octavia Hill and her friends.

iii) The Institutions of self-help

Many philanthropists had always argued that an enlarged concept of public power was unnecessary because personal effort could achieve all that was necessary. 'The battle of life is, in most cases, fought uphill; and to win it without a struggle were perhaps to win it without honour', wrote Samuel Smiles in his famous book *Self-Help* (1859).[28] The ideas of self-help and of philanthropy are complementary. The first quality offered the royal road to attaining the objectives which the philanthropists desired for working people. It was firmly linked with the idea that a sober and hard-working man could win his way to the top, though in fact most people were not likely to move very far forward, and it has been argued that between 1850 and 1880 the opportunities for moving up the social scale were actually growing less.[29] It is a mistake, however, to link the creed of self-help too closely with the prize of material reward. In the eyes of contemporaries the struggle was worth almost as much as the prize. Once again the moral imperative loomed very large as a motive for action.

Smiles' book is certainly not a paean in praise of money-making.[30] The most successful life, he argued, is not that in which a man acquires the most wealth, power or pleasure, but that in which he 'gets the most manhood, and performs the greatest amount of useful work and of human duty. Money is power after its sort, it is true; but intelligence, public spirit, and moral virtue, are powers too, and far nobler ones'.[31] The qualities, which Smiles praised were energy of will, good habits, the ability to make a wise use of time. Such qualities would certainly lead, in many cases, to financial reward. But the weight of the argument lies not on the money-making but on the personal independence which money helps to make possible. 'Any class of men', Smiles wrote, 'that lives from hand to mouth will ever be an inferior class. They will necessarily remain impotent and helpless, hanging on to the skirts of society, the sport of time and season.'[32]

The material for *Self-Help* was first prepared for young working men in Leeds who had set up an evening school for self-improvement. Its arguments are closely linked with the idea of respectability, that quality so deeply valued by the lower middle class and the skilled artisans of the day. Some of the aspects of respectability are not attractive. It tended to be linked with a stifling conventionalism and a moral bigotry which could strike harshly at those who offended against accepted habits—particularly accepted sexual habits. Yet behind the antimacassars and the lace curtains lay very solid qualities of courage, independence and hard work. For many who had won a more decent and generous standard of life for themselves and their families, the standards of respectability represented a bastion against the hand-to-mouth existence of the poor. The artisan or small shop-keeper who had achieved respectability felt that he had won a great prize—and that prize was moral as much as material.

There was a whole range of institutions to help the provident and thoughtful artisan. William Andrews of Coventry was born in 1835 and apprenticed at the age of 13 to the designing department of a silk firm. He eventually set up for himself and became a successful business man. His diary for 1854 records, in successive entries, that he had enrolled himself as a member of the Mechanics' Institution, had become a seat-holder at Vicar Lane Chapel, had opened an account at the Savings Bank, and had been presented with a medal for six ribbon designs at the annual meeting of the School of Art.[33] A better example could hardly be found of the religious, intellectual and financial guideposts which helped a young man on his way if he chose to use them.

The development of friendly societies, building societies and savings banks made saving easier. The affiliated friendly societies, made up of a national network of local branches, expanded considerably, the largest being the Manchester Unity of Oddfellows and the Ancient Order of Foresters. They developed a sound actuarial basis for the computations of sickness and mortality rates and stricter control over their local branches. An act of parliament in 1875 encouraged friendly societies to register with the Registrar of Friendly Societies, an office which had been created in 1846, though registration was not made compulsory. Affiliated societies might register as a single unit and not, as previously, branch by branch, and registered societies were required to make annual financial returns and quinquennial returns of sickness and mortality.[34]

The legal position of building societies was regulated by act of parliament in 1874.[35] The earliest of these societies had been 'terminating', that is to say, they were wound up when the particular building venture which had been undertaken was completed. This type of organization had many imperfections—for example, it was difficult to join except at the beginning, and it tended to be replaced by the 'permanent' societies which offered a fixed method of investment with much higher managerial skills. The most successful of these societies was the Leeds Permanent Benefit Building Society, founded in 1848, though other familiar names appear at much the same time like the Abbey National (1849) and the Halifax (1853). The Leeds society did not itself build houses, but it provided facilities for those who did. Its policy was flexible, and it did its best to put house purchase within the reach of working people. In the 1860's, five-sixths of its mortgage advances were for sums below £400, and for many people it acted as a savings bank, as did similar societies elsewhere.[36] The Act of 1874 placed building societies under the chief registrar of friendly societies. They were given a legal right to receive money on deposit or by loan up to an amount not exceeding two-thirds of the current value of mortgages. The act provided appropriate legal arrangements for well-conducted societies, but those which were less well-managed were not properly controlled by it, and the gaps in the law were made good by another act of 1894.[37]

The third in this trio of provident institutions was the savings bank. Many of these had been established all over the country since the beginning of the century, set up by the influential people of the area for the benefit of their poorer neighbours. This field of saving was transformed by the establishment in 1861 of the Post Office Savings Bank. The Post Office had established a successful money order department in 1838, and several proposals were made, notably by Charles Sikes of the Huddersfield Banking Company, that the system should be extended into a national bank of deposit. Such a system would be far more secure than the local savings banks and it would have the advantage of using the national network of post offices.[38] The scheme was supported by Gladstone as Chancellor of the Exchequer, but it had to face a good deal of criticism on the grounds that it was a centralizing measure and would lead to a good deal of expense.[39] The Post Office Savings Bank was an immediate success. The average total of deposits, which had been £7,000,000 in 1863-8, had risen to £29,000,000 in 1875-80 and went on rising steadily. It was believed that the P.O.S.B. touched a poorer type of contributor than the trustee savings banks had reached, and many of the latter closed down in the years following 1861.[40]

Though the efforts of working men had been assisted by legislation the main achievement had come from their own thrift and self-denial. The roots of working-class self-help had first been struck in the chapels, for it was through religion that men and women had first found their way to self-expression and self-government. The messianic notes of religion had been transmuted into worldly objectives by the Owenite movement, by the plans for self-sufficient communities, and, in more strictly political terms, by Chartism. In the period before 1850 all these movements, in their different ways, had been working to change the existing social structure and to bring about a new age. After 1850 the working-class aristocracy, at least, began to find new hope in the existing social order.

One of the outstanding examples of this accommodation was the development of the retail cooperative societies. The early phase of the movement was Owenite, aiming to bring about the creation of new communities. Many of the Rochdale Pioneers, whose society, founded in 1844, began the later phase, were themselves Owenites. They aimed to buy or rent land and to establish 'a self-supporting home of united interests'.[41] Their main break with the past was the decision to pay dividends to members according to purchases. The new policy, which was adopted by many other socities, harnessed the drive for self-improvement and self-interest to the cooperative cause. The societies developed as prosperous dividend-paying units which gave good value for money spent and a convenient method of saving. Like the friendly societies and the building societies they were an organization which operated within the existing social order to further the interests of working men. Like the other bodies which have already been dealt with they needed a defined legal status to do their work properly. The Industrial and Provident Societies Act of 1852, which had been advocated by J.M. Ludlow and the Christian Socialists, gave them a more secure legal standing, and another act of 1862 gave them incorporation with limited liability. The conferment of powers under the act of 1862 for societies to invest capital in another society, provided that the second society was itself registered under the act, made it possible to establish the English and Scottish Cooperative Wholesale Societies, which produced a wide range of goods for the whole movement.[42] When the assistant commissioner for the royal commission on popular education (1858-61) visited Rochdale, he commented as follows on the Pioneers Society:

Considering the enormous difficulties which surround a design of this kind, I consider this to be by far the most striking example of working class intelligence which came under my notice. The working class exclusively conceived the plan, contributed the capital, and conducted the management . . .[43]

iv) The Trade unions

The money which supported all these institutions came from wages earned in industry and commerce. Men tried to help themselves not only through voluntary saving but through corporate action by establishing trades unions. Some of the general problems involved in the clash between accepted doctrines of free enterprise and the collective attempts of workmen to protect themselves have already been discussed.[44] When a royal commission was set up in 1867 to enquire into the organization and rules of trades unions *The Times* wrote that its investigations 'have already shown that minute and despotic interference with the arrangement and processes of industry is more mischievous than the occasional resort to a "strike"'.[45] The workers, from their side of the argument, had three main grievances in the existing state of the law. The first was the law of master and servant, which placed a workman who broke his contract of employment (which he might do by absenting himself during a strike) in danger of more serious legal penalties than an employer who committed the same offence. The law was amended in 1867 when 'the punishment of imprisonment for breach of contract except in the case of "aggravated" breaches' was abolished.[46] The second grievance resulted from the fact that, since trades unions had no accepted legal status and could be regarded as bodies acting in restraint of trade, they had no means of protecting their property against members and officials, a problem accentuated by the decision in Hornby v. Close in January 1867.[47] Finally, working men suffered under the legal doctrine of common employment, which restricted an employer's liability for accidents suffered by one of his employees through the negligence of another. The problem of employers' liability was a peculiarly intractable one, and was only partially dealt with by an act of 1880.[48]

The principal union leaders like Allen of the Engineers and Applegarth of the Carpenters were trying to move their members away from the older traditions of conspiracy and violence and to set national standards of practice in industrial matters. In his evidence to the royal commission Applegarth dealt with three main points: the question of piece work and restrictive practices, the protection of union funds and discrimination against union members. Throughout his evidence he claimed that his society wanted nothing done in secret and totally rejected intimidation. On the question of restrictive practices he took a very moderate tone. He opposed piece work because he thought that it led to the introduction of bad material. He did not oppose the introduction of foreign carpenters' and joiners' work if it were better and cheaper. His society did not oppose its members working with non-union men and it had no rules restricting the number of apprentices. It attempted to prevent men from taking less than the average rate of wages, but it set no maximum to what could be earned. He threw off the argument that the existence of such rules would hold back the really outstanding man because, he claimed, such people would always look after themselves. 'We are not all Arkwrights, Brunels, or Stephensons. Men of such extraordinary talent soon become other than working men. We have to make rules which shall apply to workmen generally ....'[49] Of their success in that objective he had no doubt. The existence of the society had led to increased wages and shorter hours. In his evidence about restrictive practices Applegarth put comparatively little emphasis on the union's rule-book, but much more on local agreements—what were called by a commissioner 'rules adopted between the employers of labour and the working men in that locality with the sanction of the general council'.[50] There may have been something disingenuous in this argument because these local rules could well have been more restrictive than those of the union itself, but Applegarth, in placing this emphasis on local negotiations, is making a major point to which he returned later in his evidence: that masters and men should approach one another as free negotiators without discrimination on the one side or intimidation on the other.

The second part of Applegarth's evidence related to the financial side of union affairs. One major issue here was that of the security of union funds. The second was the relationship between the friendly society aspect, since the Carpenters paid their members benefits in sickness, unemployment and old age, and the industrial policy of the union, which might endanger the security of such benefits if it became involved in expensive strikes. Applegarth argued that, when a man joined the union, its trade and its benevolent purposes were not separate in his mind; he joined it as a whole. Whatever doubt might be expressed by actuaries about the financial stability of the system, it had worked well because it had been prudently managed and the members had confidence in it. Union funds, he claimed, should be protected by law, and the unions should be allowed to hold property. They did not ask for legal power to enforce their contributions or to make their rules respected. Their funds should be protected from embezzlement, and he accepted that, in order to be so protected, societies should deposit their rules and make their affairs public. He had no objection to giving full information and the power to examine the books to the registrar of friendly societies.[51]

Applegarth's final demand was for equality of treatment and the ending of discriminatory practices. He justified peaceful picketing during a strike because 'I would put the same to him [the employer] as he would do and does to me; I would adopt every means within the law to carry my strike to a successful issue'.[52] He complained of the refusal of employers to meet the men and to discuss working conditions with them, and in particular of the obnoxious rules made by the master builders' associations which had tried to blacklist union members.[53] Applegarth claimed that the unions had been successful in gaining for working men a fairer share in the total wealth of the country, and the commissioners quite naturally asked him for his views on the subject of equality. The exchange is worth quoting:

What is the share you would say that you are entitled to, is it an aliquot part of all the wealth of all the kingdom?—No: I believe that every man who is willing to toil for his bread is entitled to sufficient to feed, clothe and educate his family, and to lay by something to keep him in his old age, so that he shall not need to work after 60 or 55 years of age.
You have not got a wish to divide all the wealth equally?—No: I do not entertain any such revolutionary notions.[54]

Applegarth's arguments, though moderately and carefully expressed, went a long way towards overturning the free enterprise system of labour relations, and the majority report of the royal commission was far from accepting them. That majority report, written in terms of reluctant concession, recommended that workmen should enjoy the right to combine, but that those who wished to remain free of the combination should be allowed to do so. What the law had to do was 'to secure a fair field for the unrestricted exercise of industrial enterprise' on the part of the labourer, the capitalist and the employer.[55] There was a serious danger, it was claimed, that picketing might lead to intimidation and molestation. A bill should be introduced to relax the existing law which treated the unions as combinations in restraint of trade, but any concessions should be carefully guarded to avoid damage or loss to other persons, breach of contract or refusing to work with individuals.[56] The existing anomalous legal position about union property and funds should be ended and arrangements made for unions to be registered, but the right to registration should be hedged around with severe conditions. It should be refused where the union rules established restrictive practices at work.[57] The trade and benefit funds of unions should be kept separate.[58] The report further argued that it was doubtful whether unions had brought pecuniary advantage to their members, while a great deal of harm had certainly been done by strikes to unskilled labourers who were not union members, but who had been put out of work by industrial action.[59]

The gap between the opinions of the majority and of the trade unionists was bridged by the minority report of Thomas Hughes and Frederic Harrison, who argued—in very bold terms for that time—that the general interest of the public lay in the welfare of all the classes which composed it and not merely in the production of goods at the cheapest possible price. The public interest was not served, they argued, by a lower general level of comfort and independence, and the artisan had a right to protect himself against pauperism.[60] The minority report paid tribute to the high character of the major unions. Restrictive practices were primarily a matter of arrangement within different industries, while many union objectives, like the suppression of truck or of dangerous practices at work, harmonized with the public interest. There was no evidence that industry had been harmed by the growth of unions; indeed the practice of working to a fixed set of rules actually made industrial collaboration easier to achieve. The friendly societies aspect of union membership offered a major public service, and it would be impossible to divide the funds into 'benefit' and 'trade' sections because of the close relationship between the two sides of union activity.

The law should be changed, the minority report argued, to remove the penalties which weighed on the labouring classes.

> The whole system of special laws as applying to labour seems to us a relic of feudalism, and contrary to the spirit of modern legislation. In every way it violates the principle of the equality of all citizens before the law. We can see no ground for special laws relating to the agreements of workmen, which does not apply to the agreements made by any other order of citizens . . . .[61]

One particular grievance resulting from the position of the unions as illegal societies at common law was their inability to protect their property. Trades unions should be allowed the benefit of those portions of the Friendly Societies Act which applied to societies not fully registered. Their status would then be that of voluntary clubs, permitted to hold corporate funds and subject, so far as their expenditure was concerned, to inspection but not to regulation by the state.[62] Their property should be protected by law, and the management of their affairs conducted with full publicity. The state had no duty 'to enforce morality or to punish unsocial conduct'.[63]

The legislation of the following years represented a tussle between the 'majority' and the 'minority' view. The Gladstone government passed two acts in 1871. The first removed the possibility that unions might be liable to prosecution as conspiracies as being 'in restraint of trade'. It gave legal protection to union funds, but prohibited actions to enforce internal agreements, thus freeing unions from interference in their internal affairs. Finally it provided that unions might register with the Registrar of Friendly Societies, which gave some advantages in the management of their property, in return for his supervision of their affairs. The second act, the Criminal Law Amendment Act of 1871, tightened up the law on picketing and union activity during strikes.[64]

The courts interpreted this second act in very broad terms, and an active campaign was waged for its repeal. In 1875 Disraeli's government passed a remarkable series of measures which stabilized the legal position of the unions until the end of the century, and recognized the legality of collective bargaining. The Criminal Law Amendment Act of 1871 was repealed. The Conspiracy and Protection of Property Act 1875 laid down that no acts done by two or more persons in the course of a trade dispute should be liable to prosecution as criminal conspiracies. Such acts would henceforth be criminal only if they would have been crimes had they been committed by individuals. The new law defined much more clearly what was permissible in a trade dispute, particularly so far as picketing was concerned, and peaceful picketing was expressly permitted. Finally the Master and Servant Act of 1867 was replaced by the Employers and Workmen Act which made employer and employee equal parties to a civil contract and abolished imprisonment for breach of engagement.[65]

Perhaps the Conservatives passed this legislation because they were mindful of the political power of trade unionists who, since the Reform Act of 1867, had become voters. During the prosperous years of the early 'seventies the unions expanded considerably. In 1871-2 a Nine Hours League was formed at Newcastle and, after a five-month strike, the 54-hour week was recognized in the engineering trades of the North-East. During 1872-4 the agricultural workers' union under Joseph Arch led an active campaign in the countryside, but his initial success was short-lived. By the end of the decade there was serious economic depression. A series of strikes ended unfavourably for the workers, and the year 1879 represented a low water-mark in their fortunes.[66]

v) State control of industry: the limits of regulation

The power of the trades unions had seemed to many contemporaries to clash with the objectives of a state and society still committed to the principles of free enterprise. Yet in some ways unions and governments shared similar regulative purposes, as the state extended its control over the conditions of industrial employment. The great difference between the two sides lay in the fact that the unions wanted better conditions and shorter hours for their members who were adult males. The government still held to the idea that only women and children ought to be protected, and doubts were expressed in the 'seventies whether the protection offered to women had not been extended too far.

The acts of 1850 and 1853 had marked the end of the Ten Hours Campaign in the textile industries.[67] The next industries to be the subject of official enquiry were bleaching and dyeing and lace manufacture. Bleach and dye works came under the Factory Acts in 1860, though the law was very difficult to enforce, and the Lace Works Act of 1860 began the legislative control of that industry.[68] As in the case of the trades unions and of public health, the 'sixties and 'seventies were a period of wide-ranging public enquiry and extensive legislation. In 1861, at Shaftesbury's suggestion, a royal commission was set up to look into children's employment. Like the similar enquiry of twenty years before[69] it revealed long hours of work, bad working conditions, ignorance and immorality in a very wide range of industries. Its six volumes of reports are a mine of information on the factories and workshops of the time. Although there are many resemblances between the two enquiries of the 'forties and the 'sixties into children's employment, there are some major differences between them. The first difference is the general acceptance, by the 'sixties, that restrictions on the work of women and children are desirable in themselves, though there might be differences of opinion about particular measures to be taken. A Manchester manufacturer told the commissioners:

> Our feeling is very strong in favour of the Factory Acts, and we think that they have very much improved the condition of the people engaged in them, and also of others around, by setting a good standard to the rest so as to create a feeling against abuses of over-work of children or others.[70]

The Home Secretary, Spencer Walpole, used a similar argument in 1867 when introducing bills to extend the provisions of the factory acts. The benefits achieved by the existing acts had been very great; since serious evils still existed, it was time to extend the protection given by the law.[71]

The second major difference is related to the first. In the 'forties control of labour conditions was a new idea. Over twenty years a pattern of regulation had built up so that one change inevitably led to another. Control had begun in the textile industries because they formed the largest units of production where bad working conditions were both the most obvious and the easiest to remedy. Once textiles had been regulated, mining and manufacturing industry of other kinds followed the same path. The problems were not confined to factories because worse evils existed in workshops and in trades where women and children worked at home. The cumulative argument for restriction is illustrated in the royal commission's discussion of working conditions in the Staffordshire potteries. The law had already, they pointed out, imposed sanitary requirements on the owners and occupiers of houses. It had required mill owners and mine owners to take precautions for the health and safety of their workpeople which had cost a great deal of money. There could therefore be no valid reason against Parliament requiring from the owners and occupiers of the potteries that they shall adopt reasonable measures for the improvement of the places of work in the pottery department, and for the proper ventilation and cleanliness of all their other workrooms.[72]

Both the first and the second commissions on children's employment once again laid heavy stress on the moral evils which arose from over-work and bad conditions. Young people who began work so early were very ignorant, especially of religious subjects, a point stressed in the case both of Birmingham and of Sheffield, the two great centres of the metal trades. Since parental attitudes were unsympathetic to education and the young people were unwilling to give up their scanty leisure, there was unlikely to be much educational improvement in Birmingham.[73] The example of several of the Sheffield witnesses suggests that even those who had been to day school and to chapel had not profited very much from the experience. One of them, Henry Matthewman, aged 17, said

> One man that they preached about was Jesus Christ, but I cannot say any others, and I cannot tell anything about Him. He was not killed, but died like other people. He was not the same as other people in some ways, because he was religious in some ways, and others isn't. He was alive again, but I cannot say if he is now. He was on a cross but that is not how he was killed.[74]

Considerable emphasis was placed in the commission's reports on the beneficial effects of the system of half-time education and on the need to extend it.[75] One proposal for raising educational standards which was mentioned several times was the suggestion of a certificate to be taken at 13 years of age. No one would then be allowed to work full-time between the ages of 13 and 16 unless they could show that they had reached that standard of knowledge.[76]

Only a few examples can be given from the mass of evidence which the commissioners collected. In the Staffordshire potteries young people had to work in over-crowded and badly ventilated stoves, stove-rooms and finishing shops. There was the constant problem of dust, and some of the processes, like 'dipping' and 'scouring' were particularly unhealthy. Pulmonary diseases were therefore common, and ill-health and premature death ensued. The practice of working over-time brought many evils for young people, usually because the men with whom they worked had idled away the early part of the week and then had to strive very hard to make up the time lost.[77] Pulmonary disease was a serious hazard in other industries like the metal trades of Birmingham and the Black Country[78] and among the Sheffield grinders. A medical enquiry in 1860 had attributed the high mortality among grinders to three main causes: the liability to inhale dust, the constrained working position, and bad ventilation. The enforcement of the use of the fan in workshops would, it was claimed, effect a great improvement.[79]

In the lace manufacture some 150,000 people, a large proportion of them women, children and young persons, still had no legal protection. The warehouses and private houses in which they worked were badly ventilated, over-heated and over-crowded. Diseases like consumption were prevalent and the poor physical condition of the women led to high rates of infant mortality among them.[80] Both in lace and in hosiery, where conditions were very similar, children who worked at home were forced by their mothers to work hours as long as or longer than those required by outside employers. Young children in the hosiery trade were pinned to their mother's knee to keep them at work and slapped when they went to sleep. 'The child has so many fingers set for it to stitch before it goes to bed, and must do them.'[81]

The conviction had become general, the commissioners concluded, that excessive hours of labour were in the interest neither of employers nor of employed.[82] They helped to breed disease, to encourage ignorance, and, in some trades where young people worked in close proximity, to promote immorality. The focus of the problem had clearly shifted from the earlier concentration on the factory to the understanding that even worse evils existed in the small workshops, the warehouses and the private dwellings. This was made very clear by the enquiries into the Birmingham metal trades and the lace and hosiery manufactures, and it was thought that it might be necessary, on the grounds of expense, to put the smaller factories and workshops under local inspection rather than under the supervision of the factory inspectors.[83] The commissioners, when they looked back over their work in their fifth report, recognized that improvements had indeed taken place since the first enquiry into children's employment. Children began work at a somewhat later age. They were better treated; there were few instances of cruelty and less suffering from insufficient food and clothing. Employers had come to take a much greater interest in the welfare of their workpeople. Opportunities for education, both secular and religious, had become more widespread. Yet much remained to be done 'to which the action of the legislature may largely contribute'.[84]

Parliament was ready to legislate, though it proved very difficult to control the innumerable small workshops. In 1864 the Factory Acts had been extended to cover the pottery, lucifer match-making, percussion cap and cartridge-making, paper-staining and fustian-cutting industries.[85] In 1867 two further statutes were passed which divided workplaces according to the numbers of the people employed in them. The Factory Act covered premises in which fifty or more persons were employed in a manufacturing process and brought a large number of new industries under control—blast furnaces, iron, steel and copper mills, forges and foundaries, machine-making shops, paper and glass making, printing and book-binding. The Workshops Regulation Act applied to premises in which fewer than fifty people worked. The law protected children working with their parents, but not outworkers. Children between the ages of eight and thirteen might be employed only half-time as in factories, and young persons and women might only be employed for twelve hours a day less 1½ hours for meal times.[86]

As the commissioners had suggested, the administration of the law differed between factories and workshops. Factories naturally came under the control of the factory inspectorate. The Workshops Regulation Act made the local sanitary authorities the responsible body, but this proved to be an unworkable arrangement. Some of the local authorities refused to administer the law. In other places it was ignored or so administered as to be largely ineffective. This discrepancy in the enforcement of the law between factories and workshops caused much dissatisfaction, and in 1871 control of workshops was handed over to the factory inspectors, though they had no power to enforce sanitary regulations.[87]

The social policies of the Conservative government of 1874 covered factories as well as trades unions, housing and public health. In 1874 the working day of protected persons in the textile industry was fixed at ten hours, though Cross, the Home Secretary, in advocating the measure, still maintained that there could be no question of limiting the hours of adult males.[88] In 1876 another royal commission was appointed to consider the consolidation of the factory and workshops acts. Its principal recommendation was that workshops should be placed under the same regulations as factories and that the Workshops Act should be repealed.[89] Though control over workshops had only been partly enforced, it had already produced great benefits, particularly for milliners and children employed in unhealthy trades.[90] The commissioners did not recommend the extension of the ten-hour day, granted to textile factories in 1874, to other employments because of the different nature of the workforce in different industries. In the textile industries a large proportion of the workers were women and young persons. In the non-textile industries men were in the majority, and men were expected to negotiate their own conditions of labour. Therefore women and children might not be employed at all if their hours were further limited, and the working day should remain at 10½ hours, confined within a 12-hour period of the day.[91] The age for commencing work, at that time ten in textiles and eight in other factories and workshops, should be raised to ten and the general age for full-time employment should be thirteen.[92]

As usual, a good deal of attention was given to the education of the young workers, though the situation had changed considerably since the 'sixties as a result of the spread of compulsory education under the provisions of the 1870 Act. The commissioners recommended that children should be required to attend school before they began work as half-timers, as was not then the case,[93] and that direct compulsion to attend school should be enforced on all children whether they were at work or not. If this were done, then a half-time system would appear as a relaxation from the rules of school attendance and could be enforced much more systematically.[94]

The consolidating Factory Act of 1878 was largely based on these recommendations. The act removed the distinction between factories and workshops and defined a factory simply as a place where articles were made and repaired if mechanical power was used on the premises, though some works were included whether power was used in them or not. Conditions of work were in general to be the same in all workplaces, other than textile factories where rather shorter hours were worked, but the rules covering women's workshops and domestic workshops were left very lax. In these workplaces the working day of 10½ hours could be taken within a wide limit of time (6 a.m. to 9 p.m.), so that it was extremely difficult for the factory inspectors to check the real hours worked. Moreover they were exempted from the general provisions of the act about cleanliness and sanitation.[95] Perhaps this latitude was based on the belief that women workers should be allowed greater contractual freedom in selling their labour. It is worth noting that the royal commission of 1876 had asked the question whether the protection of adult women had not already been carried far enough, if not actually too far—though they answered their own question in the negative.[96] They did however limit—at least implicitly—the protection offered to women by deciding, after they had considered physically demanding trades like heavy nail and chain making, that they could not define the type of labour which women might be permitted to undertake.[97]

Clearly there was still in 1878 a good deal of disagreement about the appropriate limits of regulation. One of the members of the 1876 commission on the Factory Acts, the O'Conor Don, submitted a minority report in which he was critical of further labour limitations, commenting: 'I think the time has come for seriously considering how far the system of inspecting everything and everybody should be pressed. It seems to me that legislation has latterly been running ahead in this direction.'[98] He opposed any further limitations on the labour of women because he believed that they had already been kept out of trades in which they might have found employment. In his view the trades unions had done more to regulate labour than the factory acts and several women's unions were already active.[99] O'Conor's remarks, linking together state control and individual effort, bring out the point which has already been made, that these two forces, apparently contradictory in their nature, often worked towards very similar objectives.

X. The Creation of a cleaner environment

i) The Changing focus of social problems

This review of the period between 1850 and 1880 began with a study of the general process of change in English society. The three concepts of philanthropy, self-help and state power were then examined, with particular reference to conditions of industrial employment. In the two following chapters attention will be given firstly to the general problem of improving the environment and secondly to the controls and disciplines which regulated the lives of the people.

For more and more Englishmen environmental problems were urban problems, though the countryside presented plenty of its own which accelerated in gravity after the onset of agricultural depression at the end of the 'seventies. The landed interest still enjoyed great political prestige and power. Rural Conservatives tended to resist legislative measures which would increase the rates; they feared central pressures for change which were bound to be expensive.[1] On one occasion, that of the cattle plague of 1865-6, the usual roles were reversed. The landed interest demanded and got the payment of compensation for slaughtered cattle and restriction on the movement of animals against the opinions of those like Gladstone who argued that government should not be expected to make good the losses of individuals. It was, as W.L. Burn pointed out, both a striking success for the agricultural lobby and a reversal of normal roles with Tory landowners demanding national action and the government defending the autonomy of local authorities.[2]

The attitudes of both landowners and farmers towards the labourers remained rigid and unchanging. The agricultural unions of the 'seventies aroused great bitterness of feeling among the squirearchy because their leaders like Joseph Arch were Nonconformist Radicals who threatened the security of the traditional social structure of the countryside.[3] The progress of education in rural areas was very slow. There were some benevolent landlords who promoted schools, and the clergy were active, but the farmers were hostile because they wanted the ready use of child labour. The introduction of school boards after 1870 made little difference, and the educational backwardness of rural England, when so much was being achieved in the towns, added yet another handicap to the life of the village labourer.[4]

The social problem had changed its focus between the age of the first and second reform bills. In the 'thirties particular attention was given to rural pauperism. In the 'sixties the most prominent issue was that of public health, which was pre-eminently an urban problem. The change illustrates the fact that the cities and the urban interest had become the dominant element in the national life. Though poverty, especially among the unemployed and the old, raised grave questions to which no real answers had been found, concern about the evils of pauperism had diminished as the country had become richer. In practice the Poor Law of 1834 had been less effective than its advocates like Chadwick had hoped. The Poor Law Commissioners, set up by the act, had not achieved an effective administrative strategy. They were hampered by the obstructive tactics of the Guardians of the Poor, and the law was always unpopular.

Little attempt was made by the Poor Law Board, set up in 1847, to collect information—for instance, no statistics were kept of the sick,—and there was a reluctance to obtain professional advice.[5] As time went on, the number of unions in which outdoor relief was prohibited gradually declined. It was widely given to the aged and, in large centres of population, the attempt to deny it to the able-bodied had been given up by 1852.[6] The Board had adopted no particular policy for treating the sick poor and it did not appoint a medical officer until 1865.[7] Indeed, in the opinion of John Simon, the greatest mid-Victorian authority on public health, it had performed its medical duties in relation to the care of pauper children, to vaccination, to the outdoor sick poor and to workhouse infirmaries in a perfunctory way. 'This system of secretarial common sense', Simon wrote, 'had not worked successfully for the health interests of the poor'.[8]

Considerable improvements were made during the 'sixties in the treatment of the sick. The problem was considered by a select committee on poor relief in 1862,[9] and an enquiry by the Poor Law Board into the infirmaries and sick wards of London workhouses led to the Metropolitan Poor Act of 1867, which provided for the building or adaptation of separate infirmaries for the non-infectious sick. A similar act to improve the treatment of the sick poor outside London followed in 1868. These acts are of considerable importance. Under their provisions buildings were improved and better standards of medical care and nursing provided.[10] In 1875 the Public Health Act gave the new local sanitary authorities the power to provide hospitals out of the rates.[11] The policy of improving the standard of poor law infirmaries meant that the state had entered to a considerable extent into the provision of general medical care for the people. The infirmaries came to be used by non-paupers, first for infectious cases and later for non-infectious cases,[12] and an adequate medical staff was provided in poor law hospitals. The state had assumed wider responsibilities in yet another area for people who were unable to help themselves.

However, other changes in poor law policy which were made about 1870 worked towards a stricter interpretation of the regulations. The evils of the law of settlement were indeed removed by Villiers' Act of 1865 which made the responsibility for paying relief a union instead of a parish matter,[13] but in other ways tighter controls were introduced. After the commercial depression of 1866-67 the Poor Law Board and its successor, the Local Government Board, waged a long continued campaign against outdoor relief. The workhouse test was more strictly applied, partly in order to put pressure on relatives to contribute, although the various poor law unions followed very different policies about money saved or earned in other ways and about allowances to wives and widows.[14] The poor law inspectors were anxious to establish specially deterrent workhouses for the able-bodied, many of whom, it was believed, had begun to find the conditions of the ordinary workhouses not too unpleasant. In 1871 an able-bodied test workhouse of the new type was established at Poplar in East London, though after about ten years the experiment broke down because of the large numbers of the aged and infirm who had to be accommodated there. Similar experiments in other places, for example at Birmingham, met a like fate.[15] This policy of greater strictness in interpreting the poor laws should be compared with the movements in private charity which produced the Charity Organization Society and which have already been discussed.[16] By the 'eighties more and more people were beginning to doubt whether appeals to deterrent punishment on the one hand and personal effort on the other could make much impression on the hard-core problems of human destitution.

ii) Public Health: the work of John Simon

Such destitution was frequently caused by epidemic disease and aggravated by the lack of proper sanitation and water supplies. The cause of public health was at a low ebb after the fall of Edwin Chadwick in 1854, but even at that crucial point some progress was being made. In 1853 the Vaccination Act required parents and guardians to arrange for the vaccination of infants within four months of birth. As there were no provisions for enforcement the compulsory element was not effective, but about two-thirds of children born were vaccinated in this period and the death-rate from smallpox fell in consequence.[17] The Nuisances Removal Act of 1855 was a consequence of the cholera epidemic of 1853-4. It required local authorities to appoint sanitary inspectors and gave to the justices powers to order the abatement of nuisances and to the local authorities powers to enter a nuisance, with the justices' agreement, at the expense of the occupier.[18]

There was, of course, a very great difference between passing acts of parliament and enforcing an effective policy against the opposition of recalcitrant local authorities and of thousands of property owners who saw sanitary reform merely as a source of unjustified expense. For all the effort which had been made progress was very slow. Indeed the death-rate between 1841-5 and 1861-5 actually rose slightly. In 1841-5 the general death-rate for England and Wales had been 21.4 per thousand living and the infant mortality rate 148 per thousand births. In 1851-5 the figures (22.7 and 156) were slightly higher, perhaps as a result of the cholera epidemic of 1853-4. In 1861-5 the figures were still 22.6 and 151.[19] Even if some of this increase was due to better statistical recording, the general position had remained much the same, and examples which will be quoted later from some of the major cities bear this out.[20]

The public health problem was far more complex than the pioneers of the 'forties had envisaged. Chadwick had seen it primarily in terms of better sanitation and water supply, but far wider environmental issues—pressure of population, bad housing, poor nutrition—were involved. He had steadily underestimated the importance of medical questions. In a revealing passage in the Sanitary Report of 1842 he argued:

> The great preventives—drainage, street and house cleansing by means of supplies of water and improved sewerage, and especially the introduction of cheaper and more efficient modes of removing all noxious refuse from the towns—are operations for which aid must be sought from the science of the civil engineer, not from the physician, who has done his work when he has pointed out the disease which results from the neglect of proper administrative measures, and has alleviated the sufferings of the victims.[21]

Chadwick did not recognize what could be achieved by preventive medicine. The progress which was made in the twenty years after 1850 was largely on the scientific and medical side. Indeed it can be argued that by 1870 the analysis of the causes of health problems had run considerably ahead of the existence of any effective machinery for remedying them. One essential foundation for medical investigation was good statistics, and here the work of William Farr, who had been appointed compiler of abstracts in the Registrar-General's department in 1839, was of great importance. The statistics of mortality which he produced provided essential information to the medical reformers. Of particular importance was his report on the cholera epidemic of 1848-9 which contained details of cases and of deaths in every district of England and Wales.[22] Medical knowledge about the ways in which diseases were transmitted was still very imperfect, but important investigations were made during the cholera epidemics. Working at much the same time, Dr. John Snow in London and Dr. William Budd in Bristol diagnosed the cause of cholera as a living organism disseminated in drinking water and breeding in the human intestine. Snow, in his pamphlet on the subject, the second edition of which was published in 1854, emphasized the point by providing a map of one London district, showing the houses in which cholera had occurred and the pump which supplied water to most of the infected dwellings.[23]

The greatest of the medical reformers, whose rise to national celebrity coincided with the eclipse of Chadwick's career, was John Simon. Born in 1816 he had trained in London as a surgeon and had done research work in pathology. In 1848 he was appointed the first medical officer of health for the city of London, a post he retained until he became medical officer to the Board of Health in 1855.[24] His policy placed great emphasis on information and inspection. He worked closely with the poor law medical officers in collecting regular returns of sickness. He organized weekly inspections of over-crowding, insanitary conditions and offensive trades. These inspections, as he explained himself, had begun as enquiries into places where particular diseases had occurred, but, as the system developed, they became 'a methodical sanitary superintendence of all poorer parts of the city'.[25]

Simon gradually built up a co-ordinated system of public health administration. He aimed to improve water supplies, to deal with noxious trades, to purchase and destroy unsuitable houses. He early gained the influential support of *The Times*, and his work became known through his annual reports which, both in his early days and in the city of London and later at the Privy Council, were important instruments in promoting the sanitary gospel.[26] Much of his work in London was deeply affected by the cholera outbreaks of 1848-9 and 1853-4, and one of his reports, addressed to the President of the General Board of Health in 1856, set out a very important investigation into cholera deaths closely related to Snow's observations about the transmission of cholera through the water supply. Simon showed that, in an area of London supplied by two rival water companies, the Southwark and Vauxhall and the Lambeth, deaths in the 1853-4 epidemic were $3\frac{1}{2}$ times as numerous in houses supplied by the former company, which supplied filthy water, as in those supplied by the latter company which supplied water as good as any in London. In the 1848-9 epidemic the positions had been reversed, the Lambeth company supplying water even filthier than that supplied by the Southwark and Vauxhall. The tenants of the same houses supplied by the Lambeth company had suffered three times as many deaths in the first epidemic as in the second after their water supply had been improved. It was in the highest degree probable, Simon concluded, that two-thirds of the tenants of the Southwark and Vauxhall company who died in the 1853-4 epidemic would have escaped death if their water supply had been like their neighbours, and that two-thirds of the much higher number who had died in 1848-9 would have escaped if the Metropolis Water Act of 1852 had been enacted a few years earlier.[27]

The cholera epidemics, though they greatly added to Simon's problems, made his work much better known, and his scientific authority steadily grew. He claimed later that the advances made between 1848 and 1855 in the city of London had been exceptional at the time and had no parallel except in Liverpool, which had preceded the city of London in appointing a medical officer of health. Like the other sanitary reformers he saw the problems of the city as moral as well as material. He had tried, he claimed, to bring home to the corporation the personal suffering and degradation to which the poor were condemned by the conditions in which they had to live. Until these evils were removed, they could not enjoy decent family life nor acquire civilized social habits.[28] Moreover—a familiar argument by this time—the effort to remove these evils led the local authority to assume powers which they had never contemplated when they began the work. Simon wrote in his report of December 1850:

> To legislate for health was new to you. It was only through the gradual investigation of officers, appointed under the Act, that you could become adequately informed of those sanitary requirements on which your ultimate legislation for the City must found itself. Only by slow experience, only by failure as well as by success, was it possible that correct knowledge could be obtained of the powers really needful for fulfilling your sanitary intentions.[29]

Simon worked in the service of central government from 1855, when he was appointed medical officer to the second Board of Health, until his resignation in 1876. During this final and most important period of his career, he was no longer himself the executant of reforming policies as he had been in the city of London. The emphasis in his work now shifted to statistical investigation and exact scientific enquiry as head of the able medical team which he gathered around him.[30] 'We had to aim', he wrote, 'at stamping on public hygiene a character of greater exactitude than it had hitherto had.'[31] Simon and his associates believed that if the knowledge were obtained, appropriate practical action would follow, though for a decade or more the scientific knowledge of the problems which had been gained ran considerably ahead of the practical measures taken to remedy them. Between 1855 and 1858 Simon worked under the General Board of Health. The Public Heath Act of 1858 transferred the medical department to the Privy Council, though the Act was originally passed for one year only and was not made permanent until 1859. Under its provisions the medical officer was given the duty of compiling both annual and special reports which were to be presented to Parliament. It was a duty of which Simon made very good use for drawing to public attention the problems which needed to be tackled.

One remedial measure to which the reports gave regular attention was that of vaccination against smallpox, on which Simon had published his *Papers relating to the History and Practice of Vaccination* in 1857. In 1867 the law was strengthened by a new act which both tightened up procedures and provided for ways of improving the quality of the vaccine. In 1871, the year of a very serious smallpox epidemic, the Boards of Guardians were required by law to appoint a paid vaccination officer.[32] Other infectious diseases to which the reports gave attention were cholera, which re-appeared in 1865-6, typhoid, scarlatina and diphtheria. There were studies of diseases arising from industrial processes like the use of phosphorus and arsenical green and the lung conditions produced among miners, potters and steel-grinders. Unhealthy indoor trades like tailoring and dress-making were examined. There were enquiries into hospital hygiene, into the contamination of meat and milk, and into the housing of labouring people. The ninth report of 1866 examined the effects of recent measures of sanitary improvement.[33] The eleventh report of 1866 reviewed the working of the Contagious Diseases Acts and considered the need to consolidate the laws and administrative agencies relating to public health.[34] The twelfth report of 1869 returned to the old question of the links between foul water supplies and the distribution of certain epidemic diseases.[35]

When in the late 'sixties the government was again prepared to legislate for public health, Simon and his colleagues had laid a solid foundation of scientific and medical knowledge which had not existed in the Chadwick era. Theirs was a very considerable achievement which showed how much trained skill and knowledge could contribute towards improving the living conditions of society. The threat of cholera helped to produce the Sanitary Act of 1866, which extended the power of local sanitary authorities and by which, in Simon's words, 'the grammar of common sanitary legislation acquired the novel virtue of an imperative mood'. The act gave to local authorities increased powers to provide house drainage and water supplies. Stricter provisions were made for the removal of nuisances, including smoke from factories, the overcrowding of dwellings and the unhealthy conditions of places of work. Additional powers were given to regulate communicable diseases. It was made the specific duty of authorities to inspect their districts and to suppress nuisances.[36] In case of default and upon complaint being made, the Home Secretary had the power to send an inspector to enquire and, if the neglect was established, to order the defaulting authority to take the proper measures. If the authority refused, power was given to remove the order for paying the costs into the Queen's Bench. The vital section 49 of the act, giving the power to compel local authorities to comply, was not contained in the original bill which had given the local justices power to hear complaints. This clause had led to objections by the town council of Manchester which objected to being called to account before the local bench, and the revised clause, with its strong assertion of central control, was inserted. It was a accidental way of achieving an important result. The new powers were from the start quite widely used. In 1867 enquiries were made under section 49 in at least thirteen places; in 1871 in twenty five places. Complaints had been made by individuals, by groups of ratepayers, by Boards of Guardians and by Simon's own medical department.[37]

iii) The Royal Sanitary Commission and its consequences

In May 1868 the British Medical Association and the Social Science

Association, under the leadership of H. B. Rumsey of Cheltenham, asked for the appointment of a royal commission to look into sanitary law and administration, and in 1869 Gladstone set up such a commission under the chairmanship of C.B. Adderley.[38] The Royal Sanitary Commission reported in 1871. It recommended the consolidation of the sanitary laws and an administrative system which should be 'uniform, universal and imperative throughout the kingdom'.[39] What was needed at both central and local levels, the report argued, was unified control. In urban areas the sanitary authority should be the town council in boroughs, with facilities for taking over the powers of commissioners under local acts, and an elected local board in non-corporate towns. In rural areas the Guardians should be the sanitary authority.[40] Similarly there should be a single central authority under a minister, which would administer both poor law and sanitary matters because of the very close kinship between them. There should also be a unified inspectorate. In rural areas the poor law medical officer and the medical officer of health should normally be the same person and, though this would not always be possible in towns, the relationship between the two sets of medical officers should be carefully worked out. The central authority should not, it was argued, take powers from the local authorities, but it must ensure that they carried out their responsibilities. Strong central guidance would in time create a uniform public opinion in favour of good sanitary practice and would break down local apathy and obstructiveness. 'The community will first learn, and then demand, their right to protection from preventible diseases and death, in return for rates levied on them by a Local Authority responsible everywhere for public health.'[41]

There is no need to summarize the practical measures of improvement suggested by the commissioners since they were much the same as those advocated by all the reformers since Chadwick's 1842 Report.[42] Among their detailed recommendations for a consolidated statute only a few points need to be stressed.[43] The localities should be given no option of escaping from the proposed statute, the provisions of which were to apply everywhere.[44] To ensure the efficient implementation of the law every local authority should be required to appoint a medical officer of health, at least one inspector of nuisances, a clerk, a treasurer, a surveyor and other minor officials.[45] The report had previously argued that their proposals for more effective sanitary administration were bound to cost money, and, since the matter was one whose importance exceeded purely local concerns, the state ought to be prepared to assist local authorities, as it already did by contributing towards the salaries of medical officers and the expenses of the police.[46] The principle of national subvention of local expenditure was in its infancy in 1871. As it became more widely extended, it proved to be one of the main instruments of increasing the power of central government.

The recommendations of the Adderley commission were quickly embodied in legislation. In 1871 the proposed central department was established. This, the Local Government Board, took over the duties of the Poor Law Board and of the Privy Council and the Home Office for public health and sanitary matters. The Public Health Act of 1872 divided the country between local authorities, each with full powers in its own area under the sanitary acts. The 1872 act made the appointment of medical officers of health compulsory and provided that half their salaries should be paid by the Local Government Board when the officer's appointment had been approved by them. Finally in 1875 came the major consolidating Public Health Act, covering the whole field of public health, sanitation and nuisance prevention, with the preparation of which Simon had a great deal to do.[47] It was accompanied during the next few years by legislation in related fields such as an act of 1875 regulating the sale of food and drugs, an act of 1876 on the pollution of rivers, and an act of 1879 consolidating the law on contagious diseases in animals. The Factory and Workshops Act of 1878 has already been discussed.[48] Simon, looking back in his old age, claimed that this legislation 'constituted an intelligible and applicable code of law for national sanitary purposes'.[49]

Even after all this major legislation, the triumph of sanitary improvement remained incomplete. Practical reforms took a long time to implement, and the medical and scientific work, with which Simon had been so closely identified in the 'sixties, was actually cut back in the following decade. The new Local Government Board turned out to be the old Poor Law Board under a new name. The permanent secretary, John Lambert, had been a poor law inspector, and he and the other senior officials gained control of the first minister, James Stansfeld, whom we have already met in his later role as campaigner against the Contagious Diseases Acts.[50] They took an entirely different view of the duties of the new board from Simon's, and they made resolute efforts to keep him and the medical scientific view which he represented out of the policy-making side in favour of the merely administrative principles inherited from the Poor Law. The general attitude of the new Local Government Board was to contract the power of central control which had been developed in the 'sixties and to reduce national supervision over disease.[51]

Simon's own view, when he looked back many years later, was that the Local Government Board had never taken up the powers of central sanitary control which it had originally been intended to exercise. No systematic duties of supervision were given to the Medical Department, and the Board's general inspectors had no understanding of sanitary medical problems. He regarded the policy of the new ministry as one of retreat. It had failed to grasp its opportunities, and it had proved to be 'an authority of but doubtful courage for unpleasing responsibilities, an authority "be-stilled almost to jelly" at points where chief need for initiative usefulness existed'.[52] Since Simon found that he could not implement the policies in which he believed, he resigned in 1876 at the early age of fifty-nine, only one year after the passing of the consolidating Public Health Act.[53]

More stringent legislation would clearly be ineffective without more effective machinery for enforcing the law, and this took a long time to provide. One great problem was the parsimony and parochialism of local government which has already been discussed.[54] A higher standard was being set in the late 'sixties and early 'seventies at Birmingham, yet the town did not appoint a medical officer of health until it was forced to do so in 1872, and it refused the government grant of half the salary until 1875 on the ground that it wished to retain intact its control over its own officers.[55] E. C. Midwinter has shown that in the Lancashire towns progress before 1860 was slow and uneven.[56] When Manchester appointed its first medical officer in 1868, it had the highest mortality rate in the country.[57] The first medical officer, Dr. Leigh, set himself to find the reasons for this unenviable primacy. In his report for 1874 he made a comparison of deaths for children under five in a mixed population of rich and poor—the poor predominating—as compared with a group of well-to-do people. The result was 'that the average percentage of deaths of children under five in Manchester for the five years 1869-73 inclusive was 47.6, but the average percentage of deaths for the same period, amongst families belonging to the Society of Friends, was only 12.9'.[58] The figures reinforced the old lesson about the differences in mortality between groups which enjoyed different social and economic advantages. In 1877 the mortality rate had dropped to 25 per thousand, which Dr. Leigh attributed to the fact that the old ashpits and middens had been replaced by pail-closets. This was certainly an improvement, but the water supply was still too defective to enable the town to go over to water-flushed drainage. The plan to bring Lakeland water from Thirlmere was not prepared until later; the bill passed in 1879.[59]

The West Riding towns were in no better situation. In Leeds there had been a burst of activity in the early 'fifties which was not maintained. Ten years later an unfavourable report by Dr. Hunter to the medical department of the Privy Council (1865) led the corporation to improve their water supply and to appoint a medical officer of health, who launched an energetic campaign against nuisances. The increase in expenditure, by another swing of the pendulum, led to the foundation of a ratepayers' pressure group, the Leeds Municipal Reform Association, which campaigned against increased spending on the public services.[60] In the 'seventies and 'eighties the corporation's level of efficiency was very low. They pared down the payments for refuse collection, they did nothing to prevent the building of back-to-back houses, they resisted demands for the provision of public abattoirs.[61] In 1889 widespread concern was expressed over the sanitary administration of the town when a typhoid epidemic broke out.[62] In Sheffield the Housing Act of 1875[63] led to an enquiry into an area north of the old town centre. The report of this enquiry, published in 1877, revealed very bad housing conditions:

The population density was 182 per acre, rising in one sub-district to

261. There was one privy to 11.8 persons and 2.8 houses, and one privy in four was in an offensive condition. Well over two-thirds of the houses had no back doors and almost two-thirds no back windows. Most of the cellars were damp, and although they were not inhabited, they were used for keeping foodstuffs and livestock. In addition to its 23,261 persons, the area contained 112 horses, 60 cows, 12 asses, 211 pigs, 336 dogs and 844 heads of poultry. Despite the pressure by the public and the Local Government Board, the report was not followed up by any action.[64]

iv) The Housing problem: overcrowding in London

By the 'seventies it was clear that bad housing was one of the most serious elements in the public health problem, and public attention tended to concentrate on the larger cities, particularly on London which suffered problems of its own, quite apart from its sheer size. These problems, related to London's economic structure, were especially grave in the East End which by the 'eighties and 'nineties had become the standard example, used by publicists and reformers, of the moral and environmental perils produced by life in great cities.[65] London was a major port and, as such, demanded a large supply of casual labour. It was not a town of factories. Its population worked at home or in small workshops, and, by the second half of the century, its traditional industries, like the silk-weaving and ship-building of the East End, were in decline. At much the same time the clothing, footwear and furnishing trades were developing on the lines of domestic production to serve the mass market. These were the 'sweated' trades, employing large numbers of women, in which, in the latter decades of the century, wages were forced down as more and more people crowded into them. At the same time the working position for men in the East End worsened as dock labour became more and more intermittent. The introduction of steam reduced transhipments and the much quicker turn-around of steam vessels produced longer periods of slack work between the landings.[66]

These grave economic problems accentuated London's overcrowding. Poverty and low wages increased the competition for cheap living accommodation, while the casual labourer, the sempstress and the tailor had to live close to the dock-gates and to the wholesalers who put out the work. The situation, as we have already seen,[67] was worsened by the destruction of property in the inner urban areas for railway building and street improvements. These changes removed some of the slums, but they further increased the housing congestion in neighbouring areas since they did nothing to replace the stock of housing which they had destroyed.

The first attempts to improve working-class housing in London were made in the 'forties, not long after the pioneer sanitary enquiries which preceded the Chadwick Report of 1842. As was so often the case in such matters the initiative was taken by private societies. Their purpose was primarily philanthropic, but they also aimed to earn a modest dividend on the money invested, a combination of objectives neatly summed up in the title of a recent book on the subject, *Five per cent Philanthropy*.[68] The first of these societies to be established were the Metropolitan Association for improving the dwellings of the industrious classes, founded in 1841 and the Society for improving the conditions of the labouring classes, founded in 1844.[69] Some interesting pioneer work was done, but the problems were far too great for much headway to be made, and private effort did not really accelerate until the 'sixties, when housing problems elicited a great deal of interest.

A series of articles in *The Builder* in the early part of the decade condemned the filthy conditions of the larger cities,[70] and an increasing number of books on housing and public health were published, like *The Homes of the working classes with suggestions for their improvement* (1866) by the Leeds educational reformer, James Hole. Hole wanted proper legal controls over building space and the suppression of back-to-back housing. He favoured building societies to help the artisan and cheap government loans for the poor.[71] There was a considerable acceleration too in the work of the private societies in London through the foundation of new bodies operating on a larger scale. The first of these was the Peabody Trust, founded in 1862 with a benefaction from George Peabody, an American merchant, whose gift was directed at the suggestion of Lord Shaftesbury towards housing improvement. In 1863 Sydney Waterlow founded the Improved Industrial Dwellings Company, and in 1867 there followed the Artizans', Labourers' and General Dwellings Company which built suburban housing of a different type from the other two societies which concentrated on high density projects on central sites in the inner city.[72] The scale even of these larger ventures was still small in relation to the size of the problem; by 1875 the three bodies had built about 4,300 dwellings.[73] They aimed to house the artisan rather than the casual labourer, and, like the earlier societies, they aimed to make a profit.

By the mid-sixties the growing public interest in health and sanitation brought housing problems more and more under scrutiny. In 1864 and 1865 Simon's assistant, Dr. Hunter, conducted two surveys into the housing of the poor, and Simon presented them in his seventh and eighth reports to the Privy Council.[74] The Sanitary Act of 1866 stipulated that overcrowding was a nuisance and gave powers of coercion to the central authority. Two years later, in 1868, McCullagh Torrens' Act provided for compulsory power to demolish and repair houses, though the clause enabling local authorities to erect better dwellings was dropped and the act made no provision for compensating the owners for demolition. Local authorities were in consequence unwilling to take action, and the act was inoperative, though it did carry the principle of public interference into areas which had been previously regarded as the exclusive concern of private enterprise.[75] In a very few places the local authorities were beginning to act. Liverpool built a four-storey block in 1869. Glasgow took powers under a private act of 1866 to widen streets and build dwellings. Some sites were cleared, but the corporation did not themselves build houses and, when the sites were sold, the prices were too high for working-class housing to be built on them.[76]

The same difficulties were experienced in carrying through the Artizans' and Labourers' Dwellings Improvement Act of 1875 which had been promoted by Disraeli's Home Secretary, R.A. Cross, who had been much influenced by the Charity Organization Society and the City of London medical officer of health, Dr. Letheby.[77] The act of 1875 permitted authorities to prepare improvement schemes, and compulsory purchase orders might be made after confirmation by Parliament. The land thus purchased was to be offered for sale with provisions about the re-housing of the inhabitants, and the local authority could itself build only with the permission of the Home Secretary. Few provincial towns took action; one which did was Liverpool, where the corporation itself built a block of dwellings which were opened in 1885.[78] The main results of the act were, however, the schemes undertaken in London by the Metropolitan Board of Works.[79] These schemes cost a great deal of money and ran into many difficulties. Progress was slow, the conditions of sale were unpopular, and the compensation terms were fixed at a high level. The sites had to be sold at a great loss and much of the building was done by the Peabody Trust which bought a group of properties that the Board was unable to sell.

The Metropolitan Board of Works completed sixteen schemes, displacing 22,868 people. The new buildings on the cleared sites were built to very high densities because of the high cost of land and the legal requirements about the numbers to be re-housed, but they were too expensive for the labourers and casual workers who formed the core of the housing problem. It has recently been argued by Stedman Jones that the Cross Acts actually worsened the housing situation for these people.[80] One problem was the long delays involved in the process which bore hardly on the poor. Canon Barnett described the situation in Whitechapel as follows:

In 1876 the dwellings of 4,000 persons in this parish were condemned as uninhabitable ... during the ensuing 4 years compensation was agreed upon ... during all those years, landlords whose claims had been settled, spent nothing on repairs; tenants expecting their compensation put up with any wretchedness ... it was not until 1880 that the needful demolition was seriously begun. Since that date, the houses of several thousands of the poor have been destroyed without any reconstruction.

In the early 'eighties the situation worsened as the economic situation became more difficult. Building activity had reached its peak in 1876, after which construction declined and rents rose at a time of bad trade when working people had little money to spare.[81] Public concern about the housing of the poor accentuated as concern about the problems of the cities grew. There was a parliamentary select committee on housing in 1881-2, and a royal commission in 1884-5, which was much more successful in setting out the problems than in suggesting practical remedies for them. The analysis in the report of the royal commission[82] of the familiar evils—bad water supplies, epidemic disease, unhealthy trades, cellar dwellings, the difficulties of refuse disposal and of overcrowding—showed how comparatively little had been achieved in the long fight to improve the city environment. It was on city conditions that the report concentrated. In general, it was argued, housing conditions were better in provincial cities than in London, though bad cases were quoted from Bristol and Newcastle.[83] In London overcrowding was a particularly serious issue. As the report explained:

> The facts mentioned in evidence show plainly how widely the single-room system for families is established, and the statement of a clergyman from the centre of London that in his district the average is five families to six rooms will be found in certain areas to be under the mark rather than an exaggeration.[84]

The report re-affirmed some of the particular difficulties in the London situation which have already been examined. The demolitions under the Cross Acts had displaced many of the poor who could not find a home in the new model dwellings.[85] The railways had displaced many families, and had done very little to provide cheap trains from the suburbs. In any event the poor could not afford to live very far from their work. The Sanitary Acts of 1866 and 1874 had not been enforced in most of the metropolis. The report also brought out some further points of importance. One of these, which was related to the failure to enforce the sanitary code, was the strong influence on the parish vestries of the 'house farmers' and publicans who had a strong interest in preventing reforms.[86] Rents too were high, although wages were low and employment irregular, and in some areas at least the rents had been raised as a result of the demolitions. One witness testified that in Clerkenwell, St. Luke's, St. Giles' and Marylebone, 88% of the poor paid more than one-fifth of their income in rent and that 46% of the total paid between one quarter and one half.[87] These final examples came, it should be noted, from North and North-West London, and they show that the housing crisis was not confined to the East End.

The report of the 1884-5 commission provided an excellent analysis of the housing problems of the cities, and particularly of London. Having analyzed the question, they failed to provide very much in the way of answers to it. They considered the pledging of state credit to aid housing schemes, and they recommended that 'the State should lend at the lowest rate possible, without loss to the national exchequer'.[88] They suggested that railways and other bodies which cleared properties to carry out their schemes should be compelled to provide suitable new accommodation and that they should not be able to escape from this obligation by paying compensation when the old tenants were removed.[89] They proposed that the serious shortage of building land in London might be alleviated by the removal of Coldbath Fields, Pentonville, Millbank and, if necessary, Fulham prisons and the conveyance of their sites to the Metropolitan Board of Works.[90]

These recommendations were inadequate to make much impact, but the housing problem was peculiarly intractable in terms of the individualistic theories which had dominated social thought for so long. It was still generally believed that individuals must be responsible for their own lives and for those of their families. There were no better reasons therefore for subsidizing their housing than for subsidizing their food. Moreover the rights of the property owner were a particularly sacred part of the individualistic canon. On the other hand the pressures of city living and the wretched condition of the casually employed and unemployed poor were forcing some people to the conclusion that the housing question could never be alleviated, let alone solved, by the forces of the market. Sooner or later the state would be forced to take a hand in providing better homes for the poor.

The dilemma was illustrated in the supplementary memoranda which were appended to the report. G.J. Goschen and Lyulph Stanley claimed that no real progress could be made in London until its local government had been reformed. They were in favour of all possible methods of acquiring sites, but they believed that building on such sites should be left to private enterprise.[91] R.A. Cross, the author of the act of 1875, stated 'his great objections to the local authority taking upon itself the duty of providing for the housing of the working classes, except under exceptional circumstances'.[92] The Radical Jesse Collings also stressed the importance of better local government, but on the housing question he took the opposite side. Local authorities should be empowered to purchase land and dwellings in overcrowded areas as the only way of stopping the rising rents which made life increasingly difficult for the poor. As owners the local authorities would be able to prevent overcrowding and would have no incentive to raise rents beyond a point which would prevent a loss being made. If a profit did accrue, 'it would be for the benefit, not of private persons but of the whole community'.[93] In the twentieth century public housing was to be provided on a very extensive scale since it was believed that private enterprise could not meet the need.

i) The Place of religion in society

Environmental issues like sanitation and housing deeply affected Victorian Englishmen because those issues controlled the material framework of their lives. There were other less material controls which had powerful effects on the way people lived, and three of this second group—religion, education and punishment—will now be examined. All three were ideological in that they represented some principle—belief in a theology, in a concept of moral and intellectual training, in a pattern of justice and order. Yet all three expressed themselves in material forms, in churches, schools and prisons, which impinged on daily life at every point. Religion and religious influences have been one of the main threads in this book. Religion embraced social reform as one of its concerns, though all religious people were certainly not social reformers, and its sphere of activity extended far beyond the practical issues with which social reformers were concerned. It has already been argued that social reform provided a kind of substitute religion which tended to move Christianity out of the mainstream of men's interests into the more private realms of worship and faith.[1] It is certainly true that as secular agencies—central government, local government, private societies— became more active, they took over many fields of interest which the Church had claimed as its own. Nevertheless, it remained true that many of those who worked for philanthropic causes, for self-improvement, for working-class organizations, were devoutly religious men and women who saw these objectives as the manifestation of their religious calling to prayer, work and self-denial. 'By their fruits ye shall know them' was a highly apposite text, and a number of examples have already been quoted.

It was natural that there should be this close link between religion and philanthropy because personal charity had always been regarded as one of the necessary fruits of Christian faith. The religious background to many of the movements of self-help and self-improvement seems less obvious from the standpoint of the later twentieth century, though it was very important at the time. The self-help continuum stretched from the purely religious to the purely secular. At the religious end, for example, was the Young Men's Christian Association, founded in 1844 by some employees of a London drapery house and appealing particularly to young men in business. Its primary purpose was the conversion of young men to an evangelical religious faith, but its branches offered libraries, debating societies and lecture courses as well as prayer meetings. Its advocates believed that the Christian business man needed both a sound faith and and good practical abilities. One of them, W.E. Shipton, told a conference in 1855:

> Non-efficient Christian men are a hindrance to the Church, a reproach to their brethern, and a stumbling-block to the world . . . .It is the special mission of the Association to declare that everything is spiritual which God has ordained, and that we shall never be right until every calling be pursued, every duty discharged, in obedience to His will, and with distinct reference to His glory.[2]

At the other end of our suggested continuum nothing might seem more secular than the Tonic Sol-fa method of teaching singing, which was extremely popular in the second half of the century. Yet, publicized by a Congregationalist minister, John Curwen, who wanted to find a simple method of teaching music to Sunday schools, it became closely linked with Nonconformity and temperance movements and produced an increasing musical awareness among middle- and lower-class people which was as much moral and religious as aesthetic. The career of the great Sheffield choral conductor Henry Coward (1849-1944) provides an interesting example of the ideals which the tonic sol-fa movement promoted. Coward was a working cutler who first learned music from a man who was active in the Band of Hope, the children's teetotal organization. He attended a tonic sol-fa class, became a member of a chapel choir, a pupil-teacher and eventually a headmaster. He ran tonic sol-fa classes himself, gave private lessons, and became conductor of the annual Band of Hope festivals in which several thousand children sang. Eventually Coward gave up his school, became a professional musician and well known in connection with the Sheffield Triennial Music Festivals. He was knighted in 1926. Coward was clearly a remarkable man and his career was exceptional, but there were many others who shared, at a lower level, the same moral and religious aims. The tonic sol-fa movement is an interesting and little-known example of the interactions between the religious spirit and secular objectives.[3]

This strong connection between self-improvement and religious belief and sentiment must not, however, disguise the fact that organized religious faith had already, by the middle of the century, lost its hold on the majority of the urban working class, a fact constantly bemoaned by many observers. It has been estimated that, if the attendances recorded in the 1851 religious census are examined, just under 50% of the population attended services in towns of more than 10,000 people but that about 71% did so in the smaller towns and rural areas. In large towns the percentages were lower still—32% in Sheffield, 34% in Manchester, 45% in

Liverpool, 47% in Leeds. If a deduction of about one-third be made for those who attended more than once, the figure in Henry Coward's town of Sheffield falls to about 21%[4] Some of this alienation was actively secularist; the secularist ideas of Charles Bradlaugh have been described, for example, as 'part of the workshop culture of London'.[5] One particular cause of unbelief seems to have been the doctrine of hell. A correspondent wrote in 1878:

> There is no one thing which oppresses the minds of thoughtful men of the present day more than the popular idea that Christianity is committed to the affirmation of the everlasting damnation of the overwhelming majority of mankind. Among the lower class of unbelievers (I allude to such as frequent Bradlaugh's hall) there is no greater stumbling block in the way of their acceptance of Christianity.[6]

Much more widespread than active secularism was sheer indifference. The concerns of the churches made few contacts with the life of the urban worker. He was primarily absorbed in the struggle to feed himself and his family. He found his pleasures in the public house and the music hall which the churches, to a greater or lesser extent, condemned. He formed part of a mass society of the street, the factory or the workshop which created its own social patterns, from which a man was disjoined by church membership. The urban workers retained a respect for religious rituals—for example, they commonly had their children baptized—but, despite all the efforts made to build new churches, their allegiance had been lost in any deeper sense.[7]

It is dangerous, of course, to over-simplify the question of urban working-class attitudes to religious belief. One interesting strand is represented in the autobiography of the Coventry artisan, Joseph Gutteridge. He described how he became known as a free-thinker and how the consequences could be painful. 'Our little world', he wrote, 'was strictly orthodox, and it required a large amount of moral courage to publicly acknowledge oneself to be out of agreement with accepted religious beliefs.'[8] When his employer suggested that he should apply for a local charity which was given only to freemen, the clergyman trustee to whom he applied asked him what church he attended. When Gutteridge stated his disbelief in 'the doctrines of modern Christianity', he was shown the door and the clergyman complained to his employers for recommending an infidel and an atheist. Next year he was more successful with a trustee 'not so closely fettered by religious scruples'.[9] Gutteridge, however, found little satisfaction in the negative doctrines of free thought and he eventually found his way back to a form of religious belief through spiritualism to which he was led by his studies of science and of nature.[10] There was a strong dose of the same qualities of mind in many of the early trades union leaders, though in their case this was often combined with deep religious faith, as in the case of the Northumberland miners' leader, Thomas Burt, who became one of the first miners' M.P.s in 1874. His autobiography brings out very clearly the mixture of religious conviction, self-improvement and industrial activism which was a very important strand in the rise of the trades union movement.[11] Coal miners, however, were not urban workers, and Burt was a Primitive Methodist, a denomination which had an active following among rural labourers, but which was weak in the large towns.[12]

The Church of England clergy had a good record in many aspects of social reform. They had been especially active in promoting schools and many of them had supported the campaigns for better factory conditions. One village incumbent whose reforming efforts ought to be remembered is Edward Girdlestone who, when he went to Halberton in Devon as vicar in 1863, attacked the poverty and wretched living conditions of the rural labourers trying to bring up a family on a wage of 8 shillings a week. To improve the situation he organized the migration of families to the manufacturing districts, and by 1872, when he left Halberton, between 400 and 500 men had been assisted to move.[13] The country clergy came under a good deal of Radical attack during the agricultural workers' movement of the 'seventies. Their attitudes towards the Union varied a good deal, though most of them probably tried to remain neutral between men and masters. They were forced onto the defensive by the strongly anti-clerical attitude of the union leaders which led even Girdlestone to declare that he could no longer support the union because of its attacks on the clergy and on the connection between Church and State. Among the cases brought under the Criminal Law Amendment Act of 1871[14] which gained particular notoriety was the Chipping Norton case of May 1873 when two clerical magistrates sentenced sixteen women to short periods of imprisonment with hard labour because they had tried to prevent two men from breaking a strike.[15]

The agricultural depression of the late 'seventies which struck a very hard blow at agricultural unionism also gravely weakened the power—for good or ill—of the country clergy because it reduced the level of their incomes. In the towns the parish clergyman had less power but more social and professional freedom, and during the second half of the century this freedom was used to develop many different kinds of parochial ministry, some of which concentrated particularly on the social ministry of the church. One incumbent in this tradition was W.H. Fremantle, vicar of St. Mary's, Bryanston Square in West London from 1866 to 1882. Deeply concerned about the relief of distress, he worked closely with the Charity Organization Society. One of his workers was the housing reformer Octavia Hill. Among his curates was Samuel Barnett, who became vicar of St. Jude's, Whitechapel in 1873 and who was to foster social causes which have endured into the twentieth century. Barnett and his wife strongly influenced Beatrice Potter (later Mrs. Webb) in her early days as a social investigator.[16] He suggested to Charles Booth the project which became the great survey of the life and labour of the people of London.[17] His Oxford links with T.H. Green and Balliol College led eventually to the foundation in 1884 of Toynbee Hall as a settlement where educated men should live in close contact with the people of the East End.[18] Among those associated with Toynbee Hall in the twentieth century were C.R. Attlee, William Beveridge and R.H. Tawney.

ii) Elementary education and the Act of 1870

Once again it would be dangerous to over-simplify the attitudes of the Anglican clergy. The fact that some Anglican clergymen played an active part in reforming movements does not mean that an interest in social reform was characteristic of the profession as a whole. The distinctive Nonconformist contribution was strong in some areas such as temperance, weak in others like factory reform and the promotion of elementary schools. The areas of weakness and of strength tend to be related to the particular characteristics of the Nonconformist groups. They were strongly represented among the manufacturers who genuinely believed that the restriction of hours of factory work would harm the workman as much as the employer. They were keenly interested promoters of Sunday schools, but they did less to promote day schools than might have been expected from both their wealth and their numbers. There were Nonconformists like the Birmingham circles influenced by George Dawson and R.W. Dale, who held clear concepts of social action, but it was the natural result of their traditions that they tended to favour individualist rather than collectivist policies. The campaign for educational voluntaryism waged for twenty-five years by Edward Baines of the *Leeds Mercury* is an interesting example of their attitudes. Baines was a strong believer in universal education which, he thought, was essential to produce a well-informed and virtuous population. Since, however, one of the main tasks of education was to develop self-reliance and personal independence, the danger of subservience to state regulation had to be avoided and the religious bases of all education emphasized, objectives which could be achieved only by voluntary effort. Those who stressed the crucial importance of popular education normally argued that success could be achieved only if the state were to intervene. Baines turned this conventional view on its head; since education was of such vital importance, the state had no right to educate.[19]

Whatever the theoretical justification, the voluntaryist principle did not prove a success in promoting schools. The assistant commissioner for the royal commission on popular education of 1858-61 who visited Rochdale and Bradford commented on the very small contribution made by those who held this view to the education of the children of the towns:

Voluntaryism is, in truth, dead; it originates nothing, and it maintains what exists without liberality or spirit . . . . It has no positive side. It prevents persons who hold it from cooperating with their neighbours who take the opposite view, but it does nothing, or next to nothing, by its own independent action.[20]

Baines himself finally abandoned the voluntaryist platform in 1867, three years before the passing of Forster's Education Act.[21]

The Forster Act was the first government measure to effect a national solution to the problems of elementary education, and it marked a major extension of state power in an area in which voluntary activity had long been paramount. Originally elementary schools had been provided by the churches, with the Church of England, which had both the largest resources and the most effective organization, to the fore. Gradually, as the magnitude of the task had become increasingly obvious, the state had come to take a larger and larger share, though it operated not directly but through subsidies to the voluntary bodies. The first stages had been to create a central government department, an inspectorate, and a system of training teachers—a period particularly connected with James Kay-Shuttleworth, the first secretary of the Committee of Council for Education (1839-49). Under his successor Ralph Lingen (1849-69) the work of the Education Department, as it became in 1856, steadily expanded but on more formal and bureaucratized lines. The age of creative innovation was over. The department's objective was to work the system as efficiently and economically as possible. Lingen saw his job as being 'to stem the growth of a system of subsidies and to control the expansionist tendencies of inspectorate and educational public'.[22]

In 1858 a royal commission under the Duke of Newcastle was appointed to review the state of popular education. In general, it considered that the system of state aid had worked well, but it argued that the objectives had been set too high for the majority of the children who attended the schools. It would be desirable, therefore, in order to ensure that the state obtained value for money, to test the results achieved in the schools by instituting

a searching examination by competent authority of every child in every school to which grants are paid, with the view of ascertaining whether these indispensable elements of knowledge are thoroughly acquired, and to make the prospects and position of the teacher dependent, to a considerable extent, on the results of this examination.[23]

The Newcastle Commission is usually remembered—rather unjustly—by this one recommendation which was to be followed up in the system of payment by results instituted by the Revised Code of 1862. The system of paying grants to the school managers on the basis of attendance and of individual examination in reading, writing and arithmetic was not instituted in the precise form recommended by the commissioners. The plan represented the views of Robert Lowe, the minister who spoke for the department in the Commons, and it chimed in very closely with contemporary opinion which placed great emphasis on economy in public spending and which had become concerned at the rising expenditure on elementary education.[24]

The system of payment by results dominated the elementary school curriculum for thirty years. It was strongly attacked at the time and it has been the conventional opinion that it imposed upon the schools a rigid and unimaginative system of teaching. In recent years it has been argued, on the other side, that the Code emphasized secular rather than religious teaching (which was not examined) and that it thus contributed in the end to raising the general standard of work in the schools.[25] From the point of view of social policy the report of the Newcastle Commission and the controversies over the Revised Code are important because they reinforced the public interest in the subject which had been growing since the 'fifties but which was not embodied in legislation until the act of 1870.

Ever since the Reform era popular education had been regarded by many people as an essential social service, yet the necessary legislation failed over and over again to pass. There were a number of reasons for the long delay. The first and most obvious point is the involvement of educational questions with denominational rivalries at a time when these rivalries were particularly bitter. The Church of England was determined to maintain its traditional hold on the education of the people; the teaching responsibility of a national church embraced the school as well as the pulpit. The Nonconformists, growing in wealth and much more self-confident after the repeal of the old discriminatory laws, were deeply suspicious of Anglican pretensions and suspicious too that the government tended to favour their Anglican rivals. They were in the end powerful rather as a negative than as a positive force. They were not able to bring about the completely voluntary system which some of them wanted, but they could halt developments of which they disapproved. Nonconformist feeling tended to hold back state activity in education for a generation. The result of these clashing forces was to precipitate bitter collisions which sometimes led to stalemate. Good examples of this process would be the failure of the government's plan of 1839 for a normal school, after which the provision of teacher training was left to the voluntary societies, or the failure of Graham's Factory Bill of 1843.

These religious quarrels tended to make politicians and administrators wary of involvement in educational questions. Something of this caution induced by harsh experience characterized the policies of the Education Department under Lingen. There may, however, be a tendency among historians to give these religious quarrels more prominence than they really deserve as the principal reason for the tardy acceptance of full national responsibility. Whatever the arguments of publicists like John Stuart Mill, who believed that parents should be obliged to ensure that their children were educated but that the state itself should not provide the schools, the mass of public opinion was probably not convinced that universal education was necessary. Religious people made great play with the moral arguments, but the economic argument that an industrial society needs an educated work-force did not become prominent until the 'sixties, and indeed in the earlier stages of industrial development may not have been valid anyway, because industrial processes were simple and easily learned. There was particular reluctance to promote popular education in the countryside, a sentiment which endured until the end of the century. Farmers did not want their labourers to be better educated and were not prepared to spend money on the subject. Some landowners contributed generously to schools, but many did not. From the labourers' point of view education, so long as they remained in their villages, led nowhere. A man did not become a more skilled carter or ploughman because he could read and write, nor did his new skills increase his wages.

Through all this combination of reasons education was a subject which was taken up by most public men in a somewhat lethargic way—though there were always enthusiasts who spoke for it in and out of season. It has already been suggested that early Victorian governments and parliaments found it difficult to carry through long-term policies, not least because the essential administrative structures to support such policies hardly existed. The obvious example of a long-term policy which was implemented is the New Poor Law, because in this case there was a strong sense of urgency. Even in the case of the poor law, though it was not difficult to create the new machinery, it proved very difficult to put it into practice and to keep it going. In the case of education there was no such sense of urgency, and, without this sense, not much was likely to be done under the conditions of the time. Meanwhile the government contributed more or less liberally to educational development, and men of good will could feel that the voluntary societies were making good progress and that the matter could be left in their hands. This combination of voluntary activity and state support fitted admirably with the general ethos of the day.

A national system of education was a late growth, therefore, because the parliamentary and administrative will to achieve it in face of all the difficulties was lacking. The hindrances were not all concentrated in London. Another major difficulty, which was pointed out by Matthew Arnold,[26] was the absence of a structure of local government which would provide the indispensable local agencies. The municipal corporations had been reformed in 1835, but their powers were limited and their influence small. In the counties the rule of the justices of the peace lingered on until the establishment of elected councils in 1888. In the interstices of town and county proliferated a host of sanitary boards, highway boards and gas and water companies. The failure to co-ordinate all these local bodies was the greatest failure of mid-Victorian administration. No local bodies for education were set up until the School Boards were created in 1870, and even then the boards were widely divergent in size and wealth and were not set up in places where the voluntary schools were deemed sufficient.

The involvement of the state in popular education presented serious administrative problems. The first of these was that of expense. The government grant for education had grown from £30,000 in 1839 to £836,920 in 1859.[27] It was difficult enough, in terms of the financial orthodoxies of the time, to justify such an expenditure from the national exchequer, but the tensions were greatly increased as soon as the suggestion was made that, since education was a local service, it ought to be to some extent financed from the local rate. The proposal for rate-support of education emerged about 1850. It was contained, for example, in the programme of the National Public School Association of that year.[28] Local financial support would certainly mean the demand for local control, which was bound once again to bring up the denominational issue. Logically it was difficult to make a distinction between paying a national tax, some of which would help to support denominational schools, and paying a local rate for the same purpose. However, many who accepted the first were likely to baulk at the second. There was no doubt that rate aid for denominational schools would cause embittered local conflicts.

Even if these conflicts could have been resolved, the prestige of local government institutions was low, and there was little confidence that they would make good use of enlarged powers. The boroughs were generally controlled by the owners of small property who formed the bulk of the rate-payers and whose chief interest was to keep the rates down. The borough councils had a poor record as promoters of change.[29] Their record in fields like sanitation and public health had been one of parsimony, inefficiency, and occasional corruption. From what had gone before there was little reason to suppose that they would use any powers they might be given over education in an enlightened way. It is noteworthy that almost every reference to local bodies in the debates on the 1870 Education Bill is hostile. One M.P., for example, spoke of 'recalcitrant Town Councils, apathetic Vestries, hostile School Boards, and parsimonious rate-payers'.[30] It is impossible to prove that the low reputation of local government helped to delay the passing of an Education Act, but the idea is worth considering.

From the arguments which have been put forward it should now be clear that there were considerable problems involved in any national policy for education. The final difficulty was one of timing. The education issue took up a good deal of parliamentary time in the mid-fifties; in 1855 no less than three bills were before Parliament, but all were withdrawn.[31] It was not a period when the state was likely to move into a major new area of social policy because the government was tending to restrict its activities in central planning. Though the 'fifties were a decade of administrative reform, the reformers planned to achieve economies rather than to extend the range of government activity. It was likely that education, like the other social services, would have to wait for more propitious conditions to return in the later 'sixties.

Elementary education was one of the subjects where national policies were greatly influenced by local initiatives, beginning first in Manchester and later in Birmingham. The Lancashire Public School Association, founded in Manchester in 1847, was much inspired by the model of the American common school, particularly as it operated in Massachusetts.[32] The basis of the association's policy was that local districts should be given the power to tax themselves for educational purposes. A county board of education should be elected. All catechisms and creeds were to be excluded from the schools, but religious teaching might be given, based on selections from the scriptures.[33] In 1850 the society was reconstituted on a wider basis as the National Public School Association with the support of Richard Cobden and, among others, a young Bradford manufacturer named W.E. Forster. The aims of the new society were

the establishment by law, in England and Wales, of a system of Free Schools which, supported by local rates and managed by local authorities officially elected for that purpose by the ratepayers, shall impart secular education only; leaving to parents, guardians and religious teachers the inculcation of doctrinal religion, to afford opportunities for which the schools shall be closed at stated times each week.[34]

In 1851 Manchester churchmen and some Wesleyans founded the Manchester and Salford Committee on Education which also favoured the levy of an education rate, though they proposed to use the proceeds to support denominational schools. Like the N.P.S.A. the Committee wanted the money raised to be controlled by a body elected by the ratepayers. Both groups promoted bills, though neither was successful in obtaining legislation. After a few years of agitation it had become clear that the two groups had much in common. In the winter of 1856-7 denominationalists and non-sectarians agreed on a programme of rate-support and ratepayer management with the proviso that, where distinctive religious formularies were taught, parents who objected to them should be able to withdraw their children. A bill representing this common view was introduced in February 1857, but Parliament was shortly afterwards dissolved and it was not proceeded with.[35]

By that time the Manchester reformers had run out of steam. However they had publicized the idea of a public system of education, paid for by the rates and controlled by elected bodies. They had even managed to compose many of their differences about religious education. The Manchester proposals of the 'fifties did not provide a precise blue-print for the Act of 1870, but they did set out many of the basic ideas on which that act was based. The connection of W.E. Forster, who was to carry the act through the Commons, with the National Public School Association is also worth emphasizing.

During the 'sixties opinion in the cities became increasingly concerned about the large number of children who were not at school. In 1864 the Manchester and Salford Education Aid Society was founded to help pay the school fees of poor children and, if necessary, to establish free schools. The society soon discovered that the problem of school attendance was far more deep-rooted than they had supposed. When the Social Science Association met in Manchester in 1866, the society presented information, as the result of an extensive canvass, that, in every 100 children living with parents and not at work, 40 were at school and 60 were not at school. Their conclusion was that only compulsory education could deal with the apathy of parents, that if compulsion were introduced, education must be free, and that this could be provided only by a compulsory local rate.[36] In 1867 and 1868 education bills were introduced by H.A. Bruce, W.E. Forster and Algernon Egerton, and on both occasions the parliamentary initiative was strongly supported by meetings in Manchester.[37] The 1868 bill was withdrawn when it was clear that a general election was imminent. When Gladstone formed his new government, Forster became Vice-President of the Committee of Council for Education, the man who spoke for education in the Commons.

By the early days of the Gladstone government the evidence of defective educational provision was beginning to accumulate. The first and second reports of the royal commission on children's employment in agriculture brought out the poor state of education in the countryside.[38] It was clear that the half-time system, the beneficial effects of which the commission on children's employment in trades and manufactures had praised so highly,[39] could not be introduced into agricultural work. It has recently been argued, however, that the acceptance during the late 'sixties of the need for legislation arose primarily from a new realization of the extent of the urban problem, whereas previously attention had been concentrated on country areas.[40] Manchester was not the only major town to reveal its own deficiencies. Very similar conclusions were reached by the Birmingham Education Society, founded in 1867 under the presidency of George Dixon who was to play an active part in the debates on the 1870 Bill.[41] In 1869 a House of Commons return on the state of education in Birmingham, Manchester, Leeds and Liverpool showed that many children were attending no school at all and that the private schools were very inefficient.[42]

As the likelihood of an education act increased, the rival forces began to rally. The leadership which had long rested with Manchester now passed to Birmingham. Education was one of the major interests of the Birmingham municipal reformers,[43] and in 1869 they created the National Education League with George Dixon as President, Jesse

Collings as Secretary, and Joseph Chamberlain as Chairman of the committee. The League was a national movement which carried on the ideas of the National Public School Association. It aimed at the establishment of a national system for the education of all children. In order to achieve this, local authorities should be required to see that sufficient schools were founded, the cost to be met from rates and government grants. The schools aided by local rates should be managed by local authorities and subject to government inspection. They should be free and unsectarian, and attendance should be compulsory for those children who were not otherwise being educated.[44] The League represented the non-sectarian and Nonconformist view of the way ahead. In November 1869 the National Education Union was founded in Manchester, one of its main objectives being to protect the interests of the denominational schools.[45]

Although much attention has necessarily been given in this book to reforming legislation, none of the parliamentary debates have been analyzed, and this will now be done for the 1870 bill. Not only are the debates interesting in themselves, they illustrate very well the way in which the mid-Victorian House of Commons tackled a major piece of social legislation. When Forster introduced the Elementary Education Bill in February 1870, he estimated that only two-fifths of working-class children between the ages of 6 and 10 and only one-third between the ages of 10 and 12 were on the registers of government-supported schools.[46] The act, which became law on 9 August, did not design a new national system. It left the existing voluntary schools untouched and provided that, where the existing school provision was inadequate, school boards should be set up for boroughs and parishes with a single board for the whole of London, with the duty of building the schools which were necessary. These boards were to be elected, in boroughs by the burgesses and in parishes by the ratepayers, and they were given the power to issue a precept on the rating authority to be paid out of the local rate. The act, as has often been said, filled in the gaps. Indeed one discontented Radical M.P. had asked the House of Commons:

This Bill, is it a national measure such as the country demanded at your hands? You have not called it a national education measure in the title. Is it one in fact?[47]

The debates were dominated between February and the end of June by the religious question. It was finally decided that, in schools provided by the boards, 'no religious catechism or religious formulary which is distinctive of any particular denomination shall be taught in the school.'[48] In all public elementary schools a conscience clause was to apply. No child should be required to attend any religious observance or instruction from which his parent wished to withdraw him, and the timetable of such instruction was to be arranged so as to make this withdrawal possible.[49]

Elementary education was not made free. School boards might, by by-laws, make it compulsory between the ages of five and thirteen with powers for the exemption of children over the age of ten who had reached certain standards of attainment.[50] Such powers to enforce compulsion did not apply to voluntary schools.

One remarkable feature about the debates was that the major divisions of opinion were not between Conservatives and Liberals but within the Liberal majority itself. The Conservatives on the whole supported the bill, though they disagreed over some issues like the use of the ballot in School Board elections and the operation of the conscience clause. Their spokesmen, like Lord Robert Montagu, A. J. Beresford Hope and Gathorne Hardy generally spoke in favour of the denominational schools, a cause in which they were joined by some Liberals.[51] On the ministerial side Forster managed the business calmly and judiciously and won praise on all sides. However the original proposals were considerably modified by the Radical Nonconformist wing of the party, many of them recently elected M.P.s, who wanted to go further in a number of directions than the government had planned.

The Radicals themselves represented many different viewpoints. Some who were strong Nonconformists were advocates of the disestablishment of the Church of England. Prominent in this group was Forster's colleague from Bradford, Edward Miall, a former Independent minister who had founded *The Nonconformist* in 1841 and who was a leading figure in the Society for the Liberation of the Church from State Patronage and Control (or Liberation Society for short).[52] A Welsh M.P. with similar opinions was Henry Richard, who pointed out the particular difficulties raised by the religious situation in Wales and the dislike of the Welsh people for Anglican teaching in the schools. The only way out of the difficulty, Richard argued, was to make school instruction entirely secular so that religious agencies would be left to do their work outside the schools. The religious teaching given in the day schools was little more than a sham.[53]

The pressures were not all from the religious side. Compulsory education was strongly advocated by the Cambridge economist Henry Fawcett, by the Nottingham manufacturer, A. J. Mundella, who made much use of German examples,[54] and by Sir Charles Dilke, whose main contribution to the final form of the act was to propose that the school boards should be elected by the ratepayers.[55] Free education, which had also been part of the programme of the National Education League, was little discussed, and an amendment in favour of it, moved by George Dixon, was soundly defeated. The government view, as expressed by Forster, was that to introduce it would be to remove from parents a responsibility which they ought to bear and which the state could not afford.[56]

Three major modifications were made as the bill passed through the Commons. It was decided that school boards should be elected instead of nominated by town councils and parish vestries.[57] This was to prove a very important change which was to give to the major urban boards a strong popular constituency. The second organizational change was the decision to have a single board, instead of some twenty smaller boards, for London. 'If there were only one School Board', claimed the Conservative W.H. Smith, 'a degree of responsibility would be secured which, if there were a great many, it would be impossible to maintain'.[58] This again was to prove one of the most creative provisions of the act because it gave the metropolis its first genuinely representative body.

The third change, which was the most important and the most controversial, affected the religious teaching to be given in the new board schools. The bill originally provided that the boards might either establish their own schools or assist the existing denominational schools. They were left free to decide for themselves what kind of religious instruction was to be given.[59] Had such an arrangement, which would have permitted boards to give denominational instruction, passed into law, it might in time have brought voluntary and board schools together into a common system—which indeed seems to have been Forster's ultimate hope. He argued that the problem of religious teaching could not be settled on a national basis and that it was best left to the discretion of local people. They would be likely to work out a system which was religious but unsectarian, since the vast majority wanted religion taught in the schools.[60] These proposals ran contrary to the programme of the National Education League, and they raised all the Dissenting fears about the endowment of denominational teaching. George Dixon, in moving an amendment to the government's proposals, argued that they would strengthen denominationalism and would mean constant sectarian struggles for control of the boards. All rate-aided schools should be unsectarian.[61] The government view was that neighbours would be likely to reach agreement. Their opponents believed that to leave the decision to the local boards would lead to constant strife and bitterness.

The feeling aroused was so great that the government gave way.[62] Some general definition of religious teaching would have to be found if the matter was not to be left to the boards. A purely secular solution, leaving religious instruction entirely to the churches, gained very little support. Another proposal was to include terms like 'unsectarian' or 'undenominational' in the bill, though both Forster on the government side and Lord Robert Montagu for the Conservatives considered that these terms were almost impossible to define.[63] There seems to have been a strong opinion that in practice everyone knew what they meant, but that they could not be written into legislation. The solution finally accepted was the clause, proposed by Cowper-Temple, M.P. for South Hampshire, that no catechism or formulary distinctive of any denomination should be taught in the board schools. The Cowper-Temple clause was not regarded as being the same as an 'unsectarian' clause. One reason for preferring it was that it preserved the maximum possible freedom for the teacher without which he could not do his job properly.

Both Gladstone and Forster defended the Cowper-Temple clause as the best compromise available.[64] Gladstone also pointed out that, if the ties which had originally been proposed between the boards and the voluntary schools were to be severed, the voluntary schools should be provided with an augmented Exchequer grant.[65] The Bill, in its original form, would have associated the voluntary schools and the boards. The Act set a line of demarcation between them which was to grow steadily more marked as the boards acquired greater power. Had the religious clauses of the original bill been passed into law, many of the bitter conflicts of the Dual System might have been avoided if the two sides could have grown together. The historical problem remains; would this have been possible?

Much more might be said about the educational developments of the 'seventies, but the 1870 Act, in which the state accepted the responsibility of providing elementary education for all children, marks a natural point to end this account. Forster commented, during the debate on the third reading, on the extensive powers given to the Education Department and observed that 'nothing but the magnitude of the task and the arduous character of the duty we have to perform would have warranted us in asking the House to entrust us with such powers'.[66] The provisions of the act marked a major extension of state control over the lives of the people, yet another sign that the era of individual initiatives was drawing to a close.[67]

iii) Prisons and punishment

The final area of social control which will be discussed here is that of prisons and punishment. Prison discipline throughout the period was dominated by the 'separate' system about which something has already been said and which was a constant source of controversy.[68] The model established by the new prison at Pentonville, opened in 1842, was followed in a number of prisons, built throughout the country to a common pattern. After the ending of transportation in 1852,[69] the prison system had to deal with the serious problem of controlling the long-term criminal, and a new policy was laid down in the Penal Servitude Acts of 1853 and 1857. Penal servitude involved punishment in graded stages. It began with a period of 'rigorous cellular isolation and complete non-intercourse, day and night, accompanied by the plank bed, a restricted diet, a prescribed task of isolated labour, and the deprivation of all humanizing privileges'. This was followed by a period of associated labour with other prisoners, and then by conditional discharge on 'ticket of leave' under police supervision.[70]

The Home Office inspectors were strongly in favour of the physical and mental isolation of every prisoner, and during the 'fifties there was a steady movement towards making the 'separate' system universal, though the Home Office had no power to order the counties and boroughs to rebuild their prisons or amend their rules. W. L. Burn has argued that during the 'sixties public opinion was hardening against the criminal and moving towards a more rigorous and more centralized system of administration. The garrotting crimes of 1862 led to demands for severer measures against the criminal class, a demand which was clearly expressed in the report of a select committee of the House of Lords, chaired by Lord Carnarvon (1863), which proposed to increase the minimum term of penal servitude and to subject habitual offenders to longer sentences. It urged that the system of cellular isolation should be applied as completely as possible 'because it was terrible to criminals', and everything should be done to maintain its deterrent character. The committee also considered that the term 'hard labour' was too generously interpreted and thought it should be confined to the tread-wheel, the crank and shot drill.[71]

Two years later the Prisons Act of 1865 carried the quest for uniformity and rigidity a good deal further. Every prison authority was required to provide separate cells for all prisoners. All prisoners were subjected to penal labour, either first-class—at the tread-wheel, the crank, the capstan, or at shot drill and stone breaking—or second-class—such other labour as the Secretary of State might approve. Local authorities were required to frame dietaries for their prisons, which had to be approved. Governors and visiting justices were given wide powers of punishment, while the Secretary of State was given power to enforce the requirements of the act by withholding, at his discretion, the grant in aid of expenditure.[72] Two other acts of the same period increased the severity of sentences. The first, passed in 1864, enacted that five years should be the shortest period of penal servitude. The second, the Habitual Criminals Act of 1869, decreed that 'persons already twice convicted of felony, should be liable to imprisonment, if suspected either of infringing, or only of intending to infringe, the law'.[73]

The move towards centralized management of the prison service represented by the Prisons Act of 1865 was completed by the Prisons Act of 1877, which took the prisons out of the control of local authorities and vested them in the Home Secretary, who managed them through a body of commissioners under the chairmanship of Colonel (later Sir Edmund) DuCane.[74] DuCane's regime, until doubts began to be expressed in the 'nineties, was one of severity and detailed regulation, which treated every prisoner in a very mechanical way. 'The way in which offenders were treated by the first prison commissioners', wrote D. L. Howard '. . . could only exaggerate the influence of those social and psychological factors which had first made them criminal.'[75] The prison system displayed the tendencies of the time towards centralization and uniformity, which affected all the social services alike, in their most complete form. In the case of schools or public health or housing, these tendencies were balanced by a free public opinion and by the clash and conflict of everyday life. The prison world had a closed door, which was opened only by the occasional scandal or spectacular escape. For the greater part of the time its inmates gained little sympathy. They were society's failures, submitted to harsh disciplines which put deterrence above reformation. The unreformed prisons had been diseased and disorderly places. There was something tyrannical and dehumanizing about the efficient administration which had replaced them.

XII. Conclusion

The Decline of private initiative and the growth of central power

During the 'seventies major legislation was passed in all the principal areas of social policy—the Education Act of 1870, the Public Health Act and the Trades Union legislation of 1875, the Prisons Act of 1877, the Factory Act of 1878. It has been argued here that the drive towards social reform began at the end of the eighteenth century, and some of the main themes have been outlined in the first chapter.[1] Over the century which has been studied certain major points stand out. First of all, reform did not begin in 1830. It has been shown that many of the main lines had been laid down in the preceding half-century. Secondly there was a strong moralistic note among men of all schools which laid a heavy emphasis on an authoritarian approach to social policy. Much more stress was laid on coercion than on persuasion. Thirdly the reformers shared an ideological 'broad front' to which Bentham made an important contribution but for which he was not entirely responsible.

By the 'seventies the outlines began to change. The early initiatives had been private and local; by the end of our story the initiatives were becoming more and more governmental and national. The contrast can, as always, be too sharply drawn. Private endeavour and state activity interpenetrated one another, and they cooperated at least as often as they clashed. Local enterprise remained important throughout; for example, much of the power behind the campaign for an education act was generated in Manchester and Birmingham. By that date, however, central power was more and more setting the pace. Matters which would earlier have been left to local decisions were being regulated according to national standards. Local acts of parliament were replaced by national legislation; the permissive mood was replaced by the imperative. In 1856 the Home Secretary, Sir George Grey, had argued over the Police Bill that the local police 'could not be considered as an isolated question, but that it affected the whole community and not alone the county or borough in which crime was allowed to be undetected or unrepressed'.[2] The same kind of argument could be, and was, applied to epidemic disease, to public health matters, to illiteracy. Differences which left one district poorly provided with essential services in comparison with another were more and more thought to be intolerable. There were to be national standards of health and education just as there had for centuries been national standards of public order or of foreign policy.

This tendency to put social problems onto a national dimension was accompanied by an equally important change in personal attitudes. Ever since the 1780's the driving force in social change had been the doctrine of personal activity and independence which taught the individual that he was master of his own fate. It had always been clear that some individuals would be unable to help themselves, but when this was so it was expected that other individuals, either singly or in groups, would step in to provide assistance. By 1880 more and more people were beginning to doubt whether self-help and private enterprise could achieve all that had been claimed for them for so long. Perhaps the problems of society were too deep-rooted to yield to private action. Steadily, almost imperceptibly, more and more social tasks had moved from the private to the public domain and once this process had begun, it was very difficult to stop it. The provision of public utilities by municipal activity was already commonplace. If, for example, the city could provide pure water and an efficient sewage system, why should it not build houses? The secretary of the London Trades Council told the royal commission on housing (1884-5) that private enterprise and philanthropy had done a great deal, but that they could not keep pace with the demand for housing and with the increase in population . . . 'But what the individual cannot do the State and the municipality must seek to accomplish'.[3]

This movement away from individualism is clearly recorded in Beatrice Webb's account of her early career as a social investigator. There had always been plenty of critics of particular aspects of the social and economic system; what was new was the questioning of the system itself. In her book Mrs. Webb made this comment about Canon and Mrs. Barnett and their break with the Charity Organization Society:

> They had discovered for themselves that there was a deeper and more continuous evil than unrestricted and unregulated charity, namely unrestricted and unregulated capitalism and landlordism.[4]

This questioning came at a time when the world looked far less secure than it had done in the hey-day of mid-Victorian progress. The 'eighties fell in the middle of the period christened by the economists the Great Depression, though they differ among themselves a good deal about the depth of the depression.[5] Prices fell from 1873 to 1896, which meant that profits were reduced, and unemployment, at some periods, was serious. On the other hand, real wages rose and the mass of wage-earners improved their position a good deal. The export trade and home agriculture were certainly growing more slowly than before, and industrial production may have ceased to expand. One major change was that economic enterprise had become international in scale. Britain had lost its position as the premier industrial nation of the world and was confronted by strong rivals like Germany and the United States. Though the evidence is not very easy to interpret, there was certainly a widespread belief at the time in the existence of economic depression. H.L. Beales wrote:

> There was, in fact, a continuous output of discussions, speeches, books, reports and pamphlets, which prove, at least, that people thought they were depressed, whether in fact they were or not. We can, at any rate, say that the period of falling prices from 1873 to 1896 was a period when people said there was a great depression.[6]

Whatever the economic facts may have been, the belief in the existence of depression may have accentuated the sense of insecurity provoked by many other developments of the time.

Ireland was the great internal problem of the day, and Irish land legislation, designed to transfer the ownership of the soil from landlord to peasant, appeared to offer a direct attack on the principle of the sanctity of contracts and to threaten the security of property in Great Britain itself.[7] There was a growing appreciation of the problems of poverty and of the depths of class division, which reached their most extreme form in London and other great cities. Charles Booth's survey of the life and labour of Londoners, the first part of which appeared in 1889, revealed the social anatomy of the metropolis in a more complete and scientific way than had ever been attempted before. The 'bitter cry of outcast London'—to adopt the title of an influential pamphlet of 1883[8]—not only aroused men's sympathies; it also excited their dread because they began to fear that cities might produce a hereditary degeneration in the race. To cure these evils new doctrines were being preached. The American Henry George advocated the taxation of land values, since land belonged to the whole people. Socialism, proclaimed by people like H.M. Hyndman, demanded the radical reconstruction of society. Attempts to organize the unskilled worker, which gained a striking success in the London dock strike of 1889, heralded a major shift in industrial relations. The 'eighties, a decade of questioning and doubt, were a seed-time of new remedies for old ills, and the harvest planted then was to determine much of the social development of twentieth-century England.

Notes

Notes to Chapter One

1. J.R. Seeley, *Ecce Homo* (16th Ed., 1881), p. 182
2. Ibid, p.190
3. Edward Lytton Bulwer, *England and the English* (1833), vol. II, p. 171
4. 'Condition of the Working Classes and the Factory Bill', *Westminster Review*, vol. XVIII, pp. 384-5, quoted in G.L. Nesbitt, *Benthamite Reviewing. The First Twelve Years of the Westminster Review, 1824-1836* (New York, 1934), pp. 147-8
5. T. Carlyle, *Past and Present* (1891 ed.), p.2
6. See Beatrice Webb, *My apprenticeship* (2nd. ed., n.d.), especially Ch. IV.
7. J.F. Stephen, *Liberty, Equality, Fraternity* (1873), pp.241-2
8. David Ricardo, *On the Principles of Political Economy and Taxation* (Penguin ed., by R.M. Hartwell (1971) of the 3rd. Ed. (1821), p. 152
9. *Bettering Society, Reports*, vol. IV (1805), p. 4. For Bernard, see James Baker, *The Life of Sir Thomas Bernard* (1819); David Owen, *English Philanthropy 1660-1960*, (Cambridge, Mass. 1964), pp. 105-8
10. Sir James Kay-Shuttleworth, *Four Periods of Public Education as reviewed in 1832-1839-1846-1862* (1862), p.74
11. J.T. Ward, *The Factory Movement 1830-1855* (1962), p. 151
12. *A Dissertation on the Poor Laws. By a well-wisher to Mankind* (Joseph Townsend, Rector of Pewsey). (1786, reprinted 1817, pp. 104-5).
13. See below, pp.72-4, and *Eight Letters on the Management of our Poor, and the general administration of the Poor Laws;* by an overseer (George Nicholls). (Newark, 1822); J.T. Becher, *The Antipauper System; exemplifying the positive and practical good, realized by the relievers and relieved, under the frugal, beneficial, and lawful administration of the Poor Laws, prevailing at Southwell, and in the neighbouring district* (1828; 2nd Ed. 1834)
14. Richard Johnson, 'Educational Policy and social control in early Victorian England', *Past and Present*, No. 49 (Nov. 1970), pp. 96-119
15. R. Lambert, 'A Victorian National Health Service: State Vaccination 1855-1871', *Historical Journal*, Vol. 5 (1962), pp. 1-18
16. *Parliamentary Papers*, 1843, XIV, pp. 475, 481
17. See M.G. Jones, *Hannah More* (1952)
18. M.G. Jones, op. cit., p. 173
19. Robert and Charles Cuthbert Southey, *Life of the Rev. Andrew Bell* (1844) Vol. I, pp. 599-600
20. See W.W. Clay, *The Prison Chaplain; A Memoir of the Rev. John Clay, B.D., late Chaplain to the Preston Goal* (Cambridge and London, 1861)
21. See pp. 51-2
22. J. Baker, *Life of Sir Thomas Bernard*, pp. 70-71
23. W.W. Currie (ed.,), *Memoir of the Life, Writings and Correspondence of James Currie, M.D., F.R.S. of Liverpool* (1831), Vol. I, pp. 338-42
24. A.E. Clark-Kennedy, *The London. A Study in the Voluntary Hospital System*, Vol. I (1962), pp. 255-6
25. See R. Lambert, *Sir John Simon (1816-1904) and English Social Administration* (1963)
26. W.L. Burn, *The Age of Equipoise* (1964), pp. 236-7
27. S.E. Finer, *The Life and Times of Sir Edwin Chadwick* (1952), Bk. VI, Ch. II.
28. Bernard, Introductory Letter, dated 27 January 1801, to Vol. III (1802), of the *Reports of the Society for Bettering the Condition and Increasing the comforts of the Poor*, p. 41
29. E. Halévy, *The Growth of Philosophic Radicalism* (Eng. trans. reprinted 1952), pp. 405-6, 430-1
30. J. Bentham, Constitutional Code, in *Works*, ed. J. Bowring Vol. IX (1843), pp. 213-4, 257-8
31. J.H. Clapham, *An Economic History of Modern Britain. The Early Railway Age 1820-1850* (Cambridge, 1950), pp. 53-4, 536

32. R. Lambert, *Sir John Simon*, p. 59
33. E.R. Norman, *A History of Modern Ireland* (1971), pp. 116-7
34. For the development of this argument see E.R. Norman, op. cit., esp. Chs. 2, 4; Eric Stokes, *The English Utilitarians and India* (Oxford, 1959)
35. G. D. H. Cole and R. Postgate, *The Common People 1746-1946* (2nd ed., 1946), pp. 441-2, 444
36. W.H. Burston (ed.), *James Mill on Education* (Cambridge, 1969), Introduction, p. 15
37. Robert Owen, *A New View of Society: or, Essays on the Formation of the Human Character preparatory to the development of a plan for gradually ameliorating the condition of mankind* (4th ed., 1818), p.121
38. C.J. Stranks, *Dean Hook* (1954), p. 75
39. *Charles Lowder. A Biography.* By the author of 'The Life of St. Teresa' (1882), p.227

Notes to Chapter Two

1. Elie Halévy, *A History of the English People in the Nineteenth Century. England in 1815.* (Eng. trans., 2nd revised ed. 1949), p. 20
2. *The Corporation of Cambridge. A Digested Report of the Evidence* ... (Cambridge and London, 1833), pp. 61-2
3. S. and B. Webb, *The Manor and the Borough*, Part I (1908), pp. 287-8
4. Ibid, Part II (1908), p. 490; see p. 423 for the case of Leeds.
5. Ibid, Part II, p. 691
6. S. and B. Webb, *Statutory Authorities for Special Purposes* (1922), p. 103
7. S. and B. Webb, *The Parish and the County* (1906), pp. 107 ff.
8. S. and B. Webb, *Statutory Authorities for Special Purposes*, pp. 109-10
9. Ibid, pp. 219-20
10. Ibid, p. 230
11. S. and B. Webb, *English Prisons under Local Government* (1922), p. 75
12. E.C. Midwinter, 'State intervention at the local level; the New Poor Law in Lancashire', *Historical Journal*, Vol. 10 (1967), pp. 106-12
13. See Joan Simon, 'Was there a Charity School Movement? The Leicestershire Evidence', Brian Simon (ed.), *Education in Leicestershire 1540-1940. A Regional Study* (Leicester, 1968), pp. 55-100
14. 'First Report on National Education', *Quarterly Review*, Vol. VIII (1812), p. 27
15. D. Owen, *English Philanthropy 1660-1960*, pp.40-1, 43
16. See p. 21
17. C. Gill, *History of Birmingham*, Vol. I, *Manor and Borough to 1865* (1952), pp. 130-1
18. For the contrasting views, see R. Coupland, *The British Anti-Slavery Movement* (1933); Eric Williams, *Capitalism and Slavery* (Chapel Hill, N.C., 1944)
19. E. Halévy, *History of the English People in the 19th Century. England in 1815*, p. 158
20. R. Coupland, *The British Anti-Slavery Movement*, pp. 94-5
21. Ibid, pp. 121-2
22. H.J. Perkin, *The origins of Modern English Society 1780-1880* (1969), pp. 134-49
23. E.J. Hobsbawm, 'The British Standard of Living 1790-1850', and 'The Standard of Living Debate: a postscript', in *Labouring Men: Studies in the History of Labour* (1964)
24. E.P. Thompson, *The Making of the English Working Class* (1963), p.318
25. E.J. Hobsbawm, *Labouring Men*, p. 124
26. E.P. Thompson, *Making of English Working Class*, pp. 560-1
27. Quoted in D. Read, *The English Provinces c. 1760-1960. A Study in Influence* (1964), p. 47
28. See G. Wallas, *The Life of Francis Place 1771-1854* (Revised ed. 1918); *Francis Place Autobiography* ed. Mary Thale (Cambridge, 1972)
29. *History of the English People in the 19th Century. England in 1815*, p. 425
30. N. McCord, 'The Government of Tyneside 1800-1850', *Transactions of the Royal Historical Society*, 5th Ser: Vol. 20 (1970), pp. 5-30
31. E.P. Thompson, op. cit., p. 553
32. Ibid, pp. 667-8
33. Ibid, p. 670
34. See pp. 67-9
35. D. Owen, *English Philanthropy 1660-1960*, pp. 98, 101-2; see also L. Radzinowicz, *History of English Criminal Law and its administration from 1750*, vol. IV: *Grappling for Control* (1968), p. 38
36. *Westminster Review*, Vol. IX (1828), 'Life Assurances—diminution of sickness and mortality', pp. 384-421. The quotation is on p. 390
37. Francis Place, *Autobiography*, pp. 14-15
38. Place summed it all up as follows: 'The progress made in refinement of manners and morals seems to have gone on simultaneously with the improvement in Arts Manufactures and Commerce. The impulse was given about sixty years ago, it moved slowly at first but has been constantly increasing by vel-

ocity. Some say we have refined away all our simplicity and have become artificial, hypocritical, and upon the whole worse than we were half a century ago. This is a common belief, but it is a false one, we are a much better people now than we were then, better instructed, more sincere and kind hearted, less gross and brutal and have fewer of the concomitant vices of a less civilized state'. Ibid, p. 82

39.   J. C. Symons, *On the present aspect of Education. An address to the Church School Teachers' Association for the Diocese of Gloucester and Bristol at their annual meeting, Nov. 16 1855*, (1856), p.6; see also John Roach, 'Jelinger Cookson Symons 1809-1960', *Letter of the Corpus* [Christi College, Cambridge] *Association* no. 51 (1972), pp. 15-25. For a similar view expressed by the prison reformer, John Clay, see J.T. Tobias, *Crime and Industrial Society in the 19th Century* (Penguin Books ed. 1972), p. 215

Notes to Chapter Three

1.   S. and B. Webb, *The Parish and the County* (1906), pp. 603-7

2.   See p. 31

3.   A similar point is made by Asa Briggs, *The Age of Improvement* (1959), pp. 45-6

4.   R.E. Schofield, *The Lunar Society of Birmingham. A Social History of Provincial Science and Industry in 18th Century England* (Oxford, 1963), pp. 141-2

5.   This account of him is based on Thomas Percival, *The Works, Literary, Moral and Medical . . . to which are prefixed Memoirs of his life and Writings, and a selection from his Literary Correspondence* (new ed. 4 vols. 1807)

6.   Percival, 'Observations on the State of Population in Manchester and other adjacent places' (1774), in *Works*, Vol. IV, pp. 1-67

7.   *Works*, Vol. I, pp. clvii-cclviii, gives Percival's communication to the Board of Health, 7 January 1796

8.   See W. W. Currie (ed.), *Memoir of the Life, Writings and Correspondence of James Currie, M.D., F.R.S. of Liverpool*, 2 Vols. (1831)

9.   Ibid. Vol. II, pp. 221-2

10.   4 January 1797, W.W. Currie, *Memoir*, Vol. II, pp. 93-4

11.   See 'Biographical Memoirs of the late Thomas Butterworth Bayley Esq'. in T. Percival, *Works, Literary, Moral and Med-*

ical, Vol. II, pp. 287-305

12.   S. and B. Webb, *English Prisons under Local Government* p. 62

13.   *Parliamentary Papers*, 1810-11, III, pp. 601 ff (13, 15 March 1811)

14.   *Parliamentary Papers*, 1814-15, IV, pp. 985-8

15.   J.T. Becher, *The Antipauper System; exemplifying the position and practical good, realized by the relievers and the relieved, under the frugal, beneficial, and lawful, administration of the Poor Laws, prevailing at Southwell, and in the neighbouring district . . .* 2nd Ed. (1834), p. XXXII

16.   W.P. Alison, *Observations on the management of the poor in Scotland and its effects on the health of the great towns* (Edinburgh, 1840)

17.   A.N. Shimmin, *The University of Leeds: the first half-century* (Cambridge, 1954), p. 4

18.   A.W. Chapman, *The Story of a Modern University. A History of the University of Sheffield* (1955), p. 105

19.   Ibid, p. 104

20.   See G, Wallas, *Life of Francis Place*, Ch. III

21.   Halévy, *History of the English People in the 19th Century. England in 1815*, pp. 578-9

22.   G. Wallas, op. cit., pp. 95-7, 105-8

23.   C.W. Everett, *Jeremy Bentham* (1966), p. 45; E. Halévy, *The Growth of Philosophic Radicalism* (Eng. trans. 1952), p. 75

24.   The following comments on Brougham's career are taken from Chester W. New, *The Life of Henry Brougham to 1830* (Oxford 1961)

25.   C.W. New, op. cit., pp. 390, 400

26.   'William Wilberforce', 'The Clapham Sect', reprinted in Sir James Stephen, *Essays in Educational Biography* (4th ed., 1860), pp. 467-582

27.   G.O. Trevelyan, *The Life and Letters of Lord Macaulay* (popular ed. 1889), p. 49 n. 1

28.   Richard D. Altick, *The English Common Reader. A Social History of the new reading public 1800-1900* (Chicago, Phoenix Books ed. 1963), pp. 101-2

29.   Report of the Minutes of Evidence taken before the Select Committee on the state of children employed in the Manufactories of the United Kingdom. *Parliamentary Papers* 1816, III; see the evidence of George Gould, pp. 339-41; Thomas Whitelegg, pp. 382, 390; Thomas Oldmeadow Gill, p. 523

30.   See p. 15

31.   Bettering Society, *Reports*, Vol. IV (1805), p. 31

32. Thomas Bernard, *The New School; being an attempt to illustrate its principles, detail and advantages* (1809). An enlarged edition appeared in 1812 as *The Barrington School*.

33. *The Reports of the Society for bettering the condition and increasing the comforts of the Poor*. Vols. I (1798); II (1800); III (1802); IV (1805); V (1808) have prefaces by Bernard. Vol. VI (1814) has no prefatory letter.

34. Bettering Society, *Reports*, Vol. V (1808), p. 49

35. Bettering Society, *Reports*, Vol. IV (1805) p. 15

36. E. Halevy, *History of the English People in the 19th Century. England in 1815*, p. 452

37. E. Lytton Bulwer, *England and the English*, Vol. II, pp. 159-60

38. In an article of 1826; G. Wallas, *Life of Francis Place*, pp. 161-2

39. T.R. Malthus, *An Essay on the Principle of Population* and *A Summary View of the Principle of Population* (Penguin Classics edition by Antony Flew, 1970), p. 71. This reprints the first edition (1798) of the *Essay*.

40. The second edition was published in 1803. The last Edition published in the author's lifetime was the 6th (1826). I have used the re-print of this edition by G. T. Bettany (?1890).

41. Malthus, *Essay on Population* (Penguin Classics Ed.), p. 103

42. Ibid, p. 172

43. Ibid, p. 189

44. Malthus, *A Summary View of the Principle of Population*, in *Essay on the Principle of Population* (Penguin Classics), p. 249

45. Malthus, *Essay on Population*, 6th Ed. by G.T. Bettany, p. 215

46. Ibid, pp. 361-2

47. Ibid, pp. 496, 498

48. See N.W. Senior. *Two Lectures on Population, delivered before the University of Oxford in Easter Term, 1828. To which is added, a correspondence between the author and the Rev. T. R. Malthus* (1829)

49. See Malthus, *Essay on Population* (Penguin Classics ed.), pp. 95, 97

50. Malthus, *Essay on Population* (6th ed. by G.T. Bettany), pp. 357-8

51. Ibid, p. 255

52. Ibid, p. 458

53. David Ricardo, *On the principles of Political Economy, and Taxation* (Penguin ed. by R.M. Hartwell, 1971), pp. 126-7

54. Ibid, pp. 178-9

55. Ibid, pp. 331-2

56. Ibid, p. 127

57. R. Owen, *A New View of Society* (4th ed. 1818) p. 11

58. See p. 79 for his evidence to the Select Committee of 1816.

59. Owen, *A New View of Society* (4th Ed). p. 58

60. W. Lovett, *Life and Struggles* with a preface by R.H. Tawney (1967 ed.), p. 35

61. E. Halévy, *The Growth of Philosophic Radicalism*, pp. 372, 499

62. J. Bentham, *The Theory of Legislation*, ed. C.K. Ogden (1931), p. 77

63. *Encyclopedia Britannica, Supplement to the Fourth, Fifth and Sixth Editions*, Vol. VI (Edinburgh, 1824)

64. C.M. Atkinson, *Jeremy Bentham. His life and work* (1905), p. 217

65. G. Wallas, 'Jeremy Bentham', *Men and Ideas. Essays* (1940), p. 29

66. D.J. Manning, *The Mind of Jeremy Bentham* (1968), pp. 109-10

67. For an example of MacDonagh's arguments, see 'The nineteenth century revolution in government: a reappraisal', *Historical Journal*, Vol. I (1958), pp. 52-67

68. 'Climbing Boys', *Edinburgh Review*, Vol. XXXII (1819), p. 319

69. *England and the English* (1833), Vol. II, p. 166

70. For a development of this argument, see Jenifer Hart, "Nineteenth century social history: a Tory interpretation of history", *Past and Present*, no. 31 (1965)

71. S.E. Finer, "The Transmission of Benthamite ideas 1820-50", in *Studies in the growth of nineteenth century government*, ed. Gillian Sutherland (1972), p. 13

72. Ibid, p. 32

73. J. Bentham, *Works published under the superintendence of his executor John Bowring*, Vol IX (Edinburgh, 1843), p. 442 The Code is reprinted in Vol. IX of the *Works*. For an earlier and less complete version, see J. Bentham, *Constitutional Code: for the use of all nations and all governments proposing liberal opinions*, Vol. I (1830)

74. *Works*, Vol. IX, pp. 270 ff.

75. Ibid, p. 442

76. *Works*, Vol. IX, pp. 612 ff.

77. See L.J. Hume, 'Jeremy Bentham and the nineteenth-century revolution in government', *Historical Journal*, Vol. 10 (1967), pp. 361-75, which examines the views of scholars like MacDonagh and David Roberts.

Notes to Chapter Four

1. S. and B. Webb *English Local Government; English Poor Law History,* Part I, *The Old Poor Law* (1927), pp. 153-4

2. Mark Neuman, "Speenhamland in Berkshire", *Comparative Developments in Social Welfare,* ed. E.W. Martin (1972), pp. 89-90

3. Sir George Nicholls, *A History of the English Poor Law* (new ed. by H.G. Willink, 1898), Vol. II. pp. 115-6

4. M. Blaug, "The Myth of the Old Poor Law and the Making of the New", *Journal of Economic History,* Vol. XXIII (1963), and "The Poor Law Report re-examined", Ibid, Vol. XXIV (1964)

5. Sir F.M. Eden, *The State of the Poor; or, an history of the labouring classes in England, from the conquest to the present period* (3 vols. 1797), Vol. I, p. 587

6. C.M. Atkinson, *Jeremy Bentham. His Life and Work,* pp. 135-6

7. P. Colquhoun, *A Treatise on Indigence; exhibiting a general view of the national resources for productive labour* (1806)

8. Ibid, pp. 8, 13

9. Ibid, p. 43

10. Ibid, pp. 48-9

11. P. Colquhoun, *A Treatise on the Police of the Metropolis, explaining the various crimes and misdemeanours which at present are felt as a pressure upon the Community; and suggesting remedies for their prevention* (2nd. ed. 1796); see also L. Radzinowicz, *A History of English Criminal Law and its Administration from 1750,* Vol. III (1956), part IV

12. *Treatise on the Police,* p. 29

13. *Treatise on Indigence,* p. 104

14. *Treatise on Indigence,* p. 244

15. Ibid, pp. 134-5

16. Ibid, p. 177

17. T.R. Malthus, *Essay on Population* (6th ed.), pp. 494-6

18. Ibid, p. 505

19. Bettering Society, *Reports,* Vol. V (1808), p. 31

20. Ibid, p. 25

21. P.H.J.H. Gosden, *The Friendly Societies in England 1815-1875* (Manchester, 1961), pp. 173-4; see also E.P. Thompson, *The Making of the English Working Class* (1963), p. 421

22. J.C. Curwen, 'On Friendly Societies', in *Hints on the economy of feeding stock, and bettering the condition of the poor* (1808), p. 346

23. Ibid, pp. 340-1

24. J.D. Marshall, 'The Lancashire rural labourer in the early nineteenth century', *Transactions of the Lancashire and Cheshire Antiquarian Society,* Vol. LXXI (1961), pp. 124-5

25. Sir George Nicholls, *History of the English Poor Law* (1898 ed.), Vol. II, pp. 192-3

26. E. Halévy, *History of the English People in the 19th Century. The Liberal Awakening. 1815-1830* (Eng. trans., 3rd impression, 1965), pp. 40-1

27. *A Dissertation on the Poor-Laws,* by a well-wisher to mankind (Joseph Townsend, Rector of Pewsey) (1786, re-published, 1817)

28. T. Chalmers, *The Christian and civic economy of large towns,* Vol. II (Glasgow, 1823), p. 55

29. Ibid. pp. 56-60

30. Ibid. p. 350

31. Ibid, pp. 303-27, 357-60

32. Ibid, pp. 270-1, note

33. For a criticism of the Scottish Poor Law System, see W.P. Alison, *Observations on the management of the poor in Scotland, and its effects on the health of the great towns* (Edinburgh 1840). Alison argued that the system of voluntary relief had failed, and advocated the adoption of the English system.

34. Report from the Select Committee on the Poor Laws, *Parliamentary Papers,* 1817, VI, p. 29

35. S. and B. Webb, *The Old Poor Law,* pp. 273-6

36. M.E. Rose, *The English Poor Law 1780-1830* (1971), p. 64. The evidence of W.D. Evans, the Manchester stipendiary magistrate, to a House of Lords Select Committee of 1817 is quoted on p. 66

37. Ibid, p. 67

38. S. and B. Webb, *English Local Government; the Parish and the County* (1906), pp. 159-64, 274-5

39. Report from the Select Committee on Labourers' Wages, *Parliamentary Papers,* 1824, VI, p. 407

40. Report from the Select Committee on that part of the Poor Laws relating to the employment or relief of able-bodied persons from the poor rate, *Parliamentary Papers,* 1828, IV, p. 147

41. J.T. Becher, *The Antipauper System* (1828), p. 43

42. See p. 47

43. For Nicholls' career, see *Dictionary of National Biography.*

44. (George Nicholls) *Eight Letters on the management of the poor and the general administration of the poor Laws;* by an

overseer (Newark 1822). These letters had originally been published in the *Nottingham Journal*. J.T. Becher, *The Antipauper System* contains information about the influence of the Southwell system in other parts of the country.

45. Nicholls, *Eight Letters*, p. 59. The 1822-3 figures have been added in pencil in the British Museum copy by Nicholls himself.

46. Becher, *Antipauper System*, p. 9; Nicholls *History of the English Poor Law* (1898 ed.), Vol. II, p. 235

47. Becher, *Antipauper System*, p. 16

48. Ibid. p. 19

49. Ibid. p. 15

50. Nicholls, *Eight Letters*, p. 19

51. Ibid, p. 24

52. Becher, *Antipauper System*, p. 22

53. Becher, *Antipauper System* (2nd. ed., 1834), p. VI

54. J.D. Marshall, "The Nottinghamshire Reformers and their contribution to the New Poor Law", *Economic History Review*, 2nd Series, Vol, XIII (1960-1), pp. 395-6

55. Nicholls, *History of the English Poor Law* (1898 ed.) Vol. II, p. 236

56. For Malthus, see pp. 54-8; for Colquhoun, see pp. 67-9; for the Utilitarians, see pp. 59-65

57. Eden, *State of the Poor*, Vol. I, p. 429

58. "Education of the Poor", *Edinburgh Review*, Vol. XXI (1813), p. 212. For the attribution of the article to Mill, see Chester New, *The Life of Lord Brougham to 1830* (Oxford, 1961), p. 204

59. See "Education of the Poor", *Edinburgh Review*, Vol. XXX (1818), p. 489

60. Bulwer, *England and the English*, Vol. I, pp. 310-14 and appendix A (Popular Education)

61. See p. 19

62. Report on the Enquiry into the general state of the Poor. Instituted by order of the last Epiphany General Quarter Session for Hampshire, *Annals of Agriculture and other useful arts*, collected and published by Arthur Young, vol. XXV (1796), p. 380

63. For Kay's views, see also p. 15

64. "Diffusion of Knowledge", *Edinburgh Review* vol. XLV (1826-7), pp. 195-6

65. "Mechanics' Institutes and Middle Schools", *Quarterly Review*, Vol. XXXII (1825), p. 425

66. *Westminster Review*, vol. II (1824), pp. 109-10

67. See the argument in Bulwer, *England and the English*, Vol. I, pp. 233-4

68. "Scientific Education of the People", *Edinburgh Review*, Vol. XLI (1824-5); "High Church opinions on Popular Education", vol. XLII (1825); "Diffusion of Knowledge", Vol. XLV (1826-7); "Society for the Diffusion of Useful Knowledge", Vol. XLVI (1827); "Pestalozzi—Diffusion of Knowledge", Vol. XLVII (1828)

69. See pp. 49-50

70. H. Brougham, *Practical Observations upon the education of the people, addressed to the working classes and their employers* (1825)

71. Ibid, pp. 29-30

72. See, for example, "'Mr. Brougham—Education Committee", *Quarterly Review*, vol. XIX (1818), pp.492-577

73. D. Owen, *English Philanthropy 1660-1960*, pp. 189-90. This paragraph is based on Owen's discussion, pp. 182-91

74. E.P. Thompson, *The Making of the English Working Class*, pp. 340-2. See T. Percival, *Works*, Vol. I, pp. cclvii-cclviii; F.M. Eden, *State of the Poor*, Vol. I, pp. 420-2

75. *Parliamentary Papers*, 1816, pp. 554, 557, 558

76. Ibid, p. 307

77. Ibid, pp. 581, 582

78. Ibid, pp. 459-60

79. Ibid, p. 363

80. Ibid p. 523

81. Ibid, pp. 254-6, 324-5, 328-9

82. See, for example, the evidence of Kinder Wood, surgeon of Oldham, ibid, pp. 429-46, and of Matthew Baillie, M.D., pp. 263-6

83. See p. 48

84. Moss's evidence in ibid, pp. 416-23. Several other witnesses testified to his good reputation and high standing, e.g. W. Taylor, manager of Horrocks, Miller and Co. of Preston, ibid, p. 504

85. John Howard, *The State of the prisons in England and Wales, with preliminary observations and an account of some foreign prisons and hospitals* (3rd. ed., Warrington, 1784), pp. 36, 41, 469; see also S. and B. Webb, *English Prisons under local government* (1922), p. 37

86. EA.L. Moir, "Sir George Onesiphorus Paul", *Gloucestershire Studies*, ed. H.P.R. Finberg (Leicester, 1957)

87. Bettering Society, *Reports*, vol. I (1798), p. 53

88. For Becher, see pp. 47, 72-4

89. See his evidence to the select committee on the laws relating to penitentiary houses, 13, 15 March, 1811, *Parliamentary Papers*, 1810-11, III, pp. 601-7

90. S. and B. Webb, *Prisons*, pp. 47-8; W.W. Clay, *The Prison chaplain: a memoir of John Clay*, pp. 75-6

91. S. and B. Webb, *Prisons*, pp. 66-7, 71. 'Neild on prisons", *Edinburgh Review*, vol. XXII (1813-14) is a review of Neild's book.

92. L. Radzinowicz, *A History of English criminal law*, vol. I, p. 525

93. Ibid, pp. 606-7

94. H. Perkin, *The Origins of Modern English Society 1780-1880* (1969), pp. 167 ff.; J.J. Tobias, *Crime and industrial society in the nineteenth century* (Penguin Books ed., 1972), p. 295

95. See p. 67-9

96. "Police", *Quarterly Review*, Vol. XXXVII (1828), p. 503

97. ,L. Radzinowicz, *History of English criminal law*, vol. IV (1968), p. 159; E. Halévy, *The Liberal Awakening 1815-1830* (Eng. trans., 3rd. imp.), pp. 287-8

98. S. and B. Webb, *Prisons*, p. 73

99. Ibid. pp. 111-12; S. and B. Webb, *Statutory Authorities for special purposes* (1922), p. 462

100. S. and B. Webb, *Prisons*, pp. 97-8

101. "Prisons and Prison Discipline", *Encyclopaedia Britannica. Supplement to the Fourth, Fifth, and Sixth Editions*, Vol. VI (Edinburgh, 1824)

102. See also the very similar argument in "Prisons and Prison Discipline", *Westminster Review* Vol. III (1825)

103. See W.W. Clay, *The Prison Chaplain: A Memoir of the Rev. John Clay, B.D., late chaplain to the Preston gaol* (Cambridge and London, 1861)

104. Ibid, p. 148

105. Ibid, p. 120

106. S. and B. Webb, *The Manor and the Borough*, Part II (1908), p. 483

107. S. and B. Webb, *Statutory Authorities for special purposes*, pp. 242-3, 346

108. The following paragraphs are based on Conrad Gill, *History of Birmingham*, Vol. I, *Manor and Borough to 1865* (1952), chs. VIII, IX, XV

109. Ibid, pp. 183-4

110. The following is based on A. Redford and I.S. Russell, *History of Local Government in Manchester*, Vol. I, *Manor and Township* (1939), chs. IX-XIII

111. Ibid, p. 291

Notes to Chapter Five

1. 'It is impossible to be certain whether the level of crime increased in the last half of the eighteenth century and the first half of the nineteenth century. However, it seems almost certain that the upsurge of population growth in a more slowly changing economic and social environment provided great opportunities for crime and weakened many of the barriers against crime, and that reverse movement occurred as the new form of urban industrial society evolved'. (J.J. Tobias, *Crime and industrial society in the nineteenth century* (Penguin ed., 1972, p. 295

2. See pp. 35, 84-6

3. See pp. 37-8

4. Neil J. Smelser, *Social change in the industrial revolution. An application of theory to the Lancashire cotton industry 1770-1840* (1959), p. 218

5. John Foster, *Class struggle and the industrial revolution. Early industrial capitalism in three English towns* (1974), p. 83

6. Report of the Commissioners for inquiring into the condition of the unemployed hand-loom weavers in the United Kingdom, *Parliamentary Papers*, 1841, X

7. Foster, *Class struggle and the industrial revolution*, p. 95

8. Fr. Engels, *The Condition of the working class in England*, trans. and ed. by W.O. Henderson and W.H. Chaloner, (2nd. ed., Oxford: Blackwell, 1971), p. 131

9. J.T. Ward, *The Factory Movement, 1830-1855*, (1962), p. 192

10. From *Sir Thomas More: or, Colloquies on the progress and prospects of society* (2 vols. 1829), quoted in B.I. Coleman, ed., *The Idea of the city in nineteenth-century Britain* (1973), p. 61

11. E.J. Hobsbawm, *Industry and Empire. The Making of Modern English Society*, Vol. II 1750 to the present day (1968), p. 101

12. G.R. Porter, *The Progress of the Nation, in its various social and economical relations, from the beginning of the nineteenth century* (3rd ed., 1851), p. xxi (from the preface to the second edition of 1846)

13. Ibid, p. 651

14. Evidence to the select committee on criminal and destitute juveniles, quoted in B.I. Coleman (ed.), *The Idea of the city in nineteenth-century Britain*, pp. 133-4

15. *Sanitary Enquiry: England. Local Reports on the sanitary condition of the labouring population of England, in consequence of an enquiry directed to be made by the Poor Law Commissioners* (1842), pp. 138-9

16. Ibid, p. 56

17. Report from the select committee on education in England and Wales, *Parliamentary Papers*, 1835, VII, p. 797:342

18. Report from the select committee on

the education of the poorer classes in England and Wales, *Parliamentary Papers*, 1837-8, VII, p. 195:178

19. Children's Employment Commission. Second report of the commissioners (trades and manufactures), *Parliamentary Papers*, 1843, XIII, p. 507:961

20. *Sanitary Enquiry: England. Local Reports*, p. 52

21. First Report of the commissioners for inquiring into the state of large towns and populous districts, *Parliamentary Papers*, 1844, XVII, p. 43:219

22. W. Lee, *Report to the General Board of Health on a preliminary inquiry into the sewerage, drainage, and supply of water, and the sanitary condition of the inhabitants of the townships of Rotherham and Kimberworth* (1851), p. 11. This is one of a collection of reports to the General Board of Health in the University Library, Sheffield.

23. The phrase comes from *Sanitary Enquiry: England. Local Reports*, p. 191 (report of J.P. Kennedy and Edward Senior on the parish of Breadsall, Derbyshire.) See also ibid, pp. 150-1 (Edward Twistleton on labourers' cottages in Norfolk and Suffolk), 330 (Baron Howard on the poor of Manchester).

24. See S.E. Finer, *The Life and times of Sir Edwin Chadwick* (1952), book VI

25. V. Cromwell, "Interpretations of nineteenth-century administration: an analysis", *Victorian Studies*, vol. IX (1965-6), p. 253

26. D. Roberts, *Victorian Origins of the British Welfare State*. (New Haven, 1960), p. 278

27. A useful series of studies is G. Sutherland (ed.), *Studies in the growth of nineteenth-century government* (1972), which examines a number of different departments.

28. See O. MacDonagh, *A Pattern of government growth 1800-60* (1961)

29. See pp. 41-2

30. For an analsis of the inspectorate as a whole, see D. Roberts, *Victorian Origins of the British Welfare State*, pp. 152 ff.

31. See also J. Roach, "Jelinger Cookson Symons 1809-1860", *Letter of the Corpus [Christi College, Cambridge] Association*, no. 51 (1972), pp. 15-25

32. Children's Employment Commission. Appendix to the Second Report of the Commissioners (Trade and Manufactures), Part I, Reports and Evidence from sub-commissioners. *Par-*

liamentary Papers, 1843, XIV, p. 439

33. J.C. Symons, *Tactics for the times: as regards the condition and treatment of the dangerous classes* (1849), pp. 183-4

34. E. Halévy, *History of the English people in the nineteenth century—III The Triumph of reform 1830-1841*, pp. 7, 9, 15

35. See D. Williams, *John Frost. A Study in Chartism* (1939, repr. 1969)

36. J.T. Ward, *Chartism* (1973), pp. 136-7

37. S. Pollard, *A History of Labour in Sheffield* (1959), p.. 47: M. Walton, *Sheffield. Its Story and its achievements (1948)*, pp. 175-6

38. J.T. Ward, *Chartism*, pp. 162-3

39. See p. 40

40. Report from the Select Committee on Education in England and Wales, *Parliamentary Papers*, 1835, VII, p. 851: 939, 940

41. L. Robbins, *The Theory of economic policy in English classical political economy* (1952), pp. 79-80

42. William Lovett, *Life and Struggles of . . . in his pursuit of bread, knowledge and freedom, with some short account of the different associations he belonged to and of the opinions he entertained* (1967 ed., with preface by R.H. Tawney).

43. Ibid, p. 55

44. Ibid, pp. 205-7

45. Ibid, pp. 239, 279, 305

46. Ibid, p. 275 (from an address to the French Republic, 1848)

47. Ibid, p. 279

48. J. Foster, *Class Struggle and the industrial revolution*, p. 191

49. W.L. Clay, *The Prison Chaplain: A Memoir of the Rev. John Clay, B.D.*, p. 503

50. B. Harrison, "Two Roads to social reform: Francis Place and the 'Drunken Committee' of 1834", *Historical Journal* vol. 11 (1968), p. 296. Place, Harrison says, 'violently attacked temperance reformers who "instead of endeavouring to make a man have a higher notion of his own respectability and moral consequence, endeavour to make him humble—a canter—a coward, and a grovelling slave." Humility among working people was precisely the sentiment Place wished to remove . . .'

51. J.F.C. Harrison, *The Early Victorians 1832-51* (1971), p. 139

52. See Clyde Binfield, *George Williams and the Y.M.C.A. A Study in Victorian Social attitudes* (1973)

53. B. Harrison, *Drink and the Victorians. The Temperance question in England*

1815-1872 (1971), p. 117
54. Ibid, p. 150
55. Fr. Engels, *The Condition of the working class in England* (1971 ed.), p. 202
56. S. and B. Webb, *English Local Government . . . the Parish and the County*, pp. 586-8
57. For these and similar bodies see P.H.J.H. Gosden, *Self-Help. Voluntary Associations in nineteenth-century Britain* (1973)
58. A useful study is B. Harrison "Philanthropy and the Victorians", *Victorian Studies*, Vol. IX (1965-66), pp. 353-74
59. See p. 41
60. G. Kitson Clark, *Churchmen and the condition of England 1832-1885. A Study in the development of social ideas and practice from the old regime to the modern state* (1973), pp. 208-9
61. What follows about the Quakers is taken from E. Isichei, *Victorian Quakers* (1970), Part II, passim

Notes to Chapter Six

1. See pp. 59-65
2. G. Kitson Clark, *Churchmen and the condition of England 1832-1885*, p. 151
3. S.E. Finer, *The Life and Times of Sir Edwin Chadwick* (1952), pp. 48, 70-1
4. A useful modern edition is E. Chadwick, *Report on the sanitary condition of the labouring population of Great Britain*, ed. M.W. Flinn (Edinburgh, 1965)
5. D. Roberts, *Victorian Origins of the British welfare state*, pp. 31-2
6. R.A. Lewis, *Edwin Chadwick and the public health movement 1832-1854* (1952), p. 80
7. Ibid, pp. 96-7
8. Ibid, pp. 260-1
9. Finer, *Chadwick*, p. 479
10. R.A. Lewis, *Edwin Chadwick and the public health movement*, p. 373
11. See pp. 66-74
12. Report from His Majesty's Commissioners for inquiring into the administration and practical operation of the poor laws, *Parliamentary Papers*, 1834, XXVII, p. 8. The references are given to this volume of parliamentary papers. A convenient modern edition of the report is *The Poor Law Report of 1834*, ed. S.G. and E.O.A. Checkland (Penguin Books, 1974)
13. *PP*, 1834, XXVII, p. 24
14. Ibid, p. 31
15. Ibid, p. 127
16. Ibid, p. 131; for the Nottinghamshire poor law reformers, see pp. 72-4
17. *PP*, 1834, XXVII, p. 157
18. Ibid, p. 192
19. S. and B. Webb, *English Poor Law History:* Part II: *The Last hundred years*, pp. 45-6
20. *PP*, 1834, XXVII, p. 187
21. G.R. Porter, *The Progress of the Nation* (3rd ed., 1851) p. 92
22. S.E. Finer, *Chadwick*, Book VI, ch. II
23. Ibid, p. 92
24. E.W. Martin, "From Parish to Union. Poor Law Administration 1601-1865" in *Comparative Development in Social Welfare*, ed. E.W. Martin (1972), p. 40
25. See E.C. Midwinter, *Social Administration in Lancashire 1830-1860. Poor Law, Public Health and Police* (1969); R. Boyson, "The New Poor Law in North-east Lancashire 1834-71", *Transactions of the Lancashire and Cheshire Antiquarian Society*, Vol. LXX (1960), pp. 35-56
26. P. Dunkley, 'The "Hungary Forties" and the new poor law: a case study', *Historical Journal*, Vol. 17 (1974), pp. 329-46
27. E. Halévy, *The Triumph of Reform 1830-1841*, p. 120; Finer, *Chadwick*, p. 46
28. W.P. Alison, *Observations on the management of the poor in Scotland, and its effect on the health of the great towns* (1840)
29. *PP*, 1834, XXVII, p. 205
30. S. and B. Webb, *English Poor Law History*: Part II: *The last hundred years*, pp. 70-71
31. Report from select committee on the state of education; with the minutes of evidence, and index, *Parliamentary Papers*, 1834, IX, p. 106:1327. See also the evidence of William Wilson, vicar of Walthamstow, ibid, p. 173:2217, and in the report of the select committee of 1837-8, the evidence of Kay-Shuttleworth, *Parliamentary Papers* 1837-8, VII, pp. 195-6: 180 and of J.C. Wigram, secretary of the National Society, ibid, p. 244: 680, 681
32. *PP*, 1834, IX, p. 44:494
33. Ibid, p. 188:2408
34. Ibid, p. 197:2488
35. Report from the select committee on the education of the poorer classes in England and Wales: together with the minutes of evidence, and index, *Parliamentary Papers*, 1837-8, VII, p. 195:178
36. Ibid, pp. 204-5:248

37. M.W. Thomas, *The Early Factory Legislation*, pp. 168-71
38. Ibid, pp. 182-3
39. Ibid, pp. 218-9
40. *PP*, 1834, IX, pp. 224-5: 2821; 225-6:2825
41. G.R. Porter, *The Progress of the Nation* (3rd ed.), p. 684
42. Report of the Commissioners for inquiring into the condition of the unemployed hand-loom weavers in the United Kingdom, *Parliamentary Papers*, 1841, X, pp. 400-1
43. W. Lovett, *Life and Struggles*, pp. 112, 116
44. See pp. 215-18
45. E.P. Hennock, *Fit and Proper Persons. Ideal and reality in nineteenth-century urban government* (1973), p. 4
46. See E. P. Hennock, "Finance and Politics in urban local government in England, 1835-1900", *Historical Journal*, vol. 6 (1963), pp. 212-25
47. For a discussion of the position of the boroughs under the act of 1835, see S. and B. Webb, *The Manor and the Borough*, Part II (1908), pp. 753-5
48. J.J. Tobias, *Crime and industrial society in the 19th cent.*, p. 295; see also p. 90
49. G.R. Porter, *The Progress of the nation* (3rd ed.), p. 635
50. S. and B. Webb, *English Prisons under local government* (1922), pp. 111-2
51. W.L. Clay, *The Prison Chaplain*, pp. 187-8
52. Ibid, pp. 284-5, 300, 520
53. Ibid, pp. 373-5
54. D. Owen, *English Philanthropy 1660-1960*, pp. 153-6
55. C. Reith, *British Police and the democratic ideal* (1943), p. 166
56. Ibid, p. 213
57. Ibid, p. 228
58. For a general survey see Jenifer Hart, "Reform of the borough police, 1835-1856", *English Historical Review*, Vol. LXX (1955), pp. 411-27. For conditions in Lancashire see E.C. Midwinter, *Social Administration in Lancashire*, pp. 158-9, 164
59. First Report of the commissioners appointed to inquire as to the best means of establishing an efficient constabulary force in the counties of England and Wales, *Parliamentary Papers*, 1839, XIX
60. *PP*, 1839, XIX, p. 183
61. Ibid, p, 158:231
62. Ibid, p. 181:294
63. See p. 171 for the Act of 1856
64. *PP*, 1839, XIX, p. 177
65. Ibid, pp. 38-9:38
66. Ibid, p. 187:302

Notes to Chapter Seven

1. Jenifer Hart, "Reform of the borough police, 1835-1856", *English Historical Review*, Vol. LXX, pp. 426-7
2. W. Lovett, *Life and Struggles*, p. 180
3. See p. 125
4. J. Foster, *Class Struggle and the Industrial Revolution*, p. 60
5. J.T. Ward, *Chartism*, pp. 96 ff., and see A. Briggs (ed.) *Chartist Studies* (1959), passim
6. See J. Salt "Isaac Ironside 1808-1870: The Motivation of a Radical Educationist", *British Journal of Educational Studies*, Vol. XIX, pp. 183-201; and "Experiments in Anarchism, 1850-1854", *Transactions of the Hunter Archaelogical Society*, Vol. 10, pp. 37-53
7. See pp. 104-5
8. B. Harrison "Teetotal Chartism", *History*, Vol. 58 (1973), p. 214
9. *PP*, 1841, X, pp. 316-7, 322-3, 396
10. See the discussion in N. J. Smelser, *Social Change in the Industrial Revolution*, pp. 189 ff., 231 ff.
11. Ibid, p. 240
12. See p. 134
13. Smelser, *Social Change*, p. 241
14. J.T. Ward, *The Factory Movement 1830-1855*, p. 219
15. C. Driver, *Tory Radical. The life of Richard Oastler* (1946), pp. 296-8
16. Ibid, p. 225
17. Ibid, p. 328
18. See A.M. Hadfield, *The Chartist Land Company* (1970) for a general study of the Chartist estates.
19. See pp. 77-80
20. A convenient study is that of M.W. Thomas, *The Early Factory Legislation: A Study in legislative and administrative evolution* (1948)
21. Report from the Select Committee on the "Bill to regulate the Labour of Children in the Mills and Factories of the United Kingdom";—with the Minutes of Evidence, Appendix and Index, *Parliamentary Papers*, 1831-2, XV, p. 463:9852
22. Ibid, pp. 492:10280-1; 493:10284
23. An example of this is the following question to Mr. Sharp, surgeon of Bradford. 'Speaking as a medical man of considerable practice in that town and neighbourhood, do you not believe

that the long labour of the children in factories, confined as they must necessarily be to constant attention and work, and for so great a length of time, with so few and short intermissions, has a direct tendency to injure their health, to cripple their limbs, and to shorten their lives?' *PP* 1831-2, XV, p. 303:7114

24. Second Report of the Central Board of His Majesty's Commissioners appointed to collect information in the Manufacturing Districts, as to the employment of Children in Factories, and as to the propriety and means of curtailing the hours of their labour: with Minutes of Evidence, and Reports by the Medical Commissioners. *Parliamentary Papers*, 1833, XXI, p. 124

25. First Report of the Central Board of His Majesty's Commissioners for inquiring into the Employment of Children in Factories, *Parliamentary Papers*, 1833, XX, p. 36

26. *PP* 1833, XX, p. 56

27. *PP*, 1833, XX, p. 67

28. P. Gaskell, *The Manufacturing Population of England, its moral, social and physical conditions, and the changes which have arisen from steam machinery; with an examination of infant labour* (1833). His *Artisans and Machinery; the moral and physical condition of the manufacturing population considered with reference to mechanical substitutes for human labour* (1836) is really a second edition of the same. A Ure, *The Philosophy of Manufactures; or, an exposition of the scientific, moral, and commercial economy of the factory system of Great Britain* (1835). Ure's book has been reprinted in the Cass Library of Industrial Classics (1967), and *Artisans and Machinery* in the same (1968)

29. P. Gaskell, *The Manufacturing Population of England*, p. 358

30. A. Ure, *The Philosophy of Manufactures*, p. 2

31. Ibid, p. 15

32. Ibid, p. 301

33. Ibid, p. 417

34. Children's Employment Commission. First Report of the Commissioners. Mines. *Parliamentary Papers* 1842, XV, pp. 121-2: 424-5 (North Durham and Northumberland).

35. Children's Employment Commission. Second Report of the Commissioners. Trades and Manufactures, *Parliamentary Papers*, 1843, XIII, p. 374:311

36. *PP*, 1842, XV, p. 29:89

37. Ibid, pp. 50-1:167-71

38. Ibid, pp. 104:360; 106:361

39. T.C. Smout, *A History of the Scottish People, 1560-1830* (Fontana ed. 1972), p. 406

40. *PP*, 1842, XV, p. 188:744

41. Ibid, pp. 151:554-5; 155-6:578

42. Ibid, pp. 203-5:791-9, 801

43. *PP*, 1843, XIII, p. 424:560

44. Ibid, pp. 380:336; 383:346; 392:394; 419-20:535-6

45. Ibid, pp. 404-8: 455-70

46. Ibid, p. 438:623

47. *PP*, 1843, XIII, p. 468:479

48. Ibid, p. 479:830

49. Ibid, p. 578:1016

50. Ibid, p. 528

51. W.C. Lubenow, *The Politics of Government Growth. Early Victorian Attitudes towards state intervention 1838-1848* (1971), p. 116. The important question of the impact of railways on social policy will be discussed in Ch. VIII.

52. V. Cromwell "Interpretations of nineteenth century administration: an analysis", *Victorian Studies*, Vol. IX (1965-6), p. 254. She calls the period 1850-70 'One of administrative quiescence in terms of the development of new executive machinery'.

53. See p. 112

54. E. Chadwick, *Report on the Sanitary Condition of the Labouring Population of Great Britain*, ed. M.W. Flinn (1965), p. 79

55. Finer, *Chadwick*, pp. 222-4

56. Ibid, p. 221

57. Ibid, pp. 230-1; R.A. Lewis, *Chadwick and the Public Health Movement*, pp. 68-75

58. See *Sanitary Enquiry . . . Local Reports*, p. 127 on cottages in the Ampthill Union, Bedfordshire

59. Chadwick, *Sanitary Report*, p. 124

60. Ibid, pp. 147-8

61. Ibid, p. 268

62. *Sanitary Enquiry . . . Local Reports*, pp. 206-7

63. Ibid, pp. 236, 240

64. For Duncan's report on Liverpool, see ibid, pp. 283 ff. He provided a further report in First Report of the Commissioners for inquiring into the state of large towns and populous districts, *Parliamentary Papers* 1844, XVII, pp. 517 ff. Chadwick's figures of mortality in Liverpool are in *Sanitary Report*, p. 225

65. *Sanitary Enquiry . . . Local Reports*, p. 293

66. Chadwick, *Sanitary Report*, pp. 399,

405-7

67. e.g. Mr. Richard Kelsey, surveyor to the City of London Commissioners of sewers. First Report of the commissioners for inquiring into the state of large towns and populous districts, *Parliamentary Papers* 1844, XVII, pp. 229-30: 3437, 3439, 3441; 232:3486-92

68. Ibid, XVII, p. 103: 1022
69. Ibid, XVII, p. 97: 988
70. Ibid, pp. 96-7: 977
71. Ibid, pp. 89-90:923
72. Ibid, p. 97:989. Lyon Playfair made a similar comment (Second Report of the Commissioners... appendix Part II, *Parliamentary Papers* 1845, XVIII, p. 372): 'I have forwarded to you a sanatory and criminal map of Preston, in which you will see, that where the physical causes of diseases most abound, there crime also prevails to the greatest extent. The inspectors of prisons in Scotland, from separate enquiries, have also come to the conclusion, that the physical causes of disease indirectly become the causes of crime'.
73. *PP*, 1844, XVII, p. 103:1014
74. Ibid, p. 101:1010
75. Ibid, p. 348:5467
76. E.P. Hennock, *Fit and Proper Persons*, pp. 197-9. His plan was rejected in 1844 though eventually a sewerage scheme was constructed on a plan which was a modified version of his.
77. Second Report of the Commissioners for inquiring into the state of large towns and populous districts, *Parliamentary Papers*, 1845, XVIII, p. 12
78. I have taken the details of the Act from R.A. Lewis, *Chadwick and the Public Health Movement*, pp. 172-3
79. Finer, *Chadwick*, p. 324
80. Lewis, *Chadwick and the Public Health Movement*, pp. 290-1
81. E.C. Midwinter, *Social Administration in Lancashire 1830-1860*, p. 85
82. E.P. Hennock, *Fit and Proper Persons*, pp. 191 ff.
83. E.C. Midwinter, op. cit., pp. 82-3
84. See H.J. Smith, "Local Reports to the General Board of Health", *History*, Vol. 56 (1971), pp. 46-9
85. W. Lee, *Report to the General Board of Health on a preliminary inquiry into the sewerage, drainage, and supply of water, and the sanitary condition of the inhabitants of the townships of Rotherham and Kimberworth* (1851), p. 28. (From a collection of *Reports to the General Board of Health*, in the University Library, Sheffield.)

86. W. Lee, *Report . . . in Rotherham*, p. 37
87. Finer, *Chadwick*, p. 447

Notes to Chapter Eight

1. See W.L. Burn, *The Age of Equipoise. A Study of the mid-Victorian generation* (1964)
2. Ibid, p. 71
3. 'The triumph of mechanical art and of commercial associations was so complete as to furnish some excuse for the optimists, who found in the concourse of sight-seeing foreigners a pledge of universal and perpetual peace'. *Annual Summaries reprinted from the Times*, Vol. I (1851-75), (1893), p. 70
4. Quoted in Katherine Chorley, *Manchester made them* (1950), p. 182
5. Valerie E. Chancellor (ed.), *Master and Artisan in Victorian England. The Diary of William Andrews and the Autobiography of Joseph Gutteridge* (1969), p. 142 (from Gutteridge's autobiography)
6. Elizabeth Isichei, *Victorian Quakers* (1970), pp 221-4 Asa Briggs, *Victorian People* (Penguin Books ed., 1965), p. 223
7. Burn, *Age of Equipoise*, p. 82
8. John Prest, *Lord John Russell* (1972), p. 326, makes the point that, by 1851, the reformed parliament of 1832 had done as much as it could and that further changes would have to await an extension of the franchise
9. See Jo Manton, *Elizabeth Garrett Anderson* (1965)
10. E. Moberly Bell, *Josphine Butler, Flame of Fire* (1962), pp. 82-3
11. W. M. Frazer, *A History of English Public Health 1834-1939* (1950), p. 202
12. B.A. Clough *A Memoir of Anne Jemima Clough* (new ed., 1903) pp. 118-21
13. Shena D. Simon, *A Century of City Government. Manchester 1838-1938* (1938), p. 209
14. I have tried to work out this connexion in my book, *Public Examinations in England 1850-1900* (Cambridge, 1971)
15. Schools Inquiry Commission, Vol. IX, General Reports by Assistant Commissioners. Northern Counties, *PP* 1867-68, XXVIII, Pt. 8, p. 148
16. Patrick Joyce, "The Factory Politics of Lancashire in the later nineteenth century", *Historical Journal*, Vol. 18 (1975), pp. 525-53
17. See Asa Briggs, "The Language of 'Class'" in early nineteenth-century England", in Asa Briggs and John Saville

(eds.), *Essays in Labour History in memory of G.D.H. Cole* (1967). Palmerston's speech is quoted on p. 71

18. There has been a good deal of recent writing on the Act of 1867; see M. Cowling, *1867* (1967); F.B. Smith, *The Making of the Second Reform Act* (1966); R. Harrison, *Before the Socialists* (1965)

19. Paul Smith, *Disraelian Conservatism and Social Reform* (1967). The following paragraph is based on Smith's arguments.

20. Ibid, p. 98

21. Ibid, p. 160

22. Quoted in Paul Smith, *Disraelian Conservatism and Social Reform*, p. 131

23. See Ch. XII for the further development of this argument

24. E.J. Hobsbawm, *Industry and Empire. The Making of Modern English Society*, Vol. II (1750 to the present day) (1968), p. 133

25. See the evidence adduced in Geoffrey Best, *Mid-Victorian Britain 1851-1875* (1971), pp. 80-2

26. F.M.L. Thompson, *English Landed Society in the nineteenth century* (1963), p. 8. I have made extensive use of Professor Thompson's arguments in what I have said about the aristocracy.

27. See J. Roach, *Public Examinations in England, 1850-1900*, pp. 206, 212-3

28. F.M.L. Thompson, *English Landed Society in the nineteenth century*, p. 289

29. See John Simon, *Public Health Reports* (edited by the Sanitary Institute of Great Britain, 1887), Vol. II

30. B. Rodgers, "The Social Science Association, 1857-1886", *The Manchester School of Economic and Social Studies*, Vol. XX (1952), pp. 283-310. The *Transactions* of the association are a valuable source of information on all these subjects.

31. See Olive Anderson, "The Administrative Reform Association 1855-1857", in Patricia Hollis (ed.), *Pressure from without in early Victorian England* (1974)

32. Royston Lambert, *Sir John Simon (1816-1904) and English social administration*, pp. 530, 540-1, 571. The subject of public health is dealt with in Ch. X below.

33. W.M. Frazer, *A History of English Public Health 1834-1939*, pp. 98-9; Anthony S. Wohl, "Unfit for human habitation", and George Rosen, "Disease, Debility and Death", both in H.J. Dyos and M. Woolf (ed.), *The Victorian City. Images and Realities*, vol. 2 (1973)

34. Roy M. MacLeod, "The Alkali Acts Administration, 1863-84: The

emergence of the civil scientist", *Victorian Studies* Vol. IX (1965-66), pp. 85-112. See also the comment in G. Kitson Clark, *An Expanding Society* (1967), p. 169

35. Roy M. MacLeod, "Resources of science in Victorian England: the endowment of science movement, 1868-1900", in P. Mathias (ed.), *Science and Society 1600-1900* (Cambridge, 1972), pp. 111-66

36. J.F. Stephen to Lord Lytton, 1 October 1879 (J.F. Stephen MSS., Cambridge University Library)

37. There is a modern edition of *Liberty, Equality, Fraternity* edited by R.J. White (Cambridge, 1967)

38. Alistair Buchan, *The Spare Chancellor. The Life of Walter Bagehot* (1959), p. 136

39. Walter Bagehot, *Physics and Politics* (6th ed., 1883), p. 194

40. See the discussion of philanthropy in Ch. V, pp. 108-9

41. For the Charity Organization Society, see pp. 179-80

42. For the enquiry into the Sheffield outrages, see *Parliamentary Papers* 1867, XXXII. There is a modern edition, *The Sheffield Outrages*, with an introduction by Sidney Pollard (1971)

43. First Report of the commissioners appointed to inquire into the organization and rules of Trades Unions and other associations together with Minutes of Evidence, *Parliamentary Papers* 1867, XXXII, p. 14:108, 111

44. T.H. Green, *Lectures on the Principles of political obligation*, with an introduction by A.D. Lindsay (1941), p. 8

45. Ibid, p. 122

46. W.L. Burn, *Age of Equipoise*, pp. 209-10; S.W.F. Holloway, "Medical Education in England, 1830-1858", *History*, Vol. XLIX (1964), pp. 299-324

47. S. and B. Webb, *English Prisons under Local Government* (1922), p. 201. On prison policy see also pp. 223-5 below.

48. W.L. Burn, op. cit., pp. 199-202; J. Roach, *Public Examinations in England, 1850-1900*, pp. 230-1

49. Tom Taylor, "On central and local action in relation to town improvement", *Transactions of the National Association for the promotion of social science*, 1857, pp. 476, 480

50. Lord Robert Montagu argued that vestries and boards of guardians had been unwilling to provide food and medicine for the poor . . . 'How, then, was it likely that they would burden the rates in order to provide education for the children of the poor?' *(Hansard, 3rd*

ser., vol. 19°:473 and 1993)

Mr. A.F. Egerton described the election of a parish schoolmaster where three candidates presented themselves ... 'one being a very decent man, the second a drunken tailor or shoemaker, and the third a tolerably decent man. Well, a very exciting contest occurred, and it resulted in the election of the drunken shoemaker'. *(Hansard, 3rd. ser.,* Vol. 202:1021

51. E.P. Hennock, *Fit and Proper Persons. Ideal and Reality in nineteenth-century urban government,* pp. 222-3

52. Mrs. Webb's diary of autumn 1899, quoted in Shena D. Simon, *A Century of city government. Manchester 1838-1938* (1938), pp. 400-1

53. On Birmingham, see E.P. Hennock, *Fit and Proper Persons:* Asa Briggs, *Victorian Cities* (1963); C. Gill and A. Briggs, *History of Birmingham,* 2 vols. (1952)

54. See F. Adams, *History of the Elementary School Contest in England* (reprinted 1972, with an introduction by Asa Briggs)

55. Quoted in E.P. Hennock, op. cit., p. 321

56. Quoted in W. M. Frazer, *A History of English Public Health 1834-1939,* p. 139

57. See pp. 127-8

58. T.A. Critchley, *A History of Police in England and Wales, 1900-1966* (1967), p. 89

59. Ibid, pp. 110-1

60. Jenifer Hart, "The County and Borough Police Act 1856", *Public Administration* Vol. XXXIV (1956), p. 406

61. Shena D. Simon, *A Century of city government,* pp. 333-4

62. J. Hart, *Public Administration,* Vol. XXXIV, pp. 406-7; L. Radzinowicz, *A History of English Criminal Law and its administration from 1750;* Vol. 4, *Grappling for Control* (1968), pp. 295-7

63. T.A. Critchley, op. cit., p. 119

64. H. Parris, "The Home Office and the Provincial Police in England and Wales—1856-1870", *Public Law* 1961, pp. 241-2

65. Ibid, pp. 233-6

66. W.L. Burn, *Age of Equipoise,* pp. 175-6

67. T.A. Critchley, op. cit., p. 133

68. H. Parris, *Government and the railways in nineteenth-century Britain* (1965), pp. 61, 83-6

69. G.R. Porter, *The Progress of the Nation* (3rd ed., 1851), pp. 333-4

70. H. Parris, *Government and the railways,* pp. 209-10

71. See John R. Kellett, *The Impact of railways on Victorian cities* (1969)

72. J.H. Dyos, "Railways and housing in Victorian London", *Journal of Transport History,* Vol. II (1955-56), p. 14

73. See pp. 204-8 below

74. John R. Kellett, op. cit. p. 52

Notes to Chapter Nine

1. B. Harrison, *Drink and the Victorians. The Temperance question in England 1815-1872,* pp. 197-8, and see pp. 175-6 below

2. S.E. Maltby, *Manchester and the movement for national elementary education 1800-1870* (Manchester, 1918); D. K. Jones, "Lancashire, the American Common School, and the religious problem in British education in the nineteenth century", *British Journal of Educational Studies,* Vol. XV (1967), pp. 292-306

3. See p. 108

4. A good brief treatment is G. F. A. Best, *Shaftesbury* (1964). See also J.L. and Barbara Hammond, *Lord Shaftesbury* (4th ed., 1936) and the contemporary life by Edwin Hodder, *Life and Work of the seventh Earl of Shaftesbury K.G.* (3 vols., 1886)

5. See B. Harrison, "State intervention and moral reform in nineteenth-century England", in P. Hollis (ed.), *Pressure from without in early Victorian England* (1974), pp. 316-7

6. J.F. Stephen, *Essays by a Barrister* (1862), p. 43

7. B. Harrison, *Drink and the Victorians,* pp. 212 ff. The subsequent discussion of the teetotal movement is based on Harrison's book.

8. See p. 168

9. B. Harrison, op. cit., pp. 207-10

10. Ibid, p. 295; B. Harrison, "State intervention and moral reform in nineteenth-century England", P. Hollis (ed.), *Pressure from without in early Victorian England,* pp. 304-5

11. B. Harrison, *Drink and the Victorians,* pp. 357, 360

12. Ibid, pp. 277, 295

13. The following account is based on J.L. and B. Hammond, *James Stansfeld. A Victorian champion of sex equality* (1932), and E. Moberly Bell, *Josephine Butler. Flame of Fire* (1962)

14. See pp. 156-7

15. Quoted in E. Moberly Bell, *Josephine Butler,* p. 90

16. Ibid, p. 109 (Mrs. Butler's views in a letter to Henry Wilson of Sheffield,

who took an active part in organizing the campaign)

17. Ibid, p. 164
18. J.L. and B. Hammond, *James Stansfeld*, pp. 200-2, 294
19. B. Harrison, *Drink and the Victorians*, pp. 194, 222, 226
20. G. Kitson Clark argued that 'systematic philanthropy was necessarily a step away from a system based on the ordinary personal service, which anyone can render, towards the creation of a scientifically organized state whose services could only be staffed by professionals'. *(Churchmen and the condition of England 1832-1885* (1973), p. 274)
21. D. Owen, *English Philanthropy 1660-1960*, p. 141
22. Ibid, pp. 460-1; for district nursing, see W.M. Frazer, *A History of English public health 1834-1939*, p. 238
23. For the attitudes of Canon Barnett and Mrs. Webb see p. 227 below.
24. C.L. Mowat, *The Charity Organization Society 1869-1913. Its Ideas and Work* (1961), pp. 26-7 (quoting a district committee's report of 1876). This account of the C.O.S. is based on Mowat's book.
25. Ibid. pp. 48 ff.
26. Ibid, p. 81 (from a paper read by Loch in 1903)
27. See E. Moberly Bell, *Octavia Hill. A Biography* (1942)
28. Samuel Smiles, *Self-Help; with illustrations of conduct and perseverance* (new ed., 1884), p. 342
29. H. Perkin, *The Origins of modern English society 1780-1880*, (1969), pp. 425 ff.
30. For a discussion of Samuel Smiles, see Asa Briggs, *Victorian People* (Penguin Books ed., 1970), Ch. 5
31. S. Smiles, *Self-Help*, p. 312
32. Ibid, p. 293
33. Valerie E. Chancellor (ed.), *Master and Artisan in Victorian England. The Diary of William Andrews and the Autobiography of Joseph Gutteridge* (1969), p. 18
34. P.H.J.H. Gosden, *Self-Help. Voluntary Associations in nineteenth-century Britain* (1973), pp. 78-83
Paul Smith has argued that the act was marked by an unwillingness to interfere in any general way with the individual responsibility of depositors for the safety of their own money *(Disraelian Conservatism and social reform*, pp. 229-30)
35. Gosden, op. cit., pp. 163-4
36. P.H.J.H. Gosden, op. cit., pp. 156, 158; Enid Gauldie, *Cruel Habitations. A*

History of working-class housing 1780-1918 (1974) pp. 198-202
37. P.H.J.H. Gosden, op. cit., pp. 163-4, 175
38. Ibid, pp. 235-8
39. W.L. Burn, *The Age of equipoise*, pp. 152-3
40. P.H.J.H. Gosden, op. cit., pp. 239, 246-7
41. S. Pollard, "Nineteenth-century Co-operation: from community building to shop-keeping", in A. Briggs and J. Saville (eds.), *Essays in Labour history in memory of G.D.H. Cole* (1967), pp. 94-5. This paragraph is largely based on Pollard's article.
42. P.H.J.H. Gosden, op. cit., pp. 191-4
43. Education Commission. Reports of the Assistant Commissioners appointed to inquire into the state of Popular Education in England. 1861. *Parliamentary Papers*, 1861, XXI, Pt. 2, p. 241
44. See pp. 166-7
45. *Annual Summaries reprinted from The Times*, Vol. I (1851-75), (1893), p. 247
46. W.L. Burn, *Age of equipoise* p. 243; S. and B. Webb, *The History of Trade Unionism 1666-1920* (1920), p. 253
47. S. and B. Webb, ibid, p. 262; P. Smith, *Disraelian Conservatism and Social Reform*, p. 45
48. S. and B. Webb, op. cit., p. 365
49. First Report of the Commissioners appointed to enquire into the organization and rules of trades unions and other associations, together with minutes of evidence, *Parliamentary Papers* 1867, XXXII, p. 14:125
50. Ibid, p. 20:266
51. Fourth Report of the Commissioners ...*PP* 1867, XXXII, pp. 298-307
52. Ibid, p. 306:6741
53. Ibid, pp. 344:7327; 345:7337
54. Ibid, p. 354:7371-2
55. Eleventh and Final Report of the Commissioners ... Vol. I, Report, *PP* 1868-9, XXXI, p. 255:64
56. Ibid, p. 257:73-4
57. Ibid, p. 258:83
58. Ibid, p. 259:89
59. Ibid, pp. 259-60:92. The arguments of the majority were carried much further in a draft report proposed by James Booth (ibid, pp. 324-54), which suggested that picketing should be repressed by law and that unions should not be allowed to make permanent by-laws.'We see no reason,' Booth argued, 'why labour should be made an exception from the general system

of free trade, which is now the settled policy of this country; a policy under which it has flourished in a degree unexampled in the history of the world'. (p. 341:96)
60. Ibid. pp. 275-7
61. Ibid, p. 288
62. Ibid, p. 294
63. Ibid, p. 296
64. H.A. Clegg, Alan Fox, A.F. Thompson, *A History of British Trade Unions since 1889* Vol. I (1889-1910) (1964), p. 45
65. Ibid, pp. 45-6; S and B. Webb, *The History of Trade Unionism 1666-1920*, pp. 290-1
66. S. and B. Webb, op. cit., pp. 314-6, 329, 334, 345
67. See pp. 134-5
68. B.L. Hutchins and A. Harrison, *A History of Factory Legislation* (1903), pp. 133-9, 142-5
69. See pp. 138-41
70. First Report from the Commissioners on the employment of children and young persons in trades and manufactures with an appendix, *Parliamentary Papers* 1863, XVIII, p. 55:341
71. B.L. Hutchins and A. Harrison, op. cit., p. 165
72. First Report from the Commissioners . . . *Parliamentary Papers* 1863, XVIII, p. 84:139
73. Third Report from the Commissioners . . . *PP* 1867, XXII, pp. 335-6: 114
74. Fourth Report from the Commissioners . . . *PP* 1865, XX, p. 117:74
75. Sixth Report from the Commissioners . . . *PP* 1867, XVI, pp. 85-6: 78
76. Second Report from the Commissioners . . . *PP* 1864, XXII, p. XVI:121
77. First Report from the Commissioners . . . *PP* 1863, XVIII, pp. 15:72; 27:159; 28:163
78. Third Report from the Commissioners . . . *PP* 1864, XXII, pp. 326-7:35; 331:72
79. Fourth Report from the Commissioners . . . *PP* 1865, XX, pp. 108:14, 15:110-11:26; 112:42
80. Second Report from the Commissioners . . . *PP* 1864, XXII, pp. V:9; VI:13
81. Ibid, p. XXXVII:280; and see also pp. XXI:162; XXV:188
82. Ibid, p. XV:112
83. Third Report from the Commissioners . . . *PP* 1864, XXII, p. 338:145-7
84. Fifth Report from the Commissioners, *PP* 1866, XXIV, p. 26:170, 171

85. B. L. Hutchins and A. Harrison, *A History of Factory Legislation*. p. 155
86. Ibid, pp. 168-171
87. Ibid, pp. 225-31
88. Ibid, p. 176; P. Smith, *Disraelian Conservatism and Social Reform*, p. 214
89. Report of the Commissioners appointed to enquire into the working of the Factory and Workshops Acts with a view to their consolidation and amendment. Vol. I, Report, Appendix and Index, *PP* 1876, XXIX, pp. XIV:15; XVI:20
90. Ibid, p. XCIV:268
91. Ibid pp. XXVI:47; XXIX:55; XXX:58; XXXV: 75
92. Ibid, p. LVIII-LIX:150-1. The age in textiles had been raised to ten by the act of 1874.
93. *PP* 1876, XXIX, pp. LIV:139; LV:142
94. Ibid, p. LVII:147. The Agricultural Children Act (1873) had forbidden the employment of children under the age of eight but it was in practice ineffective (see P. Smith, *Disraelian Conservatism and Social Reform*, p. 177). For agricultural employment, see the First and Second Reports of the Royal Commission on the employment of children, young persons and women in agriculture, *PP* 1867-68, XVII; *PP* 1868-69, XIII
95. B.L. Hutchins and A. Harrison, *A History of Factory Legislation*, pp. 182-3, 190-1, 201
96. *PP* 1876, XXIX, p. LXXVI:210
97. Ibid, pp. LXXXII-LXXXIII:227
98. Ibid p. CXXVIII
99. Ibid, pp. CXXI, CXXII

Notes to Chapter Ten

1. P. Smith, *Disraelian Conservatism and Social Reform*, pp. 164-5
2. W.L. Burn, *Age of Equipoise*, pp. 212-6
3. H. A. Clegg, A. Fox and A. F. Thompson, *A History of British Trade Unions since 1889*, Vol. 1 (1889-1910), p. 36
4. For education in a rural county, see R.R. Sellman, *Devon Village Schools in the nineteenth century* (Newton Abbot, 1967)
5. S. and B. Webb, *English Poor Law History. Part II: The last hundred years*. Vol. I, pp. 219, 221
6. Ibid, pp. 350-1, 364-5
7. Ibid, p. 318
8. J. Simon, *English Sanitary Institutions*,

reviewed in their course of development, and in some of their political and social relations (1890), p. 350

9. S. and B. Webb, op. cit., p. 317
10. W. M. Frazer, *A History of English Public Health 1834-1939*, p. 106; P. Smith, *Disraelian Conservatism and Social Reform*, pp. 63, 114-5
11. D. Owen, *English Philanthropy 1660-1960*, p. 502
12. S. and B. Webb, op. cit., pp. 326-7
13. S. and B. Webb, op. cit., pp. 430-1
14. Ibid. pp. 351, 436, 447-53
15. Ibid, pp. 377-9, 383
16. See pp. 178-80
17. W.M. Frazer, *A History of English public health 1834-1939*, p. 72; R.J. Lambert, "A Victorian National Health Service: State vaccination 1855-71", *Historical Journal*, Vol. 5 (1962), pp. 1-18
18. W.L. Burn, *Age of Equipoise*, pp. 156-7
19. W.M. Frazer, op. cit., p. 78
20. See pp. 203-04 below
21. E. Chadwick, *Report on the Sanitary condition of the labouring population of Great Britain*, ed. M.W. Flinn, p. 396
22. W. M. Frazer, op. cit., pp. 21-2; J. Simon, *English Sanitary Institutions*, p. 240
23. W.M. Frazer (op. cit., pp. 69-70) analyzes five views held by the epidemiologists of the nineteenth century about the mode of transmission of communicable diseases. They begin with the deleterious effect of the impure atmosphere and end with infection by micro-organisms.
24. For a modern treatment of Simon's career see R. Lambert, *Sir John Simon 1816-1904 and English Social Administration* (1963). The ensuing paragraphs on Simon's work in London are based on this book (Part II).
25. J. Simon, *English Sanitary Institutions*, p. 250
26. Extracts from the reports were published in 1887 by the Sanitary Institute of Great Britain as *Public Health Reports. By John Simon, C.B., F.R.S., etc,* 2 vols. edited by Edward Seaton.
27. E. Seaton (ed.), *Public Health Reports by John Simon*, Vol. I, pp. 411-24 contains this report.
28. J. Simon, *English Sanitary Institutions*, p. 252
29. R. Lambert, op. cit., p. 168
30. See p. 164
31. J. Simon, *English Sanitary Institutions*, p. 286
32. R. Lambert, op. cit., pp. 256-7, 392, 446. See also E. Seaton (ed.) *Public*

Health Reports by John Simon, Vol. I, pp. 321-407. The other reports to which reference is made in this paragraph can be found in Vol. II of *Public Health Reports*

33. *Public Health Reports by John Simon*, Vol. II, pp. 262-72
34. Ibid, Vol. II, pp. 350-81
35. Ibid, vol. II, pp. 395-411
36. J. Simon, *English Sanitary Institutions*, pp. 299-300; W.M. Frazer, *A History of English Public Health 1834-1939*, p. 110; P. Smith, *Disraelian Conservatism and Social Reform*, pp. 65-6
37. R.M. Gutchen, "Local improvements and centralization in nineteenth-century England", *Historical Journal*, Vol. 4 (1961), pp. 91-2
38. J. Simon, *English Sanitary Institutions*, pp. 324-5; Royal Commission on sanitary laws. First Report *(Parliamentary Papers* 1868-9, XXXII) contains evidence taken up to 5 August 1869. The second report *(PP* 1871, XXXV) contains the report of the commissioners.
39. *PP*, 1871, XXXV, p. 9
40. Ibid, pp. 28-30
41. Ibid, p. 44
42. They are listed in ibid, pp. 45-57
43. 'Suggestions for a new statute' are contained in ibid, pp. 79-179. They consist of (a) a summary of the existing law and (b) recommendations for change.
44. Ibid, p. 180
45. Ibid, p. 181
46. Ibid, p. 74
47. R. Lambert, *Sir John Simon* p. 559
48. See p. 193
49. J. Simon, *English Sanitary Institutions*, p. 345. On this paragraph see also W.M. Frazer, *A History of English Public Health 1834-1939*, pp. 117, 120, 121 226 (on the adulteration of food).
50. See p. 177
51. For the early years of the Local Government Board, see R. Lambert, *Sir John Simon*, ch. XXII
52. J. Simon, *English Sanitary Institutions*, pp. 373, 386, 388, 391 (the source of the quotation), 399
53. R. Lambert, *Sir John Simon*, p. 571
54. See pp. 169-70
55. E.P. Hennock, *Fit and Proper Persons. Ideal and reality in nineteenth-century urban government*, p. 114
56. E.C. Midwinter, *Social Administration in Lancashire 1830-1860. Poor Law, Public Health and Police*: 'Public Health' passim.
57. Shena D. Simon, *A Century of city gov-*

ernment. Manchester 1838-1938, p. 165. The death-rates per 1,000 were: Birmingham 25.4; Liverpool 30.4; Manchester 33.6

58. Ibid, p. 166
59. Ibid, pp. 178-9, 351-3
60. E.P. Hennock, op. cit., pp. 204-5, 207-8, 210
61. Ibid, pp. 223-4, 226
62. Ibid, pp. 231-4
63. See p. 206 below.
64. S. Pollard, *A History of Labour in Sheffield* (1959), p. 103
65. This is briefly discussed in Ch. XII, though the debate took place after the terminal date of this book (c. 1875-80)
66. For a general discussion of these issues see Gareth Stedman Jones, *Outcast London. A Study in the relationship between classes in Victorian society* (Penguin Books ed., 1976), Part I, passim.
67. See pp. 172-3
68. J. N. Tarn, *Five per cent Philanthropy. An account of housing in urban areas between 1840 and 1914* (Cambridge, 1973)
69. Ibid, pp. 15 ff., 22 ff., D. Owen, *English Philanthropy 1660-1960*, pp. 373-8
70. J.N. Tarn, op. cit., p. 38
71. Ibid, pp. 71-2. For Hole's ideas see J.F.C. Harrison, *Learning and Living 1790-1860. A Study in the history of the English adult education movement* (1961), pp. 119-37
72. J.N. Tarn, op. cit., pp. 45, 50, 56-7
73. Ibid, p. 58
74. Enid Gauldie, *Cruel Habitations. A History of working-class housing 1780-1918*, pp. 138-9
75. J.N. Tarn, op. cit., p. 73
76. Ibid, pp. 62-4
77. The Torrens Act had been influenced by the Social Science Association. P. Smith, *Disraelian Conservatism and Social Reform*, p. 220: H.J. Dyos, in *Journal of Transport History*, Vol. II (1955-56), pp. 93-4
78. J.N. Tarn, op. cit., pp. 89-90
79. For these schemes, see Ibid, pp. 80-89
80. G. Stedman Jones, *Outcast London*, pp. 200-6, on which the ensuing passage is based.
81. E. Gauldie, *Cruel Habitations*, pp. 167, 173
82. First Report of Her Majesty's Commissioners for inquiring into the housing of the working classes, *Parliamentary Papers* 1884-85, XXX
83. Ibid, p. 12
84. Ibid, p. 11
85. Ibid, p. 58, quoting Sir Curtis Lampson

who managed the affairs of the Peabody Trust.
86. Ibid, pp. 26-27. The example quoted is that of the Clerkenwell vestry. Out of 72 members the average attendance was from 25 to 30, and the 'house farmers' and publicans had a working majority.
87. Ibid, p. 21. The witness was Mr. Marchant Williams, inspector of schools for the London School Board.
88. Ibid, p. 44
89. Ibid, p. 57
90. Ibid, p. 40
91. Ibid, pp. 66, 68-9
92. Ibid, p. 70
93. Ibid, pp. 82-3

Notes to Chapter Eleven

1. See p. 99
2. Clyde Binfield, *George Williams and the Y.M.C.A. A study in Victorian social attitudes* (1973), p. 277 and Ch. XIII, passim.
3. For the Tonic Sol-fa movement and Henry Coward, see E.D. Mackerness, *A Social History of English Music* (1964), pp. 157-64, and *Somewhere Further North. A History of music in Sheffield* (1974), pp. 86-95
4. John Kent, "Feelings and Festivals; an interpretation of some working-class religious attitudes", H.J. Dyos and Michael Wolff (eds.), *The Victorian City*, vol. 2, p. 855, and note 5 (quoting K.S. Inglis)
5. H. McLeod, *Class and Religion in the late Victorian city* (1974). p. 74
6. G. Rowell, *Hell and the Victorians. A Study of the nineteenth-century theological controversies concerning eternal punishment and the future life* (1974), pp. 147-8
7. See John Kent's article, already quoted, in Dyos and Wolff, *The Victorian City*, Vol. 2 and his article, "The Role of religion in the cultural structure of the late Victorian city", *Transactions of the Royal Historical Society*, 5th ser., vol. 23 (1973)
8. V.E. Chancellor (ed.), *Master and Artisan in Victorian England*, p. 120
9. Ibid, pp. 126-7
10. Ibid, pp. 153, 171, 236
11. T. Burt, *An Autobiography*, with supplementary chapters by Aaron Watson (1924)
12. J. Kent, in Dyos and Wolff (eds.), *The*

Victorian City, Vol. 2 pp. 857-8
13. W.G. Hoskins, *Devon* (1954), pp. 99-101
14. See p. 188
15. On the country clergy see G. Kitson Clark, *Churchmen and the condition of England 1832-1885* (1973), Ch. 9. The Chipping Norton case is dealt with on pp. 249-53
16. On Beatrice Potter, see Ch.XII, p. 227
17. See p. 228
18. G. Kitson Clark, *Churchmen and the condition of England.* pp. 276-81 (on Fremantle and Barnett); K. S. Inglis, *Churches and the working classes in Victorian England* (1963), pp. 143-55 (on the foundation of Toynbee Hall)
19. Derek Fraser, "Edward Baines", Patricia Hollis (ed.), *Pressure from without in early Victorian England* pp. 195-6
20. Report of the Commissioners appointed to inquire into the state of popular education in England, Vol. II, *Parliamentary Papers* 1861, XXI, Pt. 2, pp. 210-11
21. S.E. Maltby, *Manchester and the movement for national elementary education 1800-1870* (1918), pp. 101-2
22. R. Johnson, "Administrators in education before 1870; patronage, social position and role", G. Sutherland (ed.), *Studies in the growth of nineteenth-century government* (1972), p. 135. For the development of educational administration see A.S. Bishop, *The Rise of a central authority for English Education* (1971)
23. *PP*, 1861, XXI, Pt. I, p. 157
24. For a recent study of Lowe, see D.W. Sylvester, *Robert Lowe and Education* (1974)
25. For this argument see J. Hurt, *Education in Evolution. Church, State, Society and Popular Education* (Paladin Books ed., 1972), Ch. VI
26. M. Arnold, *Higher Schools and Universities in Germany* (1874), pp. 202-3; 'But we in England have our municipal organisation still to get; the country districts, with us, have at present only the feudal and ecclesiastical organisation of the Middle Ages, or of France before the Revolution'.
27. *PP*, 1861, XXI, Pt. I, p. 20
28. See p. 218
29. E.P. Hennock, "Finance and Politics in urban local government in England", *Historical Journal*, Vol. 6 (1963), pp. 212-25
30. *Hansard*, 3rd. ser. Vol. 203:757. The speaker was G. Melly, M.P. for Stoke.
31. S.E. Maltby, *Manchester and the movement for national elementary education*, p. 89
32. D.K. Jones, "Lancashire, the American Common School, and the religious problem in British education in the nineteenth century", *British Journal of Educational Studies*, Vol. XV (1967), p. 300
33. S.E. Maltby, op. cit., p. 69
34. Ibid, p. 80
35. Ibid, pp. 83, 91-2
36. Ibid, pp. 95-100
37. Ibid, pp. 106-7, 108-9
38. Commission on the employment of children, young persons and women in agriculture. First Report of the commissioners with appendix, Part 1, *Parliamentary Papers* 1867-68, XVII; Second Report of the Commissioners with appendix, Part I, *PP* 1868-69, XIII
39. See p. 190
40. H. Roper, "Towards an elementary education act for England and Wales 1865-1868", *British Journal of Educational Studies*, Vol. XXIII (1975), pp. 181-208
41. A.J. Marcham, "The Birmingham Education Society and the 1870 Education Act", *Journal of Educational Administration and History*, Vol. VIII (1976), pp. 11-16
42. F. Smith, *A History of English Elementary Education 1760-1902*, pp. 284-5. A different point of view from that stated here has been put forward by E.G. West (*Education and the state*, 2nd. ed., 1970). West argues that literacy was much more advanced in the mid-19th century, when it was provided by private enterprise, than is usually believed, that the introduction of the School Boards may have been unnecessary, and that it dried up private effort. See the criticism by H. Roper, *British Journal of Educational Studies*, Vol. XXIII, pp. 181-2
43. See p. 170 for a discussion of municipal reform in Birmingham.
44. Taken from the circular inviting adherence to the League in F. Adams, *History of the elementary school contest in England* (1883; reprinted 1972, with an introduction by Asa Briggs), p. 197. Adams's book tells the story of the League.
45. S.E. Maltby, *Manchester and the movement for national elementary education*, p. 114
46. *Hansard*, 3rd. ser., Vol. 199:441
47. Sir Charles Dilke, 20 June 1870 (*Hansard*, 3rd. ser. vol. 202: 518)
48. Elementary Education Act (1870), sec-

tion 14(2). A useful modern edition of the act is James Murphy, *The Education Act 1870. Text and Commentary* (1972)

49. Elementary Education Act (1870), section 7 (1 and 2)

50. Elementary Education Act, (1870), section 74

51. Like Roundell Palmer, the later Lord Chancellor Selborne. For Gathorne Hardy's views see *Hansard* (3rd. ser) Vol. 202:518-22, 534; for Palmer's vol. 199:2033, 2038

52. B.L. Manning, *The Protestant Dissenting Deputies* (1952), p. 50

53. For Richard's views, see *Hansard* (3rd ser.) Vol. 200:267-70; Vol. 202:504, 510

54. *Hansard* (3rd. ser.), Vol. 200:238

55. *Hansard* (3rd. ser.), Vol. 202:1398-9, 1414. Dilke's original amendment was narrowly defeated.

56. *Hansard* (3rd. ser.) Vol. 202:1308-10, 1312. The amendment was defeated by 257 votes to 32.

57. The story of how this change was brought about is complex. Forster announced on July 11 that the government had decided on direct election for all boards (*Hansard* (3rd. ser.), Vol. 203:267)

58. *Hansard* (3rd, ser.) Vol. 202:1478

59. See Forster's speech of 17 February 1870 (*Hansard* (3rd. ser.), Vol. 199:456-9)

60. See his speech of 14 March 1870 (*Hansard* (3rd. ser.), Vol. 199:1933-45)

61. *Hansard* (3rd. ser.) Vol. 199:1922-27

62. See Gladstone's speech of 16 June 1870 (*Hansard* (3rd. ser.), Vol. 202:270-82)

63. *Hansard* (3rd. ser.), Vol. 199: 1937; Vol. 202:655

64. *Hansard* (3rd. ser.) Vol. 202:276, 581 ff.

65. *Hansard* (3rd. ser.) Vol. 202:278-9

66. *Hansard* (3rd. ser.) Vol. 203:761

67. For developments in secondary and higher education see pp. 157-9

68. For the reformatory movement and the 'separate' system see p. 124. There is a useful discussion of prisons and penal treatment in W.L. Burn, *Age of Equipoise*, pp. 176-94

69. Except for a small number of convicts still sent to Western Australia.

70. S. and B. Webb, *English Prisons under local government*, pp. 181-2

71. D.L. Howard, *The English Prisons*, pp. 96-7; S. and B. Webb, *English Prisons under local government*, pp. 131-2, 154-5, 187-8

72. D.L. Howard, op. cit., pp. 97-8; S. and B. Webb, op. cit., pp. 189-91

73. See R. and F. Davenport Hill, *The Recorder of Birmingham. A Memoir of Matthew Davenport Hill; with selections from his correspondence* (1878), pp. 203, 207. M.D. Hill was active in penal matters and in philanthropic causes such as reformatory schools, and this book contains a good deal of interesting material on those subjects.

74. D. L. Howard, op. cit., p. 102; S. and B. Webb, op. cit., pp. 201-2

75. D. L. Howard, op. cit. p. 103

Notes to Chapter Twelve

1. See pp. 25-8

2. Quoted in L. Radzinowicz, *A History of English criminal law and its administration from 1750*, Vol. 4, p. 300

3. D. Owen, *English Philanthropy 1660-1960*, pp. 386-7

4. Beatrice Webb, *My Apprenticeship* (2nd ed., n.d.), p. 178. For Canon Barnett, see pp. 212-13

5. See H. L. Beales, "The 'Great Depression' in industry and trade", in E. M. Carus-Wilson (ed.), *Essays in Economic History* (1954), pp. 406-15; W. Ashworth, *An Economic History of England 1870-1939* (1960), ch. X; E.J. Hobsbawm, *Industry and Empire. The Making of modern English society.* Vol. II (1968), pp. 104, 135

6. H. L. Beales in E. M. Carus-Wilson (ed.), *Essays in Economic History* pp. 410-11

7. J. Roach, "Liberalism and the Victorian intelligentsia", *Cambridge Historical Journal*, Vol. XIII (1957), pp. 73-81

8. See B. I. Coleman (ed.), *The Idea of the city in nineteenth-century Britain* (1973), pp. 172-4

Notes for Further Reading

A full bibliography for a book of this kind would be very voluminous. All that I have tried to do here is to provide some guidance for further reading, and I have concentrated chiefly on books and articles which I have found useful. The place of publication of books and journals is London unless otherwise noted.

Any list of printed sources for the history of nineteenth-century England must begin with the PARLIAMENTARY PAPERS, many of which have been reprinted in the Irish University Press series of British Parliamentary Papers (chief editorial advisers, P. and G. Ford) (Shannon, Ireland), and I have cited only reports which are available in this series or in other modern reprints. Two of the most important are also to be found in a more inexpensive form—*The Poor Law Report of 1834 (Parliamentary Papers* 1834, XXVII), edited by S. G. and E. O. A. Checkland (Penguin Books, Harmondsworth, 1974), and Chadwick's *Report on the Sanitary Condition of the Labouring Population of Great Britain (PP* 1842 House of Lords XXVI), ed. M.W. Flinn (Edinburgh, 1965). On factories and industrial conditions the following are of particular note for the early period: the Report of the Select Committee of 1816 on the state of children employed in manufactures *(PP* 1816, III); the Report of Sadler's committee on the bill to regulate child labour in mills and factories *(PP* 1831-2, XV); and the first and second Reports of the Commission for enquiring into the employment of children in factories *(PP* 1833, XX, XXI). For the 1840's see the Report of the Commission on unemployed hand-loom weavers *(PP*, 1841, X); the Report of Lord Ashley's Committee on the act for the regulation of mills and factories *(PP*, 1841, IX); and the Reports of the Children's Employment Commission — Mines *(PP*, 1842, XV), and Trades and Manufactures (1843, XIII). The revived activity at the end of our period is represented by the Reports of the Commission on the employment of children and young persons in trades and manufactures—First *(PP*, 1863, XVIII); Second *(PP*. 1864, XXII); Third *(PP* 1864, XXI); Fourth *(PP*. 1865. XX); Fifth *(PP*. 1866, XXIV); Sixth *(PP*, 1867, XVI). For the parallel commission on the employment of children, young persons and women in agriculture see the First Report '... Part I *(PP*, 1867-68, XVII) and the Second Report ... Part I (PP, 1868-69, XIII). The Third and Fourth Reports *(PP*, 1870, XIII) deal with Wales and Scotland. The Commission which enquired into the organization and rules of trades unions produced a number of reports. *PP* 1867, XXXII contains the first to the fourth reports and the Report of the enquiry into the Sheffield outrages. *PP* 1867-68, XXXIX has the fifth to the tenth reports and the Report of the enquiry into the Manchester outrages. *PP* 1868-69, XXXI contains the eleventh and final Report and an appendix containing a large number of miscellaneous papers. The Commission into the working of the Factory and Workshops Acts produced two volumes of report and evidence *(PP*, 1876, XXXIX, XXX).

On public health and housing Chadwick's report of 1842 has already been mentioned. The companion to it is 'Sanitary Enquiry: England. Local Reports on the sanitary condition of the labouring population of England ...' *(PP*, 1842 House of Lords, XXVII). *PP*, 1844, XVII and 1845, XVIII contain the first and second Reports of the commissioners for inquiring into the state of large towns and populous districts. For the Report of the Royal Sanitary Commission, see *PP*, 1871, XXXV. For the housing problem see the first Report of the Commission for inquiring into the housing of working classes *(PP*, 1884-5, XXX). Environmental problems were often related to those of public order. On the police question see especially the first Report of the Commission on establishing an efficient constabulary force *(PP*, 1839, XIX).

The education of the people was considered during the 1830's by three Select Committees of the House of Commons. For their reports see *PP*, 1834, IX; 1835, VII; 1837-8, VII. During the 'sixties and 'seventies royal commissions examined most parts of the educational system; see the reports of the Newcastle Commission on popular education, 6 vols., *PP*, 1861, XXI parts I-VI; of the Clarendon Commission on the public schools, 4 vols. *PP*, 1864, XX,XXI; and of the Taunton Commission on the grammar schools, 21 vols., *PP*, 1867-68, XXVIII, parts I-XVII. Of the eight reports of the Devonshire Commission on scientific instruction and the advancement of science, the most relevant are the Second (1872) on scientific instruction in training colleges and elementary schools (*PP*, 1872, XXV) and the Eighth (1875) on the scientific work of government departments and on state support for science (*PP*, 1875, XXVIII)

I have in general cited here only those BOOKS and ARTICLES which have been published or reprinted fairly recently and are therefore not too difficult to obtain, though I have also included some works of the period where they seemed of particular importance. Two among the volumes of *English Historical Documents*, edited by David C. Douglas, are of great value: vol. XI (1783-1832), edited by A. Aspinall and E. A. Smith (1959), and vol. XII (I) (1833-1874), edited by G.M. Young and W.D. Handcock (1956). The best general introduction to the history of the period is still Élie Halévy's *A History of the English People in the Nineteenth Century* (mostly translated by E.I. Watkin), of which the relevant volumes are I, *England in 1815* (2nd ed., 1949); II, *The Liberal Awakening 1815-1830* (2nd ed., 1949); III, *The Triumph of Reform 1830-1841* (2nd ed., 1950); IV, *Victorian Years 1841-1895* (with a supplementary section by R.B. McCallum) (1951). There have been a number of recent general surveys such as G. Kitson Clark, *The Making of Victorian England* (1962) and *An Expanding Society. Britain 1830-1900* (Cambridge and Melbourne, 1967); Harold Perkin, *The Origins of Modern English Society 1780-1880* (1969); P.J. Perry, A *Geography of 19th century Britain* (1975); J.F.C. Harrison, *The Early Victorians 1832-1851* (1971); and Geoffrey Best, *Mid-Victorian Britain 1851-75* (1971). Three books by Asa Briggs are extremely useful. *The Age of Improvement* (1959) is a general study covering the years from 1783 to 1867. More specialized in their themes are *Victorian Cities* (1963) and *Victorian People. A reassessment of Persons and Themes 1851-67* (1954), which is a set of studies of leading individuals of that time. G.M. Young's long essay *Victorian England: portrait of an age* (1936) is a major work of interpretation.

General works on the economic history of the period include T.S. Ashton, *An Economic History of England. The 18th Century* (1955); William Ashworth, *An Economic History of England 1870-1939* (1960); E.J. Hobsbawm, *Industry and Empire. The Making of Modern English Society*, vol. ii; *1750 to the present day* (1968); and Sidney Pollard, *The Genesis of Modern Management. A study of the Industrial Revolution in Great Britain* (1965). J.H. Clapham's *An Economic History of Modern Britain* is on a larger scale: two volumes cover our period—*The Early Railway Age 1820-1850* and *Free Trade and Steel 1850-1886* (Cambridge, reprinted 1967-8). Among books on shorter periods or particular themes the following may be selected. W.L. Burn, *The Age of Equipoise. A Study of the mid-Victorian generation* (1964) is a magisterial re-examination of the period 1852-67. Paul Smith, *Disraelian Conservatism and Social Reform* (1967) is useful on the latter part of the period. Valuable for their own fields are F.M.L. Thompson, *English Landed Society in the nineteenth century* (1963); M.J. Cullen, *The Statistical Movement in early Victorian Britain: The foundations of empirical social research* (Hassocks, Sussex, 1975); J.A. Banks, *Prosperity and Parenthood; a study of family planning among the Victorian middle classes* (1954); and R. W. Malcolmson, *Popular Recreations in English Society 1700-1850* (Cambridge, 1973). Patricia Hollis (ed.), *Pressure from Without in early Victorian England* (1974) is a collection of essays on the influence of external pressure groups on politics.

Among the many CONTEMPORARY DIARIES, AUTOBIOGRAPHIES and WORKS OF OPINION the following are very useful to the social historian. Edward Lytton Bulwer, *England and the English* (1833), edited by Standish Meacham (Chicago and London, 1970), is a survey of the country at the time of the Great Reform Bill. Samuel Smiles, *Self-Help; with illustrations of conduct and perseverance* (centenary ed., 1958) is a famous paean to industry and hard work. Differing views of the Industrial Revolution are presented in P. Gaskell, *Artisans and Machinery. The moral and physical condition of the manufacturing population* (1836) and in Andrew Ure, *The Philosophy of Manufactures: or, an exposition of the scientific, moral and commercial economy of the factory system of Great Britain* (1835). Both of these are reprinted in the Cass Library of Industrial Classics (1968, 1967). G.R. Porter, *The Progress of the Nation, in its various social and economical relations, from the beginning of the nineteenth century* (3rd ed., 1851) reviews the economic situation at mid-century. The lives of working people and of the poor may be studied in H. Dunckley (ed.,), *Bamford's Passages in the life of a Radical and Early Days* (n.d.); William Lovett, *Life and Struggles of . . . in his pursuit of bread, knowledge and freedom*, with a preface by R.H. Tawney (1967); Valerie E. Chancellor (ed.), *Master and Artisan in Victorian England. The Diary of William Andrews and the Autobiography of Joseph Gutteridge* (1969); and, for the poor of London, Henry Mayhew, *Selections from 'London Labour and the London Poor'* (World's Classics ed., 1965) and W.H. Swan and W. Swan *The Journals of two poor Dissenters* (1970). Books by two working men who became political figures are Thomas Burt, *An Autobiography*, with supplementary chapter by Aaron Watson (1924), and Joseph Arch, *Autobiography*, edited by J.G. O'Leary (1966). Beatrice Webb's *My Apprenticeship* (2nd ed., n.d.) is very important for changing social attitudes in the 1880's.

Social history relates both to POLITICAL IDEAS and to administrative history. Bentham and the Utilitarians are dealt with below. There is a convenient Everyman's Library edition of J.S. Mill, *Utilitarianism, Liberty and Representative Government*. Mill's most percipient critic was J.F. Stephen; there is a modern edition by R.J. White of his *Liberty, Equality, Fraternity* (Cambridge, 1867, a reprint of the 2nd ed. of 1874). There are several modern reprints of Walter Bagehot, *The English Constitution* (2nd ed., 1872); see also his *Physics and Politics or Thoughts on the application of the principles of 'Natural Selection' and 'Inheritance' to political society* (6th ed., 1883). For a modern biography of Bagehot see Alistair Buchan, *The Spare Chancellor. The Life of Walter Bagehot* (1959).

A valuable introduction to ADMINISTRATIVE HISTORY is David Roberts, *Victorian Origins of the British Welfare State* (New Haven, 1960), which contains a bibliographical essay. Two useful collections of articles are Peter Stansky (ed.), *Government and Society in Victoria's Britain* (New York, 1973) and Gillian Sutherland (ed.), *Studies in the growth of nineteenth-century government* (1972). See also Oliver MacDonagh, *A Pattern of Government Growth 1800-60. The Passenger Acts and their enforcement* (1961) and *Early Victorian Government* (1977) (which I have not seen); W.C. Lubenow, *The Politics of Government Growth. Early Victorian attitudes towards state intervention* (Newton Abbot, 1971); Roger Prouty, *The Transformation of the Board of Trade 1830-1855. A Study of administrative reorganization in the heyday of laissez faire* (1957). The connections of Britain with Ireland and India are explored in Edward

Norman, *A History of Modern Ireland* (1971) and Eric Stokes, *The English Utilitarians and India* (Oxford, 1959). Among many articles of value are Jenifer Hart, "Nineteenth-century social reform: a Tory interpretation of history", *Past and Present*, no. 31 (July 1965); Valerie Cromwell, "Interpretations of nineteenth-century administration: an analysis", *Victorian Studies*, vol. IX (1965-66); R.M. MacLeod, "The Alkali Acts Administration 1863-1884. The Emergence of the civil scientist", *Victorian Studies*, vol. IX (1965-66) and "Resources of Science in Victorian England: the Endowment of Science Movement, 1868-1900" in Peter Mathias (ed.), *Science and Society 1600-1900* (Cambridge, 1972); R.M. Gutchen, "Local Improvements and centralization in nineteenth - century England". *Historical Journal*, vol. 4 (1961).

Much of eighteenth and nineteenth century history relates to LOCAL THEMES. On the earlier part of the period the classic study is still that of Sidney and Beatrice Webb, *English Local Government from the Revolution to the Municipal Corporations Act: The Parish and the County* (1906); *The Manor and the Borough*, parts I and II (1908); *Statutory Authorities for Special Purposes* (1922). For a modern treatment see Donald Read, *The English Provinces c. 1760-1960. A study in influence* (1964). On CITIES see H.J.Dyos and Michael Wolff (eds.,), *The Victorian City. Images and Realities (2 vols., 1973)*, an important series of essays on many subjects related to city life, and B.I. Coleman (ed.,), *The Idea of the City in nineteenth-century Britain* (1973), a collection of extracts from contemporary writings. There are studies of many towns and cities. On London see D.J. Olsen, *The Growth of Victorian London* (1976), G. Stedman Jones, *Outcast London. A Study in the relationship between classes in Victorian society* (Penguin Books ed., Harmondsworth, 1976), and H.J. Dyos, *Victorian Suburb. A Study of the growth of Camberwell* (Leicester, 3rd imp., 1973). on the PROVINCES see Conrad Gill and Asa Briggs, *History of Birmingham*, 2 vols. (1952); Shena D. Simon, *A Century of city government. Manchester 1838-1938* (1939); A. Redford and I.S. Russell, *The History of Local Government in Manchester*, vols. I and II (1940); E.C. Midwinter, *Social Administration in Lancashire 1830-1860. Poor Law, Public Health and Police* (Manchester 1969); Sidney Pollard, *A History of Labour in Sheffield* (1959); A. Temple Patterson *A History of Leicester 1780-1850* (Leicester, 2nd imp., 1975); R.A. Church, *Economic and Social Change in a Midland Town: Victorian Nottingham 1815-1900* (1966). E.P. Hennock, *Fit and Proper Persons,*

Ideal and Reality in nineteenth-century urban government (1973) deals particularly with Leeds and Birmingham.

Many of the books on the pre-1830 period relate to Jeremy Bentham and the Utilitarians. A very good place to start is Elie Halévy's *The Growth of Philosophical Radicalism* (English trans., reprinted 1952). Lionel Robbins, *The Theory of Economic Policy in English Classical Political Economy* (1952) is useful on the CLASSICAL ECONOMISTS and on MALTHUS as well as on Bentham. A new *Collected Works* of Bentham is in progress (general editor, J.H. Burns), of which five volumes have been published (1968-71). The most useful of these for our purposes in *An Introduction to the Principles of Morals and Legislation*, edited by J.H. Burns and H.L.A. Hart (1970). There is an edition of the same work, together with *A Fragment on Government* by W. Harrison (Oxford, 1948). Among works on Bentham are C.M. Atkinson, *Jeremy Bentham., His Life and Work* (1905); C.W. Everett, *Jeremy Bentham* (1966); D.J. Manning, *The Mind of Jeremy Bentham* (1969); L.J. Hume, "Jeremy Bentham and the nineteenth-century revolution in government", *Historical Journal*, vol. 10 (1967); and there are two useful essays on him in Graham Wallas, *Men and Ideas. Essays* (1940). Works on people related to the Benthamite circle include W.H. Burston, *James Mill on Philosophy and Education* (1973); C.W. New, *The Life of Henry Brougham to 1830* (Oxford, 1961); G. Wallas, *The Life of Francis Place* (revised ed., 1918); Francis Place, *Autobiography (1771-1854)*, edited by Mary Thale (Cambridge, 1972). Two recent articles on Place are by Brian Harrison, "Two Roads to social reform: Francis Place and the 'Drunken Committee' of 1834", *Historical Journal*, vol II (1968) and D.J. Rowe, "Francis Place and the Historian", *Historical Journal*, vol. 16 (1973). There are Penguin Classic editions of the following:—T.R. Malthus, *An Essay on the Principle of Population and A Summary View of the Principle of Population*, edited by Antony Flew (1970); David Ricardo, *On the Principles of Political Economy and Taxation.*, edited by R.M. Hartwell (1971); Robert Owen, *A New View of Society and Report to the County of Lanark*, edited by V.A.C. Gatrell (1970). On Malthus see D.V. Glass (ed.), *Introduction to Malthus* (1953), and R.M. Young, "Malthus and the Evolutionists: the common context of biological and social theory", *Past and Present* no. 43 (1969), which considers the influence of Malthus's *Essay* on some later thinkers. E.P. Thompson, *The Making of the English Working Class* (1963) puts more emphasis than

has been usual on the revolutionary strand in working-class movements. N. McCord, "The Government of Tyneside 1800-1850", *Transactions of the Royal Historical Society*, 5th ser. vol. 20 (1970) is a study of the conciliatory forces in central government and local society.

It remains to consider some of the literature on particular subjects. On the POOR LAW the basic study is that of S. and B. Webb, *English Poor Law History*: Part I, *The Old Poor Law* (1927); Part II, *The Last Hundred Years*, vol. I (1929). Among more recent works are J.R. Poynter, *Society and Pauperism: English ideas on poor relief 1795-1834* (1969); and M.E. Rose, *The English Poor Law 1780-1830* (1971). There are essays on the subject in E.W. Martin (ed.), *Comparative Developments in Social Welfare* (1972). J.D. Marshall, *The Old Poor Law 1795-1834* (Economic History Society: Studies in Economic History, M.W. Flinn (ed.) (1968) is a useful review of recent scholarship. See also the following articles: M.W. Flinn. "The Poor Employment Act 1817", *Economic History Review*, 2nd ser. vol. XIV (1961-2): Mark Blaug. "The Myth of the Old Poor Law and the making of the new", *Journal of Economic History*, vol. XXIII (1963), and "The Poor Law Report re-examined", ibid, vol. XXIV (1964); J.D. Marshall, "The Nottinghamshire Reformers and their contribution to the New Poor Law", *Economic History Review*, 2nd ser., vol XIII (1960-1); P. Dunkley, "The 'Hungry Forties' and the New Poor Law: a case study", *Historical Journal*, vol 17 (1974); R. Boyson, "The New Poor Law in north-east Lancashire 1834-71", *Transactions of the Lancashire and Cheshire Antiquarian Society*, vol. LXX (1960).

On the PENAL SYSTEM generally the standard work of reference is L. Radzinowicz, *A History of English Criminal Law and its Administration from 1750*, 4 vols. (1948-69), and J.J. Tobias, *Crime and Industrial Society in the nineteenth century* (1967) is also useful. On the Police see Charles Reith, *British Police and the Democratic Ideal* (1943) and *A New Study of Police History* (1956); T.A. Critchley, *A History of Police in England and Wales 900-1966* (1967); Jenifer Hart, "Reform of the Borough Police 1835-56", *English Historical Review*, vol, LXX (1955) and "The County and Borough Police Act 1856", *Public Administration*, vol. 36 (1956): H. Parris, "The Home Office and the Provincial Police in England and Wales 1856-70", *Public Law* (1961). On prisons see S. and B. Webb, *English Prisons under Local Government* (1922); D.L. Howard, *The English Prisons.*

Their past and their future (1960). E.A.L. Moir, "Sir George Onesiphorus Paul", H.P.R. Finberg (ed.), *Gloucestershire Studies* (Leicester, 1967) is a study of one of the pioneer prison reformers.

For PUBLIC HEALTH there is a good survey by W.M. Fraser, *A History of English Public Health 1834-1939* (1950). For Chadwick see S.E. Finer, *The Life and Times of Sir Edwin Chadwick* (1952). and R.A. Lewis, *Edwin Chadwick and the Public Health Movement* (1952). For Simon see Royston Lambert, *Sir John Simon 1816-1904 and English Social Administration* (1963). Lambert's article, "A Victorian National Health Service. State Vaccination 1855-71", *Historical Journal*, vol. 5 (1962) is also useful. Simon gave his own account in *English Sanitary Institutions, reviewed in their course of development, and in some of their political and social relations* (1890). E.W. Hope, *Health at the Gateway: Problems and international obligations of a seaport city* (Cambridge, 1931) is a study of public health in Liverpool. Articles which throw light on different parts of the subject are E.P. Hennock, "Urban Sanitary Reform a generation beforeChadwick?" *Economic History Review*, 2nd ser., vol. X (1957-8); E.M. Sigsworth, "Gateways to Death? Medicines, Hospitals and Mortality 1700-1850", in P. Mathias (ed.), *Science and Society 1600-1900* (Cambridge, 1972); H.J. Smith, "Local Reports to the General Board of Health", *History*, vol. 56 (1971).

There are two recent books on HOUSING—J.N. Tarn, *Five per Cent Philanthropy. An account of housing in urban areas between 1840 and 1914* (Cambridge, 1973) and Enid Gauldie, *Cruel Habitations. A History of working-class housing 1780-1918* (1974). The growth of RAILWAYS relates both to urban problems and to administrative history. See Henry Parris, *Government and the Railways in nineteenth-century Britain* (1965); J.R. Kellett, *The Impact of Railways on Victorian Cities* (1969); J.Dyos, "Railways and Housing in Victorian London", *Journal of Transport History* vol. II (1955-56).

INDUSTRIAL CONDITIONS and WORKING-CLASS MOVEMENTS may be treated together. For the general background, N.J. Smelser, *Social Change in the Industrial Revolution. An application of theory to the Lancashire cotton industry 1770-1840* (1959); John Foster, *Class Struggle and the Industrial Revolution. Early industrial capitalism in three English towns* (1974); Asa Briggs and John Saville (eds.) *Essays in Labour History in memory of G.D.H. Cole* (1967); E.J. Hobsbawm, *Labouring Men. Studies in the history of labour* (1968). There is a modern edition of Friedrich Engels, *The Condition of the Working Class in England* (1844), translated and edited by W.O. Henderson and W.H. Chaloner (2nd ed., Oxford, 1971). For the factory system and the movement to limit working hours see J.T. Ward, *The Factory System, 2* vols (Newton Abbot, 1970), and *The Factory Movement, 1830-1855* (1962); M.W. Thomas, *The Early Factory System. A study in legislation and administrative evolution* (Leigh-on-sea, 1948); B.L. Hutchins and A. Harrison, *A History of Factory Legislation* (1903, reprinted 1966, 1970), Cecil Driver, *Tory Radical. The Life of Richard Oastler* (New York, 1946). Chartism is dealt with in Asa Briggs (ed.), *Chartist Studies* (1959); J.T. Ward, *Chartism* (1973); David Williams, *John Frost, A study of Chartism* (Cardiff 1939, reprinted 1969). The trades unions are dealt with in S. and B. Webb, *The History of Trade Unionism 1666-1920* (1920), and in H. A. Clegg, Alan Fox, A. F. Thompson, *A History of British Trade Unions since 1889*, vol. I (1889-1910) (1964), the first chapter of which deals with the movement before 1889. Patrick Joyce, "The Factory Politics of Lancashire in the later nineteenth century". *Historical Journal*, vol. 18 (1975) is interesting on the later part of the period, as is P.L.R. Horn, "The Agricultural Children Act of 1873", *History of Education*, vol. 3 (1974) on child labour on the land.

Finally come the more personal aspects of social reform, linked with philanthropy, religion and education. On the movements for SELF-HELP. see C.L. Mowat, *The Charity Organization Society 1869-1913. Its ideas and work* (1961); P.H.J.H. Gosden, *The Friendly Societies in England, 1815-1875* (Manchester, 1961) and *Self-Help. Voluntary associations in nineteenth-century Britain* (1973); E.J. Cleary, *The Building Society Movement* (1965). For PHILANTHROPY the best place to start is David Owen, *English Philanthropy (1660-1960)* (Cambridge Mass., 1965) On the drink question see Brian Harrison, *Drink and the Victorians. The Temperance question in England 1815-1872* (1971), and his articles on related themes, "Teetotal Chartism", *History* vol. 58 (1973), and "Philanthropy and the Victorians", *Victorian Studies* vol. IX (1965-66). The greatest of the philanthropists was Lord Shaftesbury. The contemporary life is by Edwin Hodder, *The Life and Work of the seventh Earl of Shaftesbury, K.G.* (3 vols. 1886);there are modern lives by J.L. and Barbara Hammond (4th ed., 1936) and by Geoffrey Best (1964). Other valuable studies of individuals are Clyde Binfield, *George Williams and the YMCA. A study in Victorian social attitudes* (1973), and J.L. and

254

B. Hammond, *James Stansfeld. A Victorian champion of sex equality* (1932). The last title introduces the much greater role of WOMEN IN VICTORIAN SOCIETY. Many aspects of women's activities are covered by Cecil Woodham-Smith, *Florence Nightingale 1820-1910* (1950); E. Moberly Bell, *Josephine Butler. Flame of Fire* (1962); A.S.G. Butler, *Portrait of Josephine Butler* (1954); E. Moberly Bell, *Octavia Hill. A biography* (1942); Jo Manton, *Elizabeth Garrett Anderson* (1965); Barbara Stephen, *Emily Davies and Girton College* (1927).

A recent study of the relationship between RELIGION and social questions is G. Kitson Clark, *Churchmen and the Condition of England 1832-1885. A study in the development of social ideas and practice from the old regime to the modern state.* (1973). Other studies which explore similar themes are W.R. Ward, *Religion and Society in England 1790-1850* (1972); R.A. Soloway, *Prelates and People, Ecclesiastical social thought in England 1783-1852* (1969); Diana McClatchey, *Oxfordshire Clergy, 1777-1869; a study of the Established Church and of the role of its clergy in local society* (Oxford, 1960); Elizabeth Isichei, *Victorian Quakers* (1970); H.F. Mathews, *Methodism and the Education of the People 1791-1851* (1949); Hugh McLeod, *Class and Religion in the late Victorian City* (1974); K.S. Inglis, *Churches and the Working Classes in Victorian England* (1963); J.H.S. Kent, "The role of religion in the cultural structure of the later Victorian city", *Transactions of the Royal Historical Society*, 5th ser., vol. 23 (1973).

In EDUCATION the development of state activity is dealt with by A. S. Bishop, *The Rise of a Central Authority for English Education* (Cambridge, 1971) and by E.G. West, *Education and the State. A study in political economy* (2nd ed., 1970), which argues that private initiatives were much more effective than has usually been believed by historians. For the Act of 1870 see T. Wemyss Reid, *The Life of the Right Hon. W.E. Forster*, 2 vols. (4th ed., 1888); James Murphy, *The Education Act 1870. Text and Commentary* (Newton Abbot, 1972); Francis Adams, *History of the Elementary School Contest in England* (1882; edited by Asa Briggs, 1972), which tells the story from the point of view of the National Education League. Different parts of the system are handled in Mary Sturt, *The Education of the People. A history of primary education in England and Wales in the nineteenth century* (1967); John Roach, *Public Examinations in England 1850-1900*, (Cambridge, 1971), which contains a great deal about secondary education generally and about the education of women; John Spar-

row, *Mark Pattison and the Idea of a University* (Cambridge, 1967); Sheldon Rothblatt, *The Revolution of the Dons. Cambridge and society in Victorian England* (1968). There has been a good deal of writing about what is often called 'informal education'. See R.K. Webb, *The British Working Class Reader 1790-1848* (1955); R.D. Altick, *The English Common Reader. A social history of the mass reading public 1800-1900* (Chicago, 1957); J.F.C. Harrison, *Learning and Living. A study in the history of the English adult education movement* (1961).

Index

256 Index